Media Architecture

Age of Access? Grundfragen der Informationsgesellschaft

Edited by
André Schüller-Zwierlein

Volume 8

Media Architecture

Using Information and Media as Construction Material

Edited by
Alexander Wiethoff
Heinrich Hußmann

DE GRUYTER
SAUR

ISBN 978-3-11-045137-5
e-ISBN (PDF) 978-3-11-045387-4
e-ISBN (EPUB) 978-3-11-045159-7
ISSN 2195-0210

Library of Congress Cataloging-in-Publication Data
A CIP catalog record for this book has been applied for at the Library of Congress.

Bibliographic information published by the Deutsche Nationalbibliothek
The Deutsche Nationalbibliothek lists this publication in the Deutsche Nationalbibliografie; detailed bibliographic data are available on the Internet at http://dnb.dnb.de.

Typesetting: PTP-Berlin, Protago-TEX-Production GmbH, Berlin
Printing and binding: CPI books GmbH, Leck
♾ Printed on acid-free paper
Printed in Germany

www.degruyter.com

Editor's Preface

Whenever we talk about information, *access* is one of the terms most frequently used. The concept has many facets and suffers from a lack of definition. Its many dimensions are being analysed in different disciplines, from different viewpoints and in different traditions of research; yet they are rarely perceived as parts of a whole, as relevant aspects of one phenomenon. The book series *Age of Access? Fundamental Questions of the Information Society* takes up the challenge and attempts to bring the relevant discourses, scholarly as well as practical, together in order to come to a more precise idea of the central role that the accessibility of information plays for human societies.

The ubiquitous talk of the "information society" and the "age of access" hints at this central role, but tends to implicitly suggest either that information *is* accessible everywhere and for everyone, or that it *should be*. Both suggestions need to be more closely analysed. The first volume of the series adresses the topic of information justice and thus the question of whether information *should be* accessible everywhere and for everyone. Further volumes analyse in detail the physical, economic, intellectual, linguistic, psychological, political, demographic and technical dimensions of the accessibility and inaccessibility of information – enabling readers to test the hypothesis that information *is* accessible everywhere and for everyone.

The series places special emphasis on the fact that access to information has a diachronic as well as a synchronic dimension – and that thus cultural heritage research and practices are highly relevant to the question of access to information. Its volumes analyse the potential and the consequences of new access technologies and practices, and investigate areas in which accessibility is merely simulated or where the inaccessibility of information has gone unnoticed. The series also tries to identify the limits of the quest for access. The resulting variety of topics and discourses is united in one common proposition: It is only when all dimensions of the accessibility of information have been analysed that we can rightfully speak of an information society.

André Schüller-Zwierlein

DOI 10.1515/9783110453874-001

Contents

Alexander Wiethoff and Heinrich Hußmann

Introduction

Media Architecture is a new term not yet familiar to many people. It refers to the traditional discipline of architecture, as the design of buildings, cities and public locations. However, it extends this discipline by the fusion of digital information with the built environment. The basic idea is to use information as an additional construction material in architecture like glass, wood or concrete. This form of architecture enables citizens to access information through their surroundings instead of using personal devices. Umbrella terms such as "urban computing", "smart cities" or "urban informatics" also pursue the same basic idea but usually have a wider range of meaning.

Media architecture is about accessibility of information to everybody in a public location. Accessing information via the built environment can empower people to gain more knowledge on their surroundings which in turn can provoke behaviour changes. Examples included in this book exemplify the access of information through media architecture on energy consumption, public transport, pollution levels, availability of resources or sharing goods among communities. We consider it advantageous that media architecture is not only perceived as a "layer-on-top" of existing infrastructure, instead it can be considered as a new, smart construction material that can, if used wisely, enhance the communication and enable a mutual dialogue between city and citizens.

At this point we can clearly identify that the field is maturing not only within the dedicated research communities. Various projects and case studies have been documented in the past and there is a well established conference track addressing this field, however, merely for a research community. By providing this publication we aim to give an overview on the topic, its chances and opportunities, technical feasibility and practical examples in the form of case studies of using media architecture as construction material. Our goal is to reach out to people outside our core research community and to provide interested researchers with potential starting points for entering this domain. Therefore this publication is one of the first broad scientific overviews of media architecture, written by leading practitioners and researchers working in this field.

This book is dissected into three main sections. The first section provides a theoretical discourse on the topic, focusing on the context in which media architecture is applied and its functions in the organism of a city. The second part of the book then reports on practical examples derived from case studies and implementations deployed in the urban environment. The third part addresses the systematic design of media architecture in the public domain and is donated to tool

DOI 10.1515/9783110453874-002

and process models combined with technical opportunities to design the mutual dialogue between buildings and citizens. We close with a personal perspective taken from the perspective of the humanities.

Media Architecture and the Smart City

Patrick Tobias Fischer and Eva Hornecker

Media Architecture for Shared Encounters

1 Introduction

Information and Computer Technology (ICT) is weaving into the fabric of our city and becomes a pervasive medium, which accompanies our daily life. New mediums such as public displays and media façades expand the range of technology already part of the city. They also become more interactive and researchers investigate alternative uses of these technologies, which lie beyond efficiency. Human-Computer Interaction (HCI) researchers turned their interest from information displays towards more playful applications, which foster social interaction or strengthen identification with the city. Often interface designs for public displays or media architecture focused on directly accessing information provided by them, but forgot about what happens in front of the screen while the information is consumed. Does it enliven the situation? Is it preventing social interaction? In this book information is considered as constructional material on a par with traditional building materials. This emphasizes the responsibility in what way technology should be applied in our cities. Providing information access through a specific system design changes public behavior. This is similar to designing a public square. Designed in a right way it can provide the basis for a vibrant place, but done wrong it can also turn a space into a deserted area.

However, little is known about how these situated interfaces shape public space. Defining and making space is the task of urban designers and architects, but as HCI invents novel types of interfaces for the urban environment, spatial thinking as well as understanding the different types of values for public spaces becomes necessary for this research domain.

1.1 Motivation

The motivation of writing this chapter is driven by the obvious fallacy that Human-Computer Interaction scientists are able to create new media systems for public spaces without making the same mistakes urban planners and architects have done in the past. Currently, we live in an age where more and more sensors are soaking into our cities with the predominant purpose to monitor our environment and to capitalize upon it. Mobility control, smart water networks, parking space management, surveillance systems, and air pollution monitoring are only a few typical application domains for Information and Communication Technol-

DOI 10.1515/9783110453874-003

ogy (ICT) within our city. In contrast to sensing the city, actuating the city is left to digital advertisers and real estate developers. According to Hilmar von Lojewski, a Deputy of the German Städtetag, corporations currently prepare for the digital land grab by means of standardization under the flag of the "Smart City" (Lojewski 2014). In this regard only few institutions feel responsible to support cultural aspects through our new digital means. Among these are media artists who criticise the digital development of our cities (e.g. Julian Oliver with his artwork 'The Artvertiser' (Oliver 2008–2010)), hacktivists who disrupt in order to address serious deficits in the field of urban planning (e.g. TV-B-Gone by Mitch Altman (Altman 2009), Skullphone (SKULLPHONE)), parkour and skateboard practitioners who take an alternative and creative approach on architecture and culture (cf. (Borden 2001)), and freifunkers who create free wireless community networks. Surprisingly, these grassroots movements seem to contribute more positively to a digital city than city councils themselves due to the fact they maintain space, without monetary capitalisation in mind. They provide alternative views, value creativity and instead build cultural capital. Unfortunately, it seems that current master plans rarely include methods on how to increase these cultural values through todays evolving and already highly advanced digital means.

However, this chapter will not provide a tailored recommended plan of action for a good *digital* urban design, but is certainly motivated by the antiquated view of city councils on media technology. Various ICT paradigms are changing our city as shown in Figure 1.

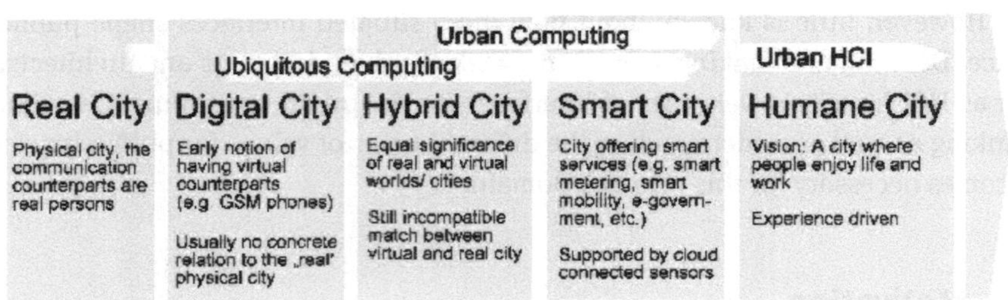

Fig. 1: ICT paradigms shaping our city (adapted from Streitz 2011).

Our research interest leans towards the idea of the *Humane City* and *Urban HCI*. Urban HCI builds on former visions of ICT merging with the city, but it also differentiates itself from it. How so, will be described in the following.

Digital displays are becoming more and more ubiquitous: they range from smaller displays, providing information such as bus schedules, to bigger ones showing latest discounts in shopping malls and retail stores, to large-scale displays covering an entire building façade (Kostakos/Ojala 2013). Although most displays act as digital signage, supporting no interaction, recent advances in technology are rapidly changing this and turn them into interactive and user-engaging technology, ultimately leading to an open and novel communications medium (Davies et al. 2012). However, most focus on spreading or gathering information efficiently and often do so by connecting to internet emergent communication technology schemes, such as social networks (Schroeter 2012) and email. System developers, however, too often forget about their situatedness, and frequently transfer global communication systems onto the streets. For example, mobile texting to a public display is a common application. By seeking out alternatives in media art and grassroots movements, innovative HCI systems can be found which enrich our everyday life (e.g. Solar Pink Pong (Assocreation 2014)). Generally, the problem is to reason what values should be preferably promoted through digital systems. City system solution developers for e.g. parking systems or out-of-home advertising can provide a monetary benefit to the city and seem to sell easier than those that develop cultural capital.

However, since 2008 the Media Façade Festival was able to gain traction in providing alternative media formats for European cities. Extending the initiative to a European festival in 2010 including seven cities, the initiative has grown to a European Urban Media Network covering the topics of the Networked City (2013), the Participatory City (2014) and the In/Visible City (2015). With being a contributing artist in 2008 and 2010, it became obvious, that great interactive projects were developed without systematic reflection. This is changing currently with the collaboration between the Media Architecture Biennale (MAB) an ACM supported conference since 2012 and the Media Façade Festival initiative, as well as the so-called "urban"-tracks in established conferences such as CHI and DIS.

2 From Ubiquitous and Urban Computing to Urban HCI

Before we begin to answer the question of which values Media Architecture should promote in the urban environment, we explain why Media Architecture requires a different thinking than the paradigms of Ubiquitous and Urban Computing and why a new paradigm is needed. For this we will focus on *conceived space*, a concept of Lefebvre's three-fold division of space (conceived space, lived space and perceived space) (Lefebvre 1991, p. 38f). Conceived spaces express a certain understanding of a place that its designers' had in mind when constructing it (Silva/Hjorth 2009). These designers typically were architects, urban planners, urban designers, etc. and nowadays with academic disciplines such as Media Architecture, architecture orients towards the digital. In the opposing direction, HCI researchers from the fields of tangible computing (which has its origins in ubiquitous computing), physical computing, computer supported cooperative work (CSCW), and mobile computing head into public space; now also constructing novel spaces, shaping experiences and behaviours. By doing so, similar problems as architects encountered on an everyday basis are also on the technologists' agenda, for example what values should be promoted in public space. A new set of design concerns arose, including managing attention, incorporating context, combining devices, the need for new physical forms and affordances and new interactive styles; all of these are aspects Ubiquitous Computing is interested in. However, these seem to miss architectural aspects that create our public space and shapes, to an extent, our public life.

We briefly attempt to argue in a similar way architectural theory might, to emphasize the role of space when designing digital systems installed in the public sphere.

The roman architect and architectural theorist Vitruvius based the definition of architecture on the three principles of stability, utility and grace. While the first two topics are also reasonable in software architecture, grace is an aesthetic concept. Stability and utility are a strongly connected to Ubicomp and Urban Computing. To quote a definition of Urban Computing of Microsoft Research:

> *Urban computing* is a process of acquisition, integration, and analysis of big and heterogeneous data generated by a diversity of sources in urban spaces, such as sensors, devices, vehicles, buildings, and human, to tackle the major issues that cities face, e.g. air pollution, increased energy consumption and traffic congestion. Urban computing connects unobtrusive and ubiquitous sensing technologies, advanced data management and analytics models, and novel visualization methods, to create win-win-win solutions that improve urban *environment*, *human* life quality, and *city* operation systems. Urban computing also helps us understand the nature of urban phenomena and even predict the future of cities.
> (Zheng et al. 2014)

In essence it rather concerned with fusing computing science with traditional fields such as transportation, civil engineering and economy in the context of urban spaces. Key challenges named by Zheng are urban sensing and data acquisition, computing with heterogeneous data and hybrid systems that blend the physical and virtual worlds (Zheng et al. 2014) (compare also to Figure 1). From that it seems Urban Computing is less concerned with the principle of grace (in the original Latin: *venustas* also translated as beauty and delight).

With the term *venustas* Vitruvius considers not only the objects of architecture as important, but already their 'audience'. This translates in architecture often to qualities of building design, scale, proportionality of visual interesting experiences, vistas, places with unique and special character, and memorable places.

For HCI, *venustas* is certainly more a concern in interaction design, interface design, user experience design and industrial design. This means Urban HCI also leans more to these disciplines rather than these of ergonomics, usability engineering, cognitive science or psychology (all disciplines of HCI). The closest discipline to architecture in this respect is Ubiquitous Computing as we can recognize from conferences research papers. However, one reason we see for developing the idea of Urban HCI is, that Yong Liu et al. found through an analysis of 15 years long publication period of HUC (Handheld and Ubiquitous Computing), UbiComp and Pervasive conferences, that Ubiquitous Computing is increasingly focusing on mobile devices (Liu et al. 2014). They also predict that sensing-related studies will become increasingly core topics given the increase of sensors available in mobile devices nowadays. This actually means that Ubiquitous Computing moves in the opposite direction. Instead of integrating (digital) beauty (*venustas* as defined above) into architecture/city, it rather abstracts space even further.

In the following, we first compare the differences in spatial thinking between architects and computer scientists. This also serves to narrow down on what scale Urban HCI should focus on to generate an integrated sense of grace as it is understood in architecture. Subsequently we will focus on additional values extracted from various disciplines, which Urban HCI should adopt to enliven and stimulate public space gracefully.

3 Scale in Architecture, Ubiquitous Computing and Urban HCI

In architecture spatial relations between the body and the built environment have been discussed at depth for thousands of years. With dimensioning being considered one of the most important tasks in architecture, it is deeply rooted in the proportions of man. The examples of the Vitruvian Man by Leonardo da Vinci (1490) based on Vitruvius writings (De architectura, 15 BC), the Modulor, devised by Le Corbusier (1934), and the human body after Ernst Neufert (1936) illustrate the relevancy. With knowledge about the Fibonacci sequence (known since ancient times ~300 BC) and an interest in proportions, Adolf Zeising (Zeising 1854) uncovered the universal law that links nature, body and art. In 1854 he for the first time described the Golden Ratio within the proportions of the human body, thus providing an objective measure and usable rule to analyse and intentionally create aesthetic relations in objects, paintings, architecture, based on nature.

Both Le Corbusier and Neufert popularized this ratio in architecture by using it as a foundation found in all nature and the human body. For example, for Neufert qualitative measures, such as harmony in architecture can be linked to the Golden Ratio within the natural body, which eventually constitutes an objective measure.

While in architecture as a discipline aesthetic reasoning through spatial relations was always present, computer science developed spatial concepts independent of aesthetic and without a bodily ground. Mark Weiser's ubiquity of the computers, which "weave themselves into the fabric of everyday life until they are indistinguishable from it" (Weiser 1999), is often envisioned or interpreted as a homogeneous digital layer on our cities rather than emphasizing different densities of digitality, which exists in relation to each other.

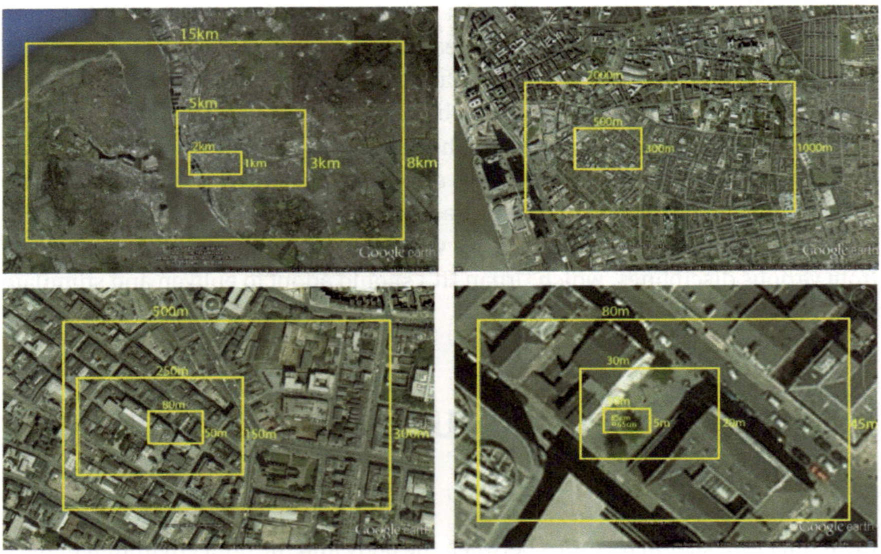

Fig. 2: Scales of the city (Liverpool).

Affecting everything rather than selected environments seemed to drive application developments in Ubiquitous Computing. With mobile phone technology becoming popular in the late 90ies, applications for the city were almost predefined in terms of spatial use. For example, large urban games were developed in HCI from ~2000 on, trying to weave technology more into the city, but actually transferring attention into the virtual realm. While researchers like Adriana de Souza e Silva aim to contextualize these urban mobile phone applications to architecture, there still seems to exist a lack of understanding of how to create harmony between technology (ICT), the body and architecture. In (Silva/Hjorth 2009) de Souza e Silva points out that modes like the haptic and aural (modes often used for urban games using mobiles) override the visual that was so important for Charles Baudelaire's flâneur. By introducing technology into the human-architecture relation, we often seem to interrupt this bond unknowingly. Consuming the city like a flâneur does seems to become secondary. This is exemplified by de Souza e Silva in an historic account (Silva/Hjorth 2009) about urban games like B.U.G (2003), Shoot me if you can (2005), Conquest (2004), Noderunner (2003), Urban Tapestries (2002–2004) (Lane et al. 2005), INP urban vibe, etc. where the city is only used as a game board. However, from her account it is also visible that relations between technology and architecture grew stronger throughout the years using location based technologies or augmented reality to create location-based mobile games (LBMG) like 'Botfight', Geo-Caching like 'Citytag' and hybrid reality games (HRG) like 'Can you see me now?', 'I like Frank', 'Uncle Roy all around you', 'Pacmanhattan' or 'MOGI' (cf. (Benford 2011)).

Fig. 3: City used as a game board for an urban mixed reality game (from Vogiazou et al. 2006).

However, these mobile approaches suffer from shortcomings on various levels to really connect to architectural qualities and promote values in public space. First and foremost it should be realized that mobile phones and the application running on them in itself are creating a space. A second reality that concurrently creates, allows, and/or demands immersion, interaction and imagination. This means that attention is shifted from the real world to the virtual. The harmony between body, architecture and technology becomes shifted in favour of the (often) private and hidden virtual space. This means that, interaction designs of the mobile games tend to exclude or separate the player from the surrounding public life. This happens especially if the game demands continuous attention to be successful in the game. Furthermore, often these LBMG designs misjudge the bodily speed and energetic effort needed to move through space. Often these designs are thought at a scale of up to 1–3 km (compare Figure 2).

However, other technologies than mobile personal computers have grown into the city and became an interest of Ubicomp research. Public displays, projections and media façades are technologies that can match the architectural scale and include the public life at the same time. They have furniture or even building size and provide a visual output at the same scale. This enables a public effect to be established because information is not hidden anymore, as was the case with a mobile phone. Putting issues of light pollution and attention grabbing content aside for the sake of constructively thinking about how to achieve harmony and grace between the body, technology and architecture we find the art form of façade mapping. An original technique fusing technology and architecture in a site-specific beautiful way by using the tactic of mapping (cf. (Urbanscreen)). However, this nowadays popular art form happening in our city has similar problems as the mobile games described by de Souza e Silva had (Silva/Hjorth 2009). It overwrites public space. In addition, the space becomes a cinema-like event, which 'freezes' public life for a moment (Figure 6). As a result, similarly to LBMG, separation among visitors is the effect even though the medium is visible to the public in contrast to the mobile phone. Balancing public life, technology and public space is a concern of Urban HCI (cf. (Urban Media Aesthetics)). Linking the bodily scale through technology to architecture without losing the aspect of public life turns out to be difficult.

In particular, one reason why balance is not achieved might be that the technological communication channel between human and architecture is underdeveloped in respect of interaction between both. Whereas today's technology provides large scale displays in the form of bright projectors, high resolution LED matrices, lighting or motorized façade elements, the input channel is somewhat underrepresented. More interfaces need to be developed which support a many-to-many communication supported by architecture and technology. This balancing seems to happen now as we see more books like this one being published. While computer scientist's lacked an understanding of space and created virtual spaces that detach people from the public space and bring them to an alternate one, architects found it hard to imagine how to gracefully integrate media technology into space. In the last ten years, both disciplines moved closer together; researchers from Ubiquitous Computing are starting to understand space at an architectural scale, public life and public space more and architects are starting to integrate interfaces to their designs (e.g. Behrens et al. (Behrens et al. 2014)) to balance out mono-directed communication channels of media architecture with novel interfaces.

Fig. 4: Site-specific façade mapping 'freezes' public life for a moment.

At a pragmatic level for Urban HCI thinking, we propose to limit the scale at which it makes sense to attempt to balance public life, technology and built environment (architectural configurations) to a maximum of a 50 × 50 meter urban setting (compare Figure 2, bottom right). This is roughly the distance at which we found social interaction supported through Media Architecture can be achieved. It is also a distance at which the human senses to perceive each other still work well. In Jan Gehl's book "Life Between Buildings" the *social field of vision*, as he calls it, is specified between 0–100 m. At a distance of 100m human individuals can be seen. Between 70–100 m it becomes possible to determine with reasonable certainty a person's approximate age, sex and what the person is doing (Gehl 2011, p. 65). To perceive people as individuals a much shorter distance of about 30 m is needed. Facial features, and hairstyle can be recognized and at 20–25 m feelings and moods of others become visible and relevant in a social context. All relevant features to be respected for a design of a lively or social situation. It also illustrates how 'absolute' measures of the body should be respected when designing space, whether being an architect or technologist.

From our experience with over 40 deployments of urban installations over the last seven years the 50 × 50 m situation is a good limitation to balance human activity, technology, and the environment, also because night time reduces the human senses (almost all of our media interventions only work in darkness as they used projection or similar) and technologies are also developed with limitations in range (e.g. WIFI, Pixel, etc.). From now, the term *50 × 50 m urban setting* refers to structures of the city (environment), which provide the space for the human activity (e.g. public life, interaction with the system, etc.). The term *50 × 50 m setting* includes the technical setup or 'interactive system' in addition to the environment and the *50 × 50 m situation* includes activity of the people in addition to environment and setup. The term marks the upper boundary of space at which we experienced a balancing of interaction to be feasible. Interaction for lager scales then moves towards crowd-computer interaction (see (Veerasawmy/Mccarthy 2014)) considering sizes of a football stadium (approx. 150–200 m) or neighbourhoods.

4 Content and Values

In the prior section we have shown what scale the idea of Urban HCI focuses on. The recalibration of Ubiquitous Computing technologies to a street level is also a concern of the architect Malcolm McCullough, who, in his book "Digital Ground" (McCullough 2005) contrasts universal technology with situated technology as follows:

Tab. 1: Universal versus situated computing (McCullough 2005, p. 67).

Universal	Situated
Anytime-anyplace	Reactive environments
Mostly portable	Integrated in the environment
Ad hoc aggregation	Accumulated aggregation
Context is location	Context is activity
Instead of architecture	Inside of architecture
Fast and far	Slow and close
Uniform	Adapted

In some respect, this comparison also summarizes the value technology creates in Ubiquitous Computing in contrast to Urban HCI. For the notion of Urban HCI and a better balance of public life, technology and built environment, the situated properties should guide new designs of interactive systems for public space. Conscious decisions regarding situatedness not only concern software and interaction design, but also interface design (physical form and hardware design). Much of Ubiquitous Computing seems to have adopted the notion of mobile phones as a universal interface.

Fig. 5: Technology creating an alternative space with limited social dynamics (from Cheok et al. 2007).

Various HCI publications focus on the combination of the mobile phone and public displays or media façades: (Boring et al. 2011), (Martin et al. 2006), (Luojus et al. 2013), (Scheible/Ojala 2005), (Böhmer et al. 2011), (Gehring/Krüger 2012). However, the mobile phone interface disembodies valuable information situated in a public space. For example, BlogWall (Cheok et al. 2007) displays a user's SMS in an animated manner and creates poetry from these. The authors describe this as "an extension of existing text messaging to a new level of self-expression and public communication using mobile phones and public displays." and "... a step into new forms of cultural computing". Although the designers of BlogWall found a smart way to create interesting content, the design stops short of thinking about the activity in front of the screen. Figure 5 shows the situation, which seems to separate the people in front of the screen by the use of the mobile. The social dynamics are shifted to an alternative space (the virtual). An interface, which is part of the physical space (e.g. a simple keyboard or touch-screen) would have created some activity around it and the social dynamics would have been more integrated into the environment. Using the mobile for this interaction design removes visible cues that provide opportunities to e.g. learn from a person or to provide fun or pleasure to watch for others. The disembodiment of information provided by an activity can be seen as reducing value for a public space. Even though the activity generated by BlogWall might be still visible and meaningful for bystanders, the reduction of information becomes more problematic at greater distances typical for urban settings.

Fig. 6: Spatial design creating multifaceted social dynamics.

The open question to ask is: Why should activity be visible? A part of the answer is already been given; "context is activity" (Table 1, right hand side). Without activity the system does not provide context. But this is important for a situation design, which aims to include people at a 50 × 50 m scale. From the urbanist William H. Whyte (Whyte 1988) we know that people like to watch other people and he names it the number one activity in public space. Furthermore, Carr et al. lists a number of *passive engagements*. For example, *observing* and *viewing* is named as providing values for public spaces (Carr et al. 1992, p. 320). They provide design recommendations for the needs of people in public places such as: "Good places to watch passing scene, people.", "Overall views, well-framed vistas." or "Good places to watch performers". The idea of designing for observers has already been translated into HCI in Reeves' account on "Designing the spectator experience" (Reeves et al. 2005) in public installations. Carr et al. (Carr et al. 1992, p. 320) also list values promoted by active engagement such as play, communication and discovery; general goals of making public space. How passive and *active engagement* and discovery can translate to HCI systems has been shown by Nemanja

Memarovic et al. in (Memarovic et al. 2012). Thus, exposing context through activity might be a better design strategy for a 50 × 50 m situation than to conceal activity. Similarly, and to summarize in McCullough's words, "architectural elements of physical space often frame and cue actions." and Ubiquitous Computing should question the sufficient representation of action; "Who is present, and what are they trying to do?" (McCullough 2005, p. 100). In a situated design, values become embedded in physical structures such as places to socialize (eating, drinking, talking), places to meet (gathering), places for seeing and being seen (cruising), places for insider (belonging) (McCullough 2005, p. 120), etc.

Designing activity in a visible way can be used to create *situations*. This is one fundamental concept in Goffman's studies of social interaction besides the two other central concepts of the *social occasion* and the *gathering* (encounter). In "Behaviour in Public Places" Goffman refers to a situation as a "full spatial environment anywhere within which an entering person becomes a member of the gathering that is (or does then become) present. Situations begin when mutual monitoring occurs, and lapse when the second-last person has left" (Goffman 1966, p. 18).

In Urban HCI this is the 50 × 50 m situation, which is to be designed. One value generated by a situation design, which goes beyond the design for the observer (Reeves et al. 2005) is based on Goffman's concept of gathering (encounter). That is, "...any set of two or more individuals whose members include all and only those who are at the moment in one another's immediate presence." (Goffman 1966, p. 18). This definition has been extended to the concept of *shared encounters*. Defined by Willis et al. a shared encounter is "the interaction between two people or within a group where a sense of performative co-presence is experienced and which is characterised by mutual recognition of spatial or social proximity." (Willis et al. 2010, p. 4).

The technological aspect for this concept is introduced by the definition of Ava Fatah gen. Schieck et al. "...a digital encounter is an ephemeral form of communication and interaction augmented by technology." (Schieck et al. 2010, p. 180).

To give an example of a shared/digital encounter we refer to two very similar situation designs. In both situations public displays were evaluated in-the-wild. However, the installations had slightly different spatial interaction/interface designs, one using touch input (Behrens et al. 2013), and the other gestural input (Mueller et al. 2012).

While both provided interesting content for the users, the emerging activity constructs different situations. In the situation shown in Figure 7 (Behrens et al. 2013) the bystanders (2) and (5) have no opportunity to enter into *immediate presence* or *co-presence* (criteria of a shared encounter) with the performers (1). They need to wait to experience the installation (actively). Figure 8 shows a

Fig. 7: Situation design limits possibilities of shared encounters (image from Behrens et al. 2013).

Fig. 8: Situation design enabling shared encounters (image from Mueller et al. 2012).

girl from group (A) noticing interactivity first, then woman (B) positions herself behind them to see what happens and also starts interacting, and later couple (C) starts to interact in a third row (Mueller et al. 2012). Even though they might not talk to each other, they experience an *ephemeral form of communication produced through technology* (digital shared encounter). This example shows space-making should also be a concern of designers of 'interactive systems'. Creating co-awareness among strangers in an ephemeral social situation is certainly a valuable asset for the public space. The value is created within the encounter, not primarily through the content. Returning to the earlier discussion of the disembodiment of information with activity created by interfaces such as mobile phones (Figure 5), these two examples show in contrast a design of embodying information into activity, which might also provide more pleasure to watch for others, similar to a situation in Figure 6, where little stories by peoples' activity within the fountain fog emerge. This also completes Goffman's framework mentioned earlier. Installations like these can create *social occasions*, "this is a wider social affair [...] bounded in regard to place and time. [...] a *social occasion* provides the structuring of social context in which many situations and their gatherings [encounters; note by the authors] are likely to form, dissolve, and re-form, while a pattern of conduct tends to be recognized as the appropriate [...]" (Goffman 1966, p. 18). Diffuse *social occasions* can develop a structure, for example be unserious, recreational, serious, regular, they can be looked forward to, looked back upon as a whole.

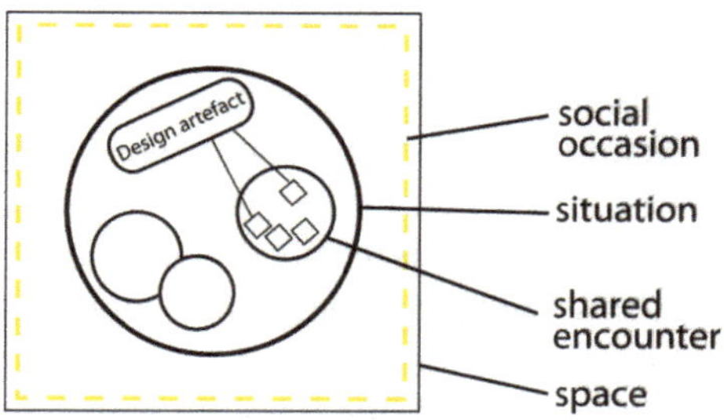

Fig. 9: Adapted concepts of social interaction (Goffman 1966).

The public display example above also shows how a careful interface/interaction design (with visible activity) can have a self-reinforcing effect even though 'only' a public display application has been designed and not a full architectural configuration. Müller's et al. (Figure 8) example demonstrated how one initial single performer can extend the situation and draw in others.

There are also greater implications to expect from a good situation design. For example, Tanenbaum's sociological studies in the subways of New York (Tanenbaum 1995) showed that crime rates tend to go down in areas where buskers regularly perform. Situation designs that promote small forms of social encounters might have similar impact. Digital designs, which foster small-talk between strangers, sharing a playful experience or creating a social occasion to play, might have similar influence, a value for our cities worth to explore.

A Shared Encounter is only one concept posing a concrete value for public space. It is a measurable and countable phenomenon which can be provoked by carefully designed Media Architecture. However, to understand at an operational level how to construct such a phenomenon, it is necessary to understand spatial design as well as how ICT influences public live within that space.

5 Summary and Conclusion

This chapter illustrated the granularity at which Urban HCI re-considers space as a resource for and product of new media artefacts in our city. It established an understanding of the difference between Ubiquitous Computing and Urban HCI by contrasting possible scales of mobile phone applications and the scale of the urban environment. To balance technology, public life, and architecture within the city, we proposed to focus on a max. 50 × 50 m situation, as it provides a scale at which this can be achieved on a practical level. Situations bigger than that tend to become mobile or distributed applications detached from the present setting. Creating a balance is a desirable endeavour to avoid an overwriting of urban places and segregating people as a result. However, there are also new strategies in the development, which might overcome the limitations of the 50 × 50 m situation. On a similar scale urban planning is operating, M. Hank Haeusler proposes in the following chapter an interaction paradigm based on the typology of the city. This provides the potential to bring ways of thinking of the architect and the computer scientist closer to each other. For architects it is abstracting from place and for creators of ICT it is reducing abstraction. This might lead to a common ground of developers and create distributed systems with an identity.

Urban design values such as providing vitality and stimulation for the dweller should lead the way. Urban design lists a plethora of ways how to increase the quality of a certain space (cf. (Carmona et al. 2010)), from which it is difficult to derive a specific direction as settings often have unique character difficult to code for as the complexity is too high and interpretation very subjective especially without formal architectural training. Here, William H. Whyte points to a valuable insight which provides focus: “People like to watch other people.” (Whyte 1988). We suggested to focus on the concept of shared encounters as a concrete value to enrich everyday life by design. In theory this could also lead to a measure of how valuable an ‘interactive system’ is, on the basis of how many shared encounters it produces. However, in the first place it has to be found out, what makes these shared encounters tick? While encounters have been explored in sociology by Goffman and other researchers, HCI currently explores how digital encounters might be produced and what types exist. Two examples of public displays showed how different interface/interaction designs create different situations with and without shared encounters happening. The reason seems to largely depend on the different spatial uses/designs of both installations and a self-reinforcing effect, where one activity sparks another activity to happen; extending a situation (sometimes also unintended). Thus the further focus of our research is directed toward understanding the 'production' of space through media interventions and the study of urban 50 × 50 m situations. With reference to Lefebvre, "If space is produced, our knowledge of it must be expected to reproduce and expound the process of production. The 'object' of interest must be expected to shift from *things in space* to the actual *production of space* [...]" (Lefebvre 1991, p. 36f).

Bibliography

Altman, M. (2009): TV-B-Gone.

Assocreation (2014): Solar Pink Pong. Dubai.

Behrens, M.; Schieck, A.F.g.; Kostopoulou, E.; North, S.; Motta, W.; Ye, L.; Schnadelbach, H. (2013): "Exploring the effect of spatial layout on mediated urban interactions". In: PerDis'13, Mountain View, California, 2013. New York: ACM, 79–84.

Behrens, M.; Valkanova, N.; Schieck, A.F.g.; Brumby, D.P. (2014): Smart Citizen Sentiment Dashboard: A Case Study Into Media Architectural Interfaces. Paper presented at the PerDis'14, Copenhagen, Denmark.

Benford, S. (2011): Performing Mixed Reality. Cambridge, MA: The MIT Press.

Böhmer, M.; Gehring, S.; Löchtefeld, M.; Ostkamp, M.; Bauer, G. (2011): "The Mighty Untouchables – Creating Playful Engagement on Media Façades". In: Mobile HCI, 2011. New York: ACM, 605–610.

Borden, I. (2001): Skateboarding, Space and the City. Oxford u.a.: Berg.

Boring, S.; Gehring, S.; Wiethoff, A.; Bloeckner, A.M.; Schoening, J.; Butz, A. (2011): "Multi-user interaction on media facades through live video on mobile devices". In: CHI, 2011. New York: ACM, 2712–2724.

Carmona, M.; Tiesdell, S.; Heath, T. (2010): Public Places Urban Spaces: The Dimensions of Urban Design. Oxford: Architectural Press.

Carr, S.; Francis, M.; Rivlin, L.G.; Stone, A.M. (1992): Public Space. Cambridge: Cambridge University Press.

Cheok, A.D.; Mustafa, A.-u.-R.; Fernando, O.N.N.; Barthoff, A.-K.; Wijesena, J.P.; Tosa, N. (2007): BlogWall: displaying artistic and poetic messages on public displays via SMS. Paper presented at the the 9th International Conference on Human Computer Interaction with Mobile Devices and Services, Singapore.

Davies, N.; Langheinrich, M.; Jose, R.; Schmidt, A. (2012): "Open Display Networks: A Communications Medium for the 21st Century". Computer 45:5, 58–64.

Gehl, J. (2011): Life Between Buildings: Using Public Space. Washington: Island Press.

Gehring, S.; Krüger, A. (2012): "Using media facades to engage social interaction". In: UbiComp'12, 2012. New York: ACM, 794–795.
Goffman, E. (1966): Behaviour in Public Places. New York: The Free Press.
Kostakos, V.; Ojala, T. (2013): "Public Displays Invade Urban Spaces". IEEE Pervasive Computing 12:1, 8–13.
Lane, G.; Thelwall, S.; Angus, A.; Peckett, V.; West, N. (2005): Urban Tapestries – Public Authoring, Place and Mobility. London: Proboscis.
Lefebvre, H. (1991): The production of space. Oxford: Blackwell Publishing Ltd.
Liu, Y.; Goncalves, J.; Ferreira, D.; Hosio, S.; Kostakos, V. (2014): Identity crisis of ubicomp?: mapping 15 years of the field's development and paradigm change. Paper presented at the the 2014 ACM International Joint Conference on Pervasive and Ubiquitous Computing, Seattle, Washington.
Lojewski, H.v. (2014): Das Thema "Smart City" richtig einordnen! Wiesbaden: Springer.
Luojus, P.; Koskela, J.; Ollila, K.; Mäki, S.-M.; Kulpa-Bogossia, R.; Heikkinen, T.; Ojala, T. (2013): Wordster: collaborative versus competitive gaming using interactive public displays and mobile phones. Paper presented at the PerDisp'13, Mountain View, California.
Martin, K.; Penn, A.; Gavin, L. (2006): Engaging with a situated display via picture messaging. Paper presented at the CHI '06, Montreal, Quebec, Canada.
McCullough, M. (2005): Digital Ground. Cambridge: MIT Press.
Memarovic, N.; Langheinrich, M.; Alt, F.; Elhart, I.; Hosio, S.; Rubegni, E. (2012): Using public displays to stimulate passive engagement, active engagement, and discovery in public spaces. Paper presented at the MAB'12 Aarhus, Denmark.
Mueller, J.; Walter, R.; Bailly, G.; Nischt, M.; Alt, F. (2012): "Looking Glass: A Field Study on Noticing Interactivity of Shop Windows". In: CHI'12, 2012. New York: ACM, 297–306.
Oliver, J. (2008–2010): The Artvertiser. Berlin.
Reeves, S.; Benford, S.; O'Malley, C.; Fraser, M. (2005): Designing the spectator experience. Paper presented at the CHI, Portland, Oregon, USA.
Scheible, J.; Ojala, T. (2005): MobiLenin combining a multi-track music video, personal mobile phones and a public display into multi-user interactive entertainment. Paper presented at the the 13th annual ACM International Conference on Multimedia, Hilton, Singapore.
Schieck, A.F.g.; Kostakos, V.; Penn, A. (2010): "Exploring Digital Encounters in the Public Arena". In: K.S. Willis; G. Roussos; K. Chorianopulos; M. Struppek (eds.) Shared Encounters. London: Springer, 179–195.
Schroeter, R. (2012): "Engaging New Digital Locals with Interactive Urban Screens to Collaboratively Improve the City". In: CSCW '12, 2012. New York: ACM, 227–236.
Silva, A.d.S.e.; Hjorth, L. (2009): "Playful Urban Spaces". Simulation & Gaming 40:5, 602–625.
SKULLPHONE X-SKULLPHONE. www.skullphone.com. 2014.
Streitz, N. (2011): "Smart Cities, Ambient Intelligence and Universal Access". In: C. Stephanidis (ed.): Universal Access in HCI. Berlin: Springer, 425–432.
Tanenbaum, S.J. (1995): Underground Harmonies: Music and Politics in the Subway of New York. New York: Cornell University Press.
Urban Media Aesthetics. urbanmediaaesthetics.org. 2014.
Urbanscreen Urbanscreen – Site specific projections. www.urbanscreen.com.
Veerasawmy, R.; Mccarthy, J. (2014): "When noise becomes voice: designing interactive technology for crowd experiences through imitation and invention". Personal and Ubiquitous Computing 18:7, 1601–1615.

Vogiazou, Y.; Raijmakers, B.; Geelhoed, E.; Reid, J.; Eisenstadt, M. (2006): “Design for emergence: experiments with a mixed reality urban playground game”. Personal and Ubiquitous Computing 11:1, 45–58.
Weiser, M. (1999): “The Computer in the 21st Century”. SIGMOBILE Mobile Computing and Communications 3:3, 3–11.
Whyte, W.H. (1988): The Social Life of Small Urban Spaces. New York: Project for Public Spaces.
Willis, K.S.; Roussos, G.; Chorianopulos, K.; Struppek, M. (2010): “Shared Encounters”. In: K.S. Willis, G. Roussos, K. Chorianopulos, M. Struppek (eds.): Shared Encounters. London: Springer, 1–15.
Zeising, A. (1854): Proportionen des menschlichen Körpers, aus einem bisher unerkannt gebliebenen, die ganze Natur und Kunst durchdringenden morphologischen Grundgesetze. Leipzig: Rudolph Weigel.
Zheng, Y.; Capra, L.; Wolfson, O.; Yang, H. (2014): “Urban Computing: Concepts, Methodologies, and Applications”. ACM Transactions on Intelligent Systems and Technology 5:3, 1–55.

Matthias Hank Haeusler

From Allopoietic Content to Autopoietic Content for Media Architecture through a Better Understanding of Architectural Typologies

1 Background

One of the pioneers of applying cybernetic thinking, architect Cedric Price, famously asserted that *"Technology is the answer, but what was the question?"*. This phrase also became the title of a 1966 lecture in which he asserted that *"architect[s] must undertake extensive research in order to truly understand and adequately respond to a project's requirements."* (Canadian Centre for Architecture 2015) The chapter recalls this lecture title and Price's views in order to highlight two topics relevant to this publication.

Firstly, but only very briefly, I will outline that while the field of media architecture has for the last decade considered 'technology' as 'the answer', more recently it has moved away from this approach to replace the quest with 'content'.

Secondly, and making this the primary focus of this chapter, I argue that 'content' alone is – as much as 'technology' was – an insufficient answer. 'Content' alone does not specify what is required from media architecture, and only describes a wide field of opportunities for moving or static text, graphics or images. Thus it is necessary to address what the question(s) might be.

1.1 Media architecture causality

For the last decade, media architecture has focused on 'technology' as 'the answer'. In my 2009 publication *Media Façades – History, Technology, Content* (Haeusler 2009) I defined through the title a causality – understood as a relation between cause and effect – that accords *Technology* as the first event that is responsible for *Content*. The motivation for establishing this causality had its origins with the development of a taxonomy that classified the new field of media architecture. Other investigations at the time, such as the Media Architecture Conference at Central Saint Martins Innovation in September 2007 in London, also confirmed the prioritisation of technology. This is expressed by the Media Architecture Conference homepage that stated:

DOI 10.1515/9783110453874-004

> Developments in display technology and building materials are leading to new forms of hybrid architecture that break away from existing conceptions of surface, structure, lighting and moving imagery. Light Emitting Diode (LED) displays integrated with the fabric of built structures allow prominent imagery to be integrated with the façade, even in direct sunlight. Although energy requirements are practical only when displays are used in less bright conditions, there remain significant consequences for the townscape and urban environment; cinematic utopias as pervasive as Minority Report and Blade Runner have become technically feasible. (Mediaarchitecture.com 2007)

One could argue that media architecture's initial pre-occupation with technology lay principally in its novelty, as by the end of the 20th century it was possible to produce large-scale RGB LED screens. In other words, the technology was new and hence offered a large area of exploration and development (Simpson 1997).

Within the first decade of the 21st century, a vast majority of economic and technological challenges of building large-scale RGB LED screens were overcome. The 2012 book *New Media Facades – A global survey* (Haeusler et al. 2012) documented how one could build media facades in virtually any part of the world. Here the aspect of the title 'global survey' suggests that *Space* had taken an important role as the book aimed to study cultural and regional differences in the design of media facades. I would therefore argue that after *Technology*, *Space* has become increasingly critical to the way media architecture is understood – and consequently developed by architects and designers.

Subsequently as no media façade can operate without *Content*, one could argue for the causality of *Technology* (existence of LED screens) → *Space* (applying LED screens in built environment) → *Content* (designing visual imagery) as a common way of designing media architecture in the first decade of the 21st century.

Recent debates in media architecture at conferences, summits from 2010 onwards, and in several discussions amongst the authors represented in this publication, have highlighted that this causality prevents more meaningful progress in the field. The reason for this is manifold. Firstly, the focus on technology as a driver for media architecture is in contradiction with the construction process of the AEC (Architecture Engineering Construction) industry. Most buildings that incorporate large LED screens in their building skin take years from preliminary design to completion; hence state of the art LED technology specified at the preliminary design stage is outdated by the completion date of the project. Secondly, and as a further argument against technology, is that cities, and particular those located in Asia, now host an increasing number of large screens, rendering media architecture as no longer novel but rather ubiquitous. While the sensation and spectacle of the new and novel large screen, as for example the Fremont Street Experience Las Vegas which opened in 2004 with 12.5 million LEDs, might continue to be effective in a casino city context, this is not necessarily the case in most other everyday places and cities.

Consequently, the view of many stakeholders and scholars in the media architecture field has been to 'flip' the accepted causality of *Technology* → *Space* → *Content*. This flip productively reorganizes the design process as *Content* (to design experiences that reflect the needs and interests of citizens) → *Space* (to reflect location, cultural and political parameters) → *Technology* (to use appropriate technologies to achieve the first two goals).

2 The challenge of content

The following discussion lays out the argument that for media architecture, 'content' alone is, as much as 'technology' was, the wrong answer. To do this I will briefly outline both what has been meant by content in the context of media architecture and new content methods. In *Media Facades – History, Technology, Content* (Haeusler 2009) I defined three key forms of content: Pre-recorded Content (dynamic text, graphic, or images displayed by the media façade), Live Content (dynamic images – i.e. sports events in real time) and Interactive Content. While the first two require little explanation, the later category of Interactive Content is often misunderstood in the context of media architecture projects. Often media architecture projects are described as 'interactive', when in reality they are simply 'participatory', or 'reactive'. In these projects, participation is enabled through sensors, cameras, microphones or devices such as a Microsoft Kinect. In various ways, these technologies allow the viewer to 'participate' in the media architecture content, such as by changing its appearance, i.e. the colour or the image, by registering the user's movement, such as with a camera or Kinect system that translates such movement to media content, or translating the detection of sound into images, similar to an equalizer in sound to different and visualise frequencies. Interactivity on the other hand is defined by a series of responses, and critically, a relationship between these responses. Rafaeli (1988) describes interactivity as,

> ... an expression of the extent that in a given series of communication exchanges, any third (or later) transmission (or message) is related to the degree to which previous exchanges referred to even earlier transmissions.

Regardless of these clarifications of content type, in many media architecture projects design discussions with clients often centre on the notion of interactive content, yet the outcomes are more likely to be participatory or responsive. In either case, the intense focus on interaction, interactivity, participation and responsiveness, overlooks the potential to specify what the media architecture project might actually display. This approach merely aims for participation and a potential feedback loop to alter the content's appearance through information communication technologies. Typically this is a change of media screen colours enabled through a web cam or a Kinect sensor, which as well as technology before, has often lost its 'novel' factor in contemporary fixed installations or temporary light festivals such as the annual Vivid Lights Festival in Sydney.

In any case, content in all forms – pre-recorded, live, participatory or interactive has one main challenge, particularly for fixed media facades; one needs a lot of content to run a screen successfully. In either the 'traditional' causality of *Technology → Space → Content* or when placing *Content* at the forefront of the discussion – a media façade needs approximately 8000 hours of content per year to display an engaging program (as is the case at Federation Square, Melbourne). The main challenge of the content issue becomes then curation and management, and thereby the requirement for a type of TV production studio associated with each screen. Achieving this for each single media facade or urban screen in a city, country or globally is extremely challenging for any designer or design team. Consequently screens often display the same content repeatedly, causing the public to pay limited attention, or even to completely ignore the screen (Huang; Koster; Borchers 2008) a phenomenon that has been previously described as display blindness (Müller et al. 2009).

3 From allopoietic to autopoietic content

3.1 Autopoietic content

To overcome these challenges a question to ask is how content is conceived and produced? In most cases of pre-recorded, live, participatory or interactive content, content is generated and designed by something *other than itself*, to be precise a designer or a team of designers, film producers, artists, etc. As already mentioned, the design of sufficient content for media architecture can be time and cost intensive, hence it is sensible to investigate other methods of design in generating a large amount of content. One approach to this, it is argued here, is to take better advantage of the already high saturation of sensors, actuators, and computers in media architecture and through sensors to transform each media façade into a machine that can generate content *by itself*. The two concepts of *other than itself* and *by itself* are briefly explained in the following.

In science, engineering or designing a shift from a 'system', 'object' or 'form' that is developed or created by something other than itself is often referred by the Greek *allos (ἄλλος)*, meaning 'other, different, strange' in comparison to the Greek *autós (αὐτός)*, meaning 'self'. Exemplary for this use of *allos* or *autós* is an essay in architecture named *Aegis hyposurface: autoplastic to allo-plastic* by Mark Goulthorpe (1999) where he adds the suffix *plastós (πλαστός)*, meaning 'formed or molded' to discuss a "continuity of creative process into manufacture" which "offers a precision without determinism or without auto-determinism" hence defining

> Autoplastic [as] being a determinate, fixed environment – one 'designs', auto-dictates – and alloplastic [as] an indeterminate, open description, a reciprocal relation between environment and self. (Goulthorpe 1999)

Given this, one can argue in the case of media architecture to date, that various types of content have been primarily designed by someone *other than itself* (i.e. a designer) and could therefore be classified as *allopoietic content*, using the suffix *poiesis* (ποίησις), etymologically derived from the ancient term (ποιέω), which means "to make". If on the other hand content is generated *by itself*, one would refer to this as *autopoietic content.*[1]

In the publication *Autopoiesic content: A conceptual model for enabling situated self-generative content for public displays*, Langheinrich et al. (2011) introduced the idea of autopoietic content as a conceptual model for enabling situated self-generative content for public displays. Here they traced the concept of autopoiesis back to cognitive biology where in the early 1970s two biologists, Maturana and Varela, discussed autopoiesis as a system capable of reproducing and maintaining itself (Maturana and Varela 1980). For Maturana and Varela the autopoietic machine is,

> ... a machine organized (defined as a unity) as a network of processes of production (transformation and destruction) of components which: (i) through their interactions and transformations continuously regenerate and realize the network of processes (relations) that produced them; and (ii) constitute it (the machine) as a concrete unity in space in which they (the components) exist by specifying the topological domain of its realization as such a network.

---

1 I will continue using the 'poietic' as an adjective for 'poiesis' as Maturana and Varela used this form of spelling in their publication in 1973, Langheinrich et al. on the other hand used the adjective 'poiesis' in their writing.

The term of autopoeisis was also adopted in the mid-1970s by the German sociologist Niklas Luhmann to explain aspects of his systems theory. Maturana later disagreed with Luhmann on the correct use of the term. In the context of this chapter the sociological adaptation of autopoeisis in relation to communication is considered to more closely aligned with the interests of media architecture than its origin in cognitive biology. Consequently this chapter adopts Luhmann's reading of the term autopoiesis.

For Luhmann (1975) a system is defined by the boundary between itself and the environment. A system in its interior is reduced in its complexity; the exterior (environment) on the other hand is defined through its infinitive complex and chaotic nature. Important for Luhmann is that communication within a system operates by selecting only a limited amount of all information available in the environment, a process he calls the "reduction of complexity" (Luhmann 1982). Luhmann stresses the importance of the reduction of complexity as he associates with each system a 'distinctive identity of the system' that is constantly reproduced in its communication. The aspect of identity also helps to identify what is meaningful for the system and what is not. Consequently if a system fails to maintain that identity, it ceases to exist as a system and dissolves back into the environment. This process is what Luhmann defines as autopoiesis, a reproduction from elements previously filtered from an over-complex environment.

This is important to this discussion of directing media architecture towards autopoietic content generation as this 'reduction of complexity' is useful in (1) limiting what system we want to establish; (2) in what environment the system operates and (3) what information the system selects from its environment. Again when moving from allopoietic to autopoietic content a "reduction of complexity" and a "distinctive identity of the system" (Luhmann 1982) help to define the boundary, an aspect I will return to shortly.

Returning to the research of Memarovic, Langheinrich and Elhart (2011a, b) on autopoietic content, the authors acknowledge that their motivation for moving to an autopoietic content model follows the argument presented here concerning cost and time factors. They state that,

> One of the reasons these displays are not showing customized information that resonates with their particular location and surrounding space is the high cost associated with creating tailored content (Alt et al. 2011).

They further assert that,

> We believe that the idea of [such] self-sufficiency can also be used to shape future public display systems, be offering an economic way of turning today's often ignored large pub-

> lic display systems into more appreciated (and more noticed) services (Langheinrich et al. 2011).

In two subsequent key papers a conceptual model for enabling situated self-generative content for public display is set out by Langheinrich et al. (2011), and initial experiences with autopoietic content are described by Memarovic et al. (2011). More specifically, Langheinrich (2011) outlines a framework for categorizing autopoietic content into three classes as:
- "*Content visualization*, i.e. content created from local context information,
- *Content connection*, i.e. content created by either sourcing or exchanging content from/with related spaces, and
- *Content integration*, where content is created by combining local context streams with existing content fragments using matching templates". (Langheinrich 2011)

In a follow-up paper the research team acknowledges that in developing a first autopoietic content,

> The first two classes of autopoiesic content, i.e., context visualisation and context connection, have been explored to a certain extent. (Memarovic 2011)

Previously, Schmidt and Gellersen (2001) have described content visualisation examples including coloured orbs showing stock trends (ambient orb), water fountains indicating exchange rates (Datafountain), or lamps indicating web site access numbers. Yet, it is argued here that the aforementioned content visualisation examples are those that contribute to the phenomena of public display blindness as outlined by Müller et al. (2009) and Huang et al. (2008). According to Memarovic et al. (2011), people increasingly seek to see "personalised and situated content". While it could be debated that the above mentioned content visualisations could be 'personalised', it is argued here that they do not consider the following two points.

Firstly, the authors state that,

> This [personalised and situated content] could be provided through a menu where people could choose their preferred category in addition to choosing if content type should be local or global. (Memarovic et al. 2011)

This reference to "local or global content type" contradicts Luhmann's (1982) understanding of autopoietic as a 'reduction of complexity'. Equally, Luhmann associates with each system a 'distinctive identity of the system' that is constantly reproduced in its communication – a key point in generating an autopoietic system.

Secondly, this overlooks how public space and the surrounding building typologies already provide a distinctive identity to be used to generate autopoietic content. Memarovic et al. (2011) acknowledge that,

> While some ... [large public displays] are presenting contextualized information that reflects their surroundings, e.g. train schedules and university talks, a large majority is simply displaying traditional advertising, such as short commercials, slideshows, or simple images. (Memarovic et al. 2011)

Yet in their own case study of the development of the Fun Square Project, the same authors indicate they failed to present sufficient "contextualized information that reflects their surroundings" (Memarovic et al. 2011). This project instead collected local fun facts that locals associate with places or objects nearby, or in the immediate area, a point they state in the discussion of the paper as,

> Although autopoiesic content connects local information from the display surrounding with information from without, some people wanted to get content that is even more connected within the locality. Some people even wanted to get *localized content on specific topic*, e.g., information about local politics, events, or history. With two parameters, topic and locality, categorizing content becomes difficult. (Memarovic et al. 2011)

At this point I want to point out two assumptions in order to extend the research undertaken by Memarovic et al. (2011). Firstly, media architecture and media facades are by definition part of architecture and the urban condition. Secondly, and the primary focus of the following section of this chapter, is that architecture can be defined through typology, and typologies produce the local condition in an urban setting (i.e. the business district through the 'office' typology or the shopping district through the 'shops and retail' typology). Based on this, Memarovic et al.'s (2011) problem of categorizing content via two parameters, topic and locality, can be reimagined through the concept of typology, where typology is understood to also define locality. Yet, how is typology defined in the context of the architectural discipline and what is its relationship to autopoietic content?

3.2 Typology in architecture

Typology is defined as a classification according to general type. In architecture and urban design typology functions as a taxonomic classification of types. Moore and Wilson (2014) argue that

> The modern concept of type has alternately been used as a method to classify both building functions – hospital, bank, house, museum, etc. – as well as building morphologies – courtyards linear, tower, block, ziggurat, etc.

The concept of architectural type has been subject of many studies spanning at least four hundred years and includes architectural scholars such as J. F. Blondel (1705–1774), Quatremère de Quincy (1775–1849), and Gottfried Semper (1803–1879). Modern typologies have been discussed and articulated as system by Nikolaus Pevsner in *A History of Building Types* around 1930 (Pevsner, 1979). On Pevsner's account, Moore and Wilson (2014) argue that,

> The significance of Pevsner's insight is a major contribution to the formation of sociotechnical codes – it is to recognise that buildings are an index of changing *social organisations* as well as changing *social tastes*. Buildings are, then, technologies [...] designed to assist us in our effort to make the world a better or richer place.

Further they note that

> [t]he adoption of a recognised building typology by a patron is, then, to accept the social agenda of that type as a tool necessary to satisfy normal social activities ... That the existence of architectural types that emerge over time – in response to changing social, ecological, and economical conditions – precedes the agency of individual designers.

Thus both Pevsner's (1979) and Moore and Wilson's (2014) positions support the argument that typology solves Memarovic et al.'s (2011) problem of categorizing content via the two parameters of topic and locality – as one can equal "social organisations" and "social activities" with topic and "buildings function" as a driver to the local character or locality.

Yet, how can applying the concept of typology in the context of autopoietic content for media architecture prove productive? Seen through the lens of both typology and autopoeisis, the following three observations regarding media architecture can be made:

1) Media architecture can be more than just a screen when augmented by other digital technologies such as sensors, actuators, and ICT systems (Haeusler 2009, 2011).

2) When equipping building skins with screens and digital technologies one can argue that a building equals an autonomous system, able to sense and collect data. This data can then be processed into information to communicate to other buildings or humans to generate new knowledge about the building itself or the urban context (Haeusler 2011).

In the case of media architecture currently, communication occurs mainly from the building to humans, but not yet from a building to a building. Yet if systems become increasingly autonomous and buildings can be autonomous systems – where buildings communicate with buildings – the argument here is that their dialogs can constitute autopoietic content. The implementation of this autopoietic strategy for media architecture, however, requires addressing further questions. In order to communicate information between buildings, buildings need not only to know what data to collect, and how to process this data into productive information. More importantly, a building should know and understand what another building is interested in and what a building does not need or want to know. To further outline this point, consider an example from a human context, presented in a simplified story taken out of a situation in daily life. Imagine a social gathering where a soccer fan and a fine arts lover want to discuss and communicate their interests to each other. Each party may seek to stimulate interest in their specific subject from the other party, yet they remain talking about their specific focus, perhaps obstructing the potential for a longer conversation. The reason for this, ignoring here for a moment communication theoretical concerns and argumentations, is that there is no *common* topic of interest to discuss. Being aware that this statement might imply a entire set of assumptions regarding the structure of human communication, for simplifying the argument we can argue that if the fine art lover is substituted with another soccer fan, and even if both soccer fans support different teams, a *conversation* can occur through the common foundation of soccer itself.

Consider now the example of the fine art lover and soccer fan as buildings that are differentiated by typology, the fine art lover is an office building and the soccer fan is a train station. While it seems reasonable to assume two train stations can exchange information, to what advantage, and further, how can an office building 'talk' to a train station? Things that are relevant for train stations such as timetable updates, passenger numbers, ticket information and so on, may or may not be of value to the office building. Yet, between various buildings of the same typology, such as two train stations, or a bus stop and a train station (akin to the two soccer fans who support different teams), common topics can be readily established and productive interaction is made more feasible. This brings us to the third and last observation.

3) Communication, and rules about language and the use of language, has been argued by William Allman (1995) to be relevant to the formation of a civil society. Given this, if buildings can communicate, so it follows that they require a set of rules – not to generate a society, but rather to establish and maintain a self-generating system. Two possible rules for communication between buildings are considered here.

In a city system, and based on the previously discussed topic of typologies – *non-typology specific rules* and *typology specific rules* can define an interaction between systems.[2] As argued prior with Moore and Wilson (2014) "buildings are an index of changing *social organisations* as well as changing *social tastes*" These *social organisations* define what users expect from a building (in transport environments the notion that the user will be transported from A to B and is informed about how to start his/her journey from A to B via a set of information such as customer information [what mode of transport]; wayfinding information [where does my journey start]; time table information [when does my journey start] and ticketing information [how much is my journey]). Hence it is not the typology as such that has communication capacities but the social organisation that can be communicated from one type (a bus stop or taxi station) to another similar type as all types within the same typology provide the same "index of changing *social organisations* as well as changing *social tastes*". In outlining the difference between the two sets of rules two comparison cases are discussed in the following to show the difference between *non-typology specific rules* and *typology specific rules.*

Non-typology specific rules can, for example, describe the potential communication between the typology of an office building and an apartment block. The second *typology specific rules* can describe the communication within a typology, such as transport. The first, non-typology specific rule, can be compared, as discussed in the chapter on observations, with a conversation between a soccer fan (i.e. office building typology) and a fine art lover (i.e. apartment block typology) where both have very clear rules (passion) within their system (hobby), but one has to first establish and understand rules (a common discussion point) amongst both systems to achieve a holistic phenomenon (a long lasting conversation). The second, typology specific, on the other hand is similar to two gardeners (i.e. bus stops) who have both the same interest (rules of interaction amongst parts) talking to each other about horticulture (timetable information and bus arrivals).

Furthermore, it is argued that *non-typological and typology-specific rules* can form the basis for generating autopoietic content as they follow Luhmann's (1982) argument of "reduction of complexity" and a "distinctive identity of the system".

To illustrate this point further the following section discusses a research example of a typology specific rule set applied within the context of a public transportation system.

---

2 I am using 'typology' in favour of the term 'type' as the typology of i.e. transport it would include types such as bus stops, train stations, etc., who all respond the same, as Wilson and Moore (2014) noticed, "changing social, ecological, and economical conditions".

3.3 'Bus Stop of the Future'

In the context of public transport infrastructure research (train station, bus stops, ferry terminals), the concept of typology has been operatively adopted in the following research example to achieve a reduction of complexity and to make the social, economic and operational demands of public transport more comprehensible and manageable. This follows the argument that – as Gardner et al. (2010) argued on the topic of responsive environments in *Infostructure: A Transport Research Project* – the pressure on public transport systems can be addressed in three key ways: by improving the proximate access to a transport service (physical and contextual), by improving access to service frequency (operational and demand led), and by facilitating and managing better access to information (commuter interface). In discussing typology in the context of autopoietic content the research has favoured and followed the last point on improving access to information, and to be precise, enabling this through the application of digital technologies.

This research topic has been the focus of an Australian Research Council project funded since 2010. This has culminated in the production of a mock-up bus stop as a test set-up for future autopoietic content development. While the scope of this chapter does not allow for an extensive outline of the development process, the publication *Interchanging – Future Designs for Responsive Transport Environments* (Gardner et al. 2014) further details the conceptual framework employed in the development of the bus stop mock-up. Furthermore, the chapter entitled, 'Responsive Transport Environments – System thinking as a method to combine media architecture into a digital ecology to improve public transport' in the book *Digital Futures and the City of Today – New Technologies and Physical Spaces* (Clift; Smith; Caldwell 2016) frames this approach from a theoretical perspective.

In short the developed bus stop made use of a range of number of ICT components such as screens; Mac Minis; Microsoft Kinect sensor; LEDs and control systems; and WiFi; Bluetooth, etc. Intentionally, all components were purchased from a large local electronics supplier, and subsequently nothing 'exotic' was specified for the project. This was an important point for the team as we aimed to demonstrate that Urban ICT does not require expensive state of the art technology, but rather can be achieved with 'everyday' consumer electronics.

The bus stop design concept was developed in January 2014 at the University of New South Wales as part of a design studio for 3rd and 4th Bachelor students from Architecture, Computational Design, Interior Architecture, Landscape Architecture, Industrial Design and Construction Management. In parallel, Masters of

Design Computing students at the University of Sydney developed a series of apps to be displayed on the screens of the 1:1 prototype.

With the bus stop's design finalized the team commenced production using the facilities available at each of the universities. Based on the optimization phase, the team fabricated the bus stop out of 18mm plywood panels using a 3-axis CNC mill.

Fig. 1: Bus stop side view with LED panel © Xavier Ho.

Fig. 2: Interacting with location information © Xavier Ho.

Fig. 3: Active surveillance content of 60 inch screen © Xavier Ho.

Ideas and concepts for apps were based on shifts in the day-to-day engagement with digital technology, and how such apps might better influence how we commute and travel. A key objective and challenge was to translate interaction design concepts that work on a personal device with a small-scale screen, to a public device used by potentially many users concurrently on a larger-scale screen. In detail these were: real-time bus timetable and seat availability information (displayed on the large LED screen); active surveillance system (displayed on the 60″ screen facing inward) and local business information (displayed on the 42″ screen facing inwards) (see Figures 1–3).

Notably, the design of the hardware and the software had a key research constraint worth mentioning here and elsewhere in other publications before. As there was only one bus stop prototype, and as this mock-up was situated, first in a museum, and secondly outdoor on university campus, testing and evaluating of apps and hardware was not possible and constraints and findings will be published shortly.

4 Conclusion and discussion

Returning to the opening quote by Cedric Price that has framed this discussion, that *"architect[s] must undertake extensive research in order to truly understand and adequately respond to a project's requirements"* (Canadian Centre for Architecture 2015) it is argued that for media architecture, adopting the concept of typology provides a trajectory into a mode of "extensive research". This seeks to enable a reduction of complexity as outlined by Luhmann (1982) and a means towards better understanding the conditions that influence and define the typology as a system.

In our research on responsive transport, we have mapped this understanding of the conditions that influence a system to treatment approaches that are designed to heal and enhance the performance of the human body, namely syndromes, symptoms, signs and studies, as a methodology to study and design intervention. In medicine, syndromes are a collection of signs and symptoms that are observed in, and characteristics of, a single condition. In our research these conditions (syndromes) were noticed through subjective experiences between stakeholders (symptoms), and objective observation (signs), through in vitro examinations (studies). In vivo studies[3] were conducted through observations in situ, while ex vivo studies[4] are conducted to test isolated elements. Based on the in vivo and ex vivo studies the depth and systemic nature of the syndromes could be treated through digital design interventions. The design and development of the *bus stop of the future* is an exemplary model of such a digital design intervention.

In adopting the concept of typology as a seed for autopoietic content, this research builds on Memarovic et al. (2011) to propose a method to develop autopoietic content for public transport.

Similarly, the *bus stop of the future* project has aimed to address context sensitivity through the integration of various digital components intended to collect

3 Latin for "within the living", thus within the public transport environment.

4 Latin for "out of the living", thus outside the public transport environment.

dynamic information about the surrounding environment, and to translate this into 'context streams'. As discussed, given the bus stop mock-up has only been showcased in an indoor and outdoor exhibition set-up, establishing a content fragment database has not yet been possible. Developing this further, and establishing a "content fragments database" to achieve an "[...] autopoiesic matching engine that combines content fragments and context streams into new content" (Memarovic et al. 2011), constitute the next critical steps for our research.

What the *bus stop of the future* has already achieved is a mock-up of what Memarovic et al. (2011) refer to as the "user interface", to be precise, the real-time bus timetable and seat availability information; active surveillance system; and local business information.

Through the combined methods of the reduction of complexity via the concept of typology, and developing an understanding of the conditions that influence a system, the *bus stop of the future* project established the framework for content to be displayed on the screens. The next step for the mock-up is, following Memarovic et al. (2011), the generation of autopoietic content.

To conclude, the opening quote has reframed Cedric Price's famous dictum as *Content is the answer but what was the question*? For media architecture, it is argued here that content can be the answer and typology is the question.

Bibliography

Allman, W. (1995): Stone Age Present: How Evolution has shaped modern life – From Sex, Violence and Language to Emotions, Morals and Communities. New York, USA: Touchstone Press.

Canadian Centre for Architecture, Cedric Price: Fun Palace Collection available from: http://www.cca.qc.ca/en/collection/283-cedric-price-fun-palace (accessed: July 2015).

Clift, E.; Smith, C.; Caldwell, G. (2016): Digital Futures and the City of Today – New Technologies and Physical Spaces. Bristol, UK: Intellect Books.

Gardner, N.; Haeusler, M.; Tomitsch, M. (2010): Infostructure – A Transport Research Project. Christchurch, New Zealand: Freerange Press.

Gardner, N.; Haeusler, M.; Mahar, B. (2014): Interchanging – Future Scenarios for Responsive Transport Infrastructure Design. Bamberg, Germany: Spurbuch.

Goulthorpe, M. (1999): "Aegis hyposurface: autoplastic to alloplastic; Architects: dECOi Architectes". AD Profile 140 (Hypersurface Architecture II) Architectural Design 69:(9–10), 60–65.

Haeusler, M. (2009): Media Facades – History, Technology, Content. Ludwigsburg, Germany: avedition.

Haeusler, M.; Beilharz, K. (2011): "[Architecture = Computer] – from computational to computing environments". In: Proceedings of the 14th CAAD Futures Conference, CAAD Future, University of Liège, Liège, Belgium, 217–231.

Haeusler, M.; Tscherteu, G.; Tomitsch, M. (2012): New Media Facades – A global survey. Ludwigsburg, Germany: avedition.
Huang, E.; Koster, A.; Borchers, J. (2008): "Overcoming assumptions and uncovering practices: when does the public really look at public displays"? In: Pervasive Computing: Proceedings of the 6th International Conference, Pervasive 2008, Sydney, Australia. Heidelberg, Germany: Springer Verlag, 227–243.
Langheinrich, M.; Memarovic, N.; Elhart, I.; Alt, F. (2011): "Autopoiesic content: A conceptual model for enabling situated self-generative content for public displays". In: Proceedings of the 1st International Workshop on Pervasive Urban Applications, 2011, available from: https://www.pervasive.wiwi.uni-due.de/uploads/tx_itochairt3/publications/PURBA-7_cr.pdf (accessed: September 2016).
Luhmann, N. (1975): "Systemtheorie, Evolutionstheorie und Kommunikationstheorie". Sociologische Gids 22:3, 154–168.
Luhmann, N. (1982): "The World Society as a Social System". International Journal of General Systems 8:3, 131–138.
Maturana, H.; Varela, F. ([1st edition 1973] 1980): Autopoiesis and Cognition: the Realization of the Living (Boston Studies in the Philosophy of Science 42). Dordecht, The Netherlands: D. Reidel Publishing Co.
Media Architecture Conference Central Saint Martins London 11.–12. September 2007: Mediaarchitecture.com (accessed: October 2015).
Memarovic, N.; Elhart, I.; Langheinrich, M. (2011): "FunSquare: First experiences with autopoiesic content". In: Proceedings of the 10th International Conference on Mobile and Ubiquitous Multimedia, ACM Digital Library, 175–184.
Moore, S.A.; Wilson, B. (2014): Questioning Architectural Judgment: The Problem of Codes in the United States. Abingdon, UK: Routledge, 33–39.
Müller, J.; Wilmsmann, D.; Exeler, J.; Buzeck, M.; Schmidt, A.; Jay, T.; Krüge, A. (2009): "Display blindness: the effect of expectations towards digital signage". Pervasive Computing: 7th International Conference, Pervasive 2009. Nara, Japan, May 11–14, 2009, Proceedings. Heidelberg, Germany: Springer Verlag, 1–9.
Pevsner, N. (1979): A History of Building. Princeton, NJ: Princeton University Press.
Rafaeli, S. (1988): "Interactivity: From new media to communication". In: R.P. Hawkins; J.M. Wiemann; S. Pingree (eds.): Advancing Communication Science: Merging Mass and Interpersonal Processes (Sage Annual Reviews of Communication Research 16). Beverly Hills, LA: Sage, 110–134.
Schmidt, A.; Gellersen, H. (2001): "Visitor Awareness in the Web". In: WWW 2001 Proceedings of the 10th International conference on World Wide Web. New York, NY, USA: ACM Publisher, 745–753.
Simpson, R. (1997): Videowalls: The Book of the Big Electronics Image. Waltham, MA, USA: Focal Press.

Nanna Verhoeff

Interfaces of Media Architecture

1 Approaching Media Architecture

In my contribution I want to approach media architecture – specifically media façades and urban screens – as urban interfaces. In particular, I want to do justice to the social ("inter") and dynamic ("-ing") aspect of interfac*ing*: in time – "historical", temporary, and processual – and place – located, positioning, communicating. When departing from the question of "access" – the question raised by this book series – in my consideration of the specificities of media architecture, I wish to combine two perspectives. On the one hand, I consider the medium-specificity of architecture, and on the other, the architectural specificity of location-based and public forms of urban media. Hence, I take interface, or to be more precise, the verb interfacing as a concept that allows us to grasp the role of media architecture (and architectural media) in today's information society – driven by the ambitions of shared access and of public participation: an open society of access for all. In particular, interfacing as a concept theorizes how "access" is always already an active form of exchange. Indeed, in the *Age of Access*, access is also a social issue, especially when taking place, literally, in urban public spaces. This literal, concrete "taking place" focuses the attention on the temporality as well as materiality of interfacing. The interface thus functions as a material object as well as a concept. We can call it an object-concept.

The interface as object-concept is connected to a set of other object-concepts that share overlapping traits. This overlap we find in comparison helps us to understand the specificity of the object we study. We can discern understandings of the interface as a material object via the metaphorical relationship with other objects, such as a membrane or skin, a surface or zone of simultaneous separation and contact.[1] Moreover, as the concept developed in light of new, digital technologies, we can see how the interface is often understood within frameworks of older, technologies of vision, most notably *the screen.* (Bolter/Grusin 2000; Manovich 2001) Indeed, as Shannon Mattern (2014) has more recently pointed out, the urban interface is most often imagined as a flat display or screen. It is not a coincidence

1 In a related but slightly different vein, Marianne van den Boomen (2009) has pointed out how digital interface – via the Graphical User Interface, or GUI – are often operated by means of, what she calls, material metaphors. Her examples are on-screen icons of, for example, mailboxes with which we use to operate email software on our computers with. She calls these sign-tools. The image of the mailbox, then, is between a Peircian sign (icon) and a Heideggerian operating tool.

DOI 10.1515/9783110453874-005

but significant that these metaphorical objects – membrane, skin, mirror, or the architectural surface, window or aperture – are recurring terminology and central to our conception of both interface and screen. (Bolter/Gromala 2003; Friedberg 2006; Bruno 2014) In her work on media installation art, Kate Modloch phrases this double function of object and concept succinctly:

> Screens themselves have the curious status of functioning simultaneously as immaterial thresholds onto another space and time and as solid material entities. The screen's objecthood, however, is typically overlooked in daily life. (Modloch 2010: 4)

In other words, the quintessential and ubiquitous example for these overlapping and sometimes paradoxical qualities of the visual interface, the screen can be considered a material element of media architecture, and a metaphor, or metonym, for the larger and abstract interface quality of architecture, and a model for investigating the specific interactive spectatorial engagement with media architecture.

As such, I will develop my consideration of media architecture as material, communicative and performative architectural media, by examining the interfacing aspect of architecture via the screen as a model to think with. Hence, the term object-concept. Not only are urban screens, in their wide diversity, the most exemplary and visible instances of media architecture. Also, through the example of the screen and a theoretical approach to the screenic property of media architecture, I argue, we can analyze how media architecture as a wider category contributes to the social fabric of contemporary urban life.

But when we consider its status as between material object and concept, "screen" is too general a term. Traditionally conceived of as a framed surface on which to project selected and composed images, or from a realist perspective, a transparent window from which we can view the world, augmented digital screens come to us already replete with images. Moreover, in the course of watching them these images (can) continuously change and transform, under the influence of the actions we call interactions – whether human interactions, mediations between technologies or the processing of flows of data pushing and pulsing on our screens. In the following, I will explore the differentiated functions and manifestations of interfacing through analyzing a set of metaphors for, or meanings of the screen that foreground the object-concept status of the screen as interface: the screen as mirror, as interlocutor, and as surface for display. The interactive, digital screen requires a reconsideration of the formalist model of the picture frame, the realist model of the window, and the poststructuralist model of the mirror, as Kate Modloch summarizes (Modloch 2010, IV), that have been reigning for the cinematic and electronic, or televisual screen. In my book on screens and what I have called, the visual regime of navigation (Verhoeff, 2012a),

I have analyzed the diversity of (digital) screens – whether fixed and architectural, or small and mobile – as a map, the screen as a (portable) gadget and the screen as skin, or site of touch, to investigate the mobile, haptic, interactive engagements afforded and invited by digital technologies and how this impacts screenic spectatorship. From this comparative approach and the question of the specificity of, what we may call urban spectatorship here I zoom in on some recent examples, each innovative, experimental and emphatically self-reflexive in its use of (media) technologies in their architectural design, and probe how they operate as mirrors, as interlocutors, as surfaces of display, and in this variety demonstrate how digital architectural screens operate as consoles for interfacing.

2 Interface / Screen

But first, let's return to the interface – the starting point of this inquiry in media architecture. We speak of interfaces easily, when pondering interactive and digital media technologies. A pioneer in thinking about the impact of digital technologies on, what he terms, our interface culture, Steven Johnson summarizes the interface as follows:

> In its simplest sense, the word refers to software that shapes the interaction between user and computer. The interface serves as a kind of translator, mediating between the two parties, making one sensible to the other. In other words, the relationship governed by the interface is a semantic one, characterized by meaning and expression rather than physical force." (Johnson 1997: 14)

This is close, if not identical to the essence of mediation. In her rich study on surfaces and the materiality of media, Giuliana Bruno reminds us about the etymological root of the word medium which

> ... refers to a condition of "betweenness" and a quality of "becoming" as a connective, pervasive, or enveloping substance. As an intertwining matter through which impressions are conveyed to the sense, a medium is a living environment of expression, transmission and storage. (Bruno, 2014: 4)

Following these ideas about the mediality of interfaces – whether as translation, expression, transmission or storage – and the materiality of media technologies – whether software, surfaces, substance or matter – I situate the term interface between abstract concept (interfacing) and material manifestation (interfaces), or object. "Interface" as a noun begets a remarkable concreteness in its use. Indicative of the ubiquity of the digital in our visual and material culture, we speak of mobile interfaces, architectural interfaces, digital interfaces, or haptic interfaces, etc. We speak in those terms when we indicate the material technologies that, in a stricter sense *produce* the interface between technology – whether digital, analogue or material – and subject.

This is perhaps where Alexander Galloway (2012) speaks of the interface *effect* – a set of processes rather than a (singular and fixed) object. His focus shifts the attention from media (fixed) *objects* to (on-going) *practices* of mediation:

> Interfaces are not simply objects or boundary points. They are autonomous zones of activity. Interfaces are not things, but rather processes that effect a result of whatever kind. For this reason I will be speaking not so much about particular interface objects (screens, keyboards), but *interface effects*. And in speaking about them I will not be satisfied just to say an interface is defined in such and such a way, but to show how it exists that way for specific social and historical reasons. Interfaces themselves are effects, in that they bring about transformations in material states. (Galloway 2012: vii)

Here we can recognize an intersection of a spatial ("zones of activity") and performative conception of the interface ("processes that effect"). Moreover, Galloway underscores the material and inherently social and historical nature of interfaces and of interfacing.

Branden Hookway (2014) also emphasizes that interfaces are inherently about interfacing. In his approach to interfacing as process, he stresses that interface is a form of relation. In his words, interfacing is essentially about the duality of relationality:

> [...] the interface is that form of relation which is defined by the simultaneity and inseparability of its processes of separation and augmentation, of maintaining distinction while at the same time eliding it [...] (Hookway 2014, 5)

This double logic of the interface – the distance implied in connection, and vice versa – is operative at the threshold of materiality or technology, which Hookway also describes in spatial terms:

> The interface is a liminal or threshold condition that both delimits the space for a kind of inhabitation and opens up otherwise unavailable phenomena, conditions, situation, and territories for exploration, use, participation, and exploration. (Hookway 2014, 5)

While not conceived of as material object – the interface does "take place": it has a spatial and temporal quality, which we recognize in Galloway's words as well ("zones of activity") above. Moreover, Hookway's conception is architectural ("delimits the space for a kind of inhabitation").

We can recognize the spatial thinking intersecting with the emphasis on (time-based) practice and process in the way in which Galloway points out both the essential layeredness of the interface:

> While readily evident in things like screens and surfaces, the interface is ultimately something beyond the screen. It has only a superficial relationship to the surfaces of digital devices, those skins that beg to be touched. Rather, the interface is a general technique of mediation evident at all levels; indeed it facilitates the way of thinking that tends to pitch things in terms of "levels" or "layers" in the first place. [...] Hence the interface is above all an allegorical device that will help us gain some perspective on culture in the age of information. (Galloway 2012, 54)

This layeredness implies both access and separation, and the self-referentiality of specific interfaces – here: architectural screens or surfaces – with respect to this layering. By means of allegory, Galloway then underscores the fundamental role these processes and practices of "interfacing" play in our culture. In this line, philosopher Jos de Mul also adds a fundamental aspect of interfacing that leads to a critical perspective from which to evaluate actual instances of interfaces:

> Media are interfaces that mediate not only between us and our world (designation), but also between us and our fellow man (communication), and between us and ourselves (self-understanding). (De Mul 2009, 95)

From this viewpoint interfaces operate as means to communicate but also to self-reflect – on ourselves and our relation to the world around us. This points out the fundamental role of interfaces and processes of interfacing in the construction of the cultural fabric of our cities. Moreover, it suggests the way we navigate our cities, our world, via interfaces: by communicating with, and relating to our environment, we position ourselves in relation to the world, to others, and in this process we construct our conception of where and who we are.

This makes it not only relevant but also urgent to consider the architectural aspect of the interfacing use of screen. Architecture itself can be seen as interface – and interface as architecture, for that matter – including the possibility to offer a critical analysis of it:

> As technology is about to take the next step and turn ubiquitous, the problems and prospects of computer interfaces will become relevant to the whole built environment. However, architecture has always had its human interface: building façades have communicated their function, their social prestige, their history, and their aesthetics. (Teräväinen 2014, 7)

I propose to follow this perspective on architecture as medium, rather than on media embedded within architecture. In the following, let us look at the way the architectural screen can work to reflect, to connect and to project.

3 Reflections: The Screen as Mirror

Let me begin with the "face" of interface. I want to start with what is, perhaps, a rather unexpected example of media architecture-as-screen: a moving façade that we can consider as somewhat between a traditional screen and a moving, 3-dimensional, kinetic surface. To frame this example as a screen is already a conceptual move. So is the comparison to the screen that I aim to shed light on in its functioning as a mirror.

MegaFaces is a temporary façade designed by Asif Kahn and engineered by iArt, for the pavilion of the Russian telecom network MegaFon, set-up during the 2014 Winter Olympic and Paralympic Games in Sochi. This cross-platform work comprised a façade with 11.000 moving so-called actuators, each equipped with an LED light. Like the children's pin point impression toy called a "pin art board" or "pinscreen" the "mirror" images are given 3D shapes on the façade. In small, individual 3D photo booths, set up on location and throughout the country, participants could upload their mirror images. Captured by camera, translated to code, and uploaded to a database comprised of thousands of faces, the self images were displayed, large-scale, via the façade/screen, creating a private-yet-public, and individual-yet-anonymous, delayed and (literally) pro-jected mirror image.

Fig. 1: By-standers taking pictures of the *MegaFaces* projections. Image from the video *MegaFaces Pavilion and kinetic* façade, *Sochi Winter Olympics 2014* available at www.vimeo.com/99547933, a film by Marcus McSweeney.

Indeed, this system demonstrates a directionality of the image as "information" that is perhaps reminiscent of, yet also somewhat exceeds the viewing model of the mirror. The mirror as interface already has two sides. It reflects but also transforms the self into an "other". As the installation includes the capture and transmission of the mirror image – the reflection self becomes a projection of the selfie. Moreover, in his case, by its sheer size but also its public positioning in public space, it blows up the individual and private mirror image to the scale of a public monument.

Asif Kahn articulates his ambition with the work as to construct an "inclusive monument to people, regardless of their status as athletes or spectators, their age, nationality, sexuality or gender."[2] This speaks to a participatory ideal of inclusion that is in tension with, even problematic in light of, the façade as large-scale monument. Inherently, due to its non-human scale and spectatorial arrangement or dispositif, in the process of making a monument, these "people" become a de-individualized part of a large data-set, that is not so much accessed as it is displayed. Moreover, the data translation and processing involved, and the delay in presentation works towards a distancing effect within the exchange between the subject and his or her image – not only in space but also in time. This delayed and extended public-ness reframes the mirror's intimate self-portrait as a display of the self-as-other – out of reach of the subject to communicate with.

The interfacing quality of the mirror – as an exemplary spectatorial arrangement or dispositif of screen-based visuality – is the possibility to enact different versions of the self; to be in touch, so to speak, with the self as other. In this case, however, the allusion to the mirror also demonstrates the discrepancies that always-already exist in the mirror. Like a pseudo-mirror – similar but not quite the same as the model – this work can indeed be better conceived of as a mega-mirror. It demonstrates though its excess to what extent the mirror is not a reflection making a duplication but an estrangement of the self. In line with psychoanalyst Jacques Lacan's view of the mirror, this work, then, puts a critical gloss to our common conception of the mirror as a tool for self-exploration, demonstrating that what we see in the mirror is our self image as other; as seen by others.

This gloss has particular relevance in the present cultural moment. Perhaps more than a monument for the people, the screen-façade of *MegaFaces* is a monument for the flawed communication of the mirror image as self-portrait in the selfie culture of today. As the designer points out, "The 'Emoticons', 'Selfies', 'Facebook', 'FaceTime' etc. have become universal tools for communicating and expressing emotion and affect, and the face persists as the prevalent shorthand in these new mediums". This particular, but now, ironic monument to the new media of today uses the face of the mirror image as selfie to demonstrate some

2 See his website at http://www.asif-khan.com/project/sochi-winter-olympics-2014/.

crucial paradoxes of today's ideals and pitfalls of digital communication: to be disconnected in connection; to lose privacy and ownership of one's self-image by ubiquitous forms of surveillance, yet have unprecedented access to, but little control over all kinds of data; and to have technologies and platforms for individual expression and visibility, yet be anonymous and de-individualized on the global scale of our public culture; and to lose agency in the midst of the proliferation of interactive technologies and participatory platforms.

4 Connections: The Screen as Interlocutor

After considering the "face" of interface via the intimate individuality and frontality of the mirror in a shift to a public projection of self via the façade, the next case is an example that shows us the ambition of using architectural screens for dialogue, for exchange, foregrounding the "inter" of interface.

Connectivity, a hallmark of digital and networked culture, both sparks and is resulting from the ideal of communication, or the dialogic exchange of information. (De Vries 2012) While more defined in communicative terms than accessibility, as a more one-sided form of retrieval and a form of ownership, connectivity is not necessarily dialogic. Here, I wish to invoke the linguistic conception of the interlocutor – as a partner, co-present instance within a dialogic exchange. This position of the "you" that together with the "I" is included in the "we" is not so much already present as it is constructed at the interface, or via the screen, in the present (and presence) of the encounter.[3]

Recently I have discussed this principle of connections and encounter via interactive screens set up in public spaces. There, I discussed some instances of mobile media architecture – screens that are temporarily set up in public spaces, or temporary uses of more permanent screens. These screens, albeit in different ways, all worked for viewers in different cities to "connect" on screen, by waving, or by joining in virtual game spaces via avatars that are controlled by Kinect cameras (Verhoeff 2015). All these dispositifs or technological and spectatorial arrangements comprised a set of screens, cameras (webcam or Kinect), and internet

3 This is the deictic nature of dialogue. In film theory, the linguistic concept of deixis – or the relative positing of speaker (the "I"), addressee (the "you") and the third instance, of which is spoken (he, she or it) – has played an important role in describing filmic enunciation and spectatorial address. As I have argued, this deictic essence is also at the heart of interactive installations and mobile screens for navigation (Verhoeff 2012a). For a discussion of deixis in film theory, see also (Hesselberth, 2014).

connectivity. Whether individually controlled or larger, public set-ups, these instances constructed virtual bridges between the two locations. Inspired perhaps by earlier projects, such as the 2009–2013 project *Large Screens and the Transnational Public Sphere* that established a connection between large screens in Melbourne and Seoul (Papastergiadis et al. 2013), the Dutch company Dropstuff provided the case study of *The Bridge* – a traveling screen-based connection between different cities in Europe. On the screens of *The Bridge*, local publics can play different games by sharing game space on screen, or witness each other "on location" via video stream.

In my discussion of this project and some related ones that work with connected screens, I wanted to raise the question of connectivity – are people truly connecting in a dialogic exchange or rather witnessing the other when sharing screen space? Moreover, if they are in connection, what does this connection produce? What struck me, looking at the playful engagement with the games on screen, and the encounter of the spectator/participant/engager seems to allow, first and foremost, an encounter with the self on screen – whether in photographic likeness (via video stream), or in the form of a responding avatar in the case of video games. When looking at strangers looking back at us, and acknowledging our presence by waving, also, our presence within our direct environment is marked. Somewhat between mirror image and the image of another – the participants play with their presence in front of the screen. The bi-locality of the set-up – a two-way connection between locations – does not necessarily lead to a bi-directional, dialogic exchange. Or more precisely, this exchange, in its fleeting, playful form, is perhaps not so very different from the mirror of our first example in how the responsiveness of the screen invites markings of presence. The screen mediation this as a third space by triangulating these connections perhaps always absorbs connected locations.

A project that creatively exploits this space between the screen as mirror and the screen as interlocutor, between one- and two-directionality, is *Occupy the Screen*, developed in 2014 by Brighton-based Paul Sermon and Charlotte Gould. Curated as part of Connecting Cities, it makes use of existing, public urban screens that, as the artist himself states, people can "approach on their own terms", without a scripted narrative or game design.[4] The technology of camera and chroma key technique are used for a collage of background – a colorful environment reminiscent of game aesthetics – a middle ground (audience in location A) and foreground (audience in location B). One can see people playfully engaging with

4 For a presentation and description of his project see the artist on video on https://vimeo.com/118602716.

the screen, within the space they occupy in front of the screen, in response to their representation and that of others, elsewhere, in the virtual space in front of them. The merging of spaces on the screen simultaneously expands and shrinks one's direct urban surroundings, extending these in connection with elsewhere, but by merging this into a fictitious screenspace also cutting this off from continuity with the immediately connecting the urban space. After the mirror's transformation of self into other, this is perhaps another paradox of interfacing – that in connection there is always also a loss, much as in expansion there is always also separation.

Fig. 2: *Occupy the Screen* during Connecting Cities event #3 *Urban Reflections* in September 2014 connecting audiences in Riga and Berlin. Image from the video on https://vimeo.com/107784956.

5 Projections: Between Access and Display

Taking a comparative approach to the diversity that the category of media architecture comprises, perhaps the most eye-catching are those projects that work with the possibility of using existing building façades as large surfaces of display, As added screens or light-emitting installations embedded in or built on the skins of buildings, these surfaces operate by essentially visualizing all kinds of data, whether in the form of recognizable images or more abstract, colorful light effects. The following example of media architecture demonstrates a double functioning of media facades as sites for (interactive) access to, and surfaces of (spectacular) display of data.

Firstly, as our analytical object it is layered in the sense that it is both permanent and temporary. It is permanent, as far as buildings ever are permanent, because of the fact that it uses the pre-existing interactive LED façade of the Ars Electronica Center. At the same time, it is temporary in the way that it is one of several changing projects designed to make use of the façade. Secondly, on the thematic level, this project itself is in a sense also about the layering of urban space. Called *Deep City*, it is developed by Ursula Feuersinger, who articulates her ambition to visualize and bring to the surface hidden layers of data, about urban spaces – Linz, Vienna, Berlin and New York – their inhabitants, and recourses – the city's *big data*, if you will. These data sets were grouped in pairs (growth/diversity, green spaces/bike paths, water usage/waste and density/noise exposure). As explained on the Ars Electronica web page:

> Just as a city's history can be uncovered by an archeological dig, the collective information that defines its present and potential future can be represented as a digital cross-section, emerging from underneath its concrete, visible structures. The Ars Electronica Center façade will put these underground samples on display: Observers of the project transform into participants by physically extracting hidden artifacts from the deep, bringing them to the surface, and examining them. The resulting layers of visualized data emphasize various political, sociological, cultural, or even personal characteristics of an urban space, encouraging the inhabitants of that space to critically engage with their surroundings.[5]

Proposed here is the use of the building's surfaces as site of access to data by means of visualization. The underlying premise is that visual technology can provide a form of (physical) contact with real-life experiences and "personal characteristics" of urban space, as well as the urban archive of collective information.

Indeed, the layered and hybrid interface of the work is sophisticated. The arrangement comprises a separate-but-connected terminal, or console, by means of which the participants can browse and select data sets and have some input in what is shown on the building's façade. It invites distant observers (Crary 1990) to become more attentive (Crary 1999) and even active engagers – "participants" in the quote here – by playfully browsing and combining data sets from different cities and composing a colorful show of lights on the building's façade. In the very act of making visible by the processing data into information, generating knowledge, and translating this into colorful lights, however, "data" becomes a spectacle – for both observers and participants. This perhaps makes the otherwise distracted observer a more attentive spectator.

5 From the announcement of Ars Electronica's Future Lab, 2015, available at http://www.aec.at/futurelab/en/residency-network/connectingcities/. See also http://www.aec.at/postcity/en/deep-city/ for a video impression of the project.

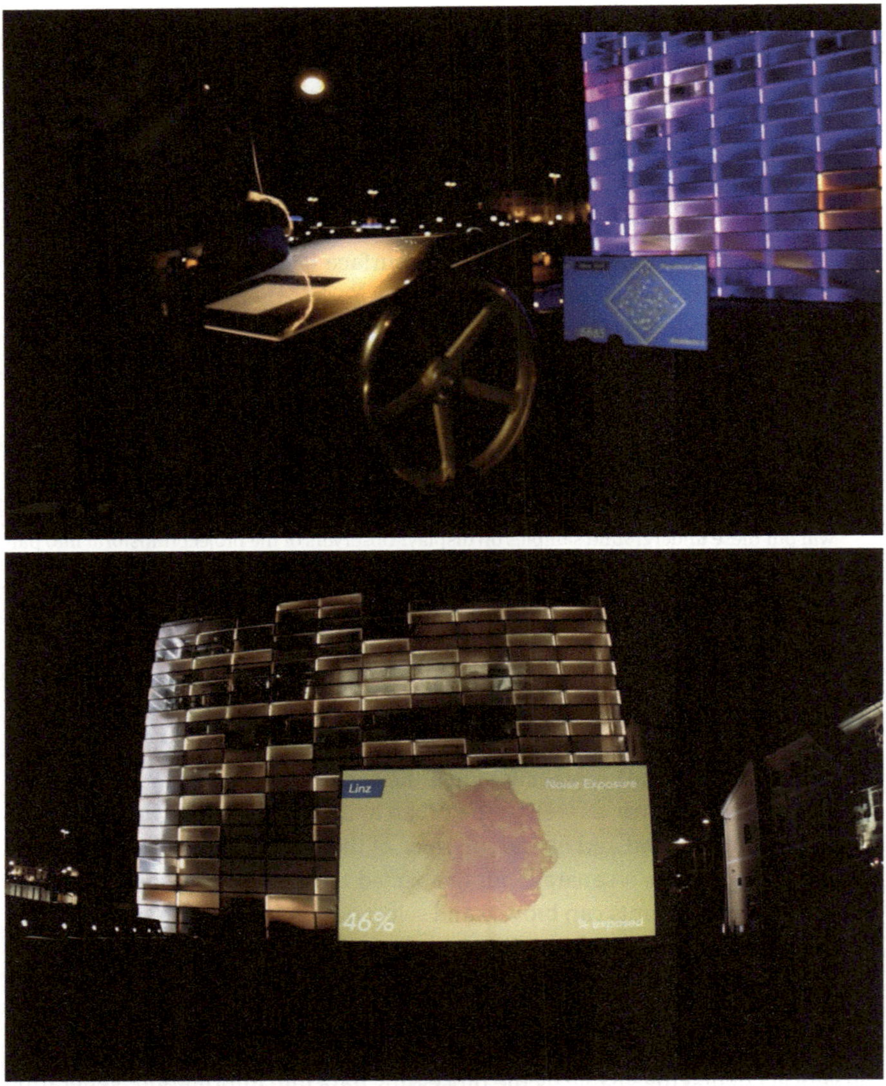

Fig. 3: Images from the *Deep City Documentary* (2015), available at www.vimeo.com/128586188. Camera: Benjamin Skalet, Claudia Schnugg, Veronika Pauser, Sigrid Nagele. Editing: Christian Haas, Ursula Feuersinger.

In his analysis of Lozanno Hemmer's urban installation, *Body Movies*, Scott McQuire (2008) describes a similar shift, which he registers in the public present at the night-time event. He interprets the attention focused onto the building in its illuminated state as comparable to our usual, everyday distracted relation to architecture. This is result of the openness, or "incomprehensibility", of the interface, that invites engaged and playful experimentation of the participants:

> Here it is worth recalling Benjamin's argument that the radical impact of cinema in the context of the modern city depended – like architecture – on the fact that it was consumed in a 'distracted' state. Since the film image acted at the margins of conscious perception, it was able to circumvent the habitual defence shield each city dweller erected so as to protect themselves from the excessive sensory demands of urban life. *Body Movies* occupies a similar liminal terrain. Passers-by aren't sure what to make of it; the interface is striking but not immediately comprehensible. Habit is suspended in favour of experimentation. Unexpected conjunctions emerge. (McQuire 2008, 153–154)

McQuire values the affective experiences brought about by these installations/ events that function as tactical urban interventions by setting-up, designing "unexpected", interactive encounters in public space.

The unexpected and experimental nature of these works – temporary by necessity – may invite playful interactions, however, its visual spectacle also positions the public in the position of a more distant spectatorship. Access in the form of visual display, in this way, both reveals and problematizes the possibilities for, and limitations of open access to big data for exploration, examination and analysis. In this sense, the work makes a good case for the 2015 program of *Visible Cities*, curated by the Connecting Cities Network for which *Deep Cities* was developed in a Research Residency. The questions central in the *Visible Cities* theme advocate a role of façades and screens as "black boards" and "visualization zones" for information:

> How can we make social, environmental and intercultural processes visible and use the screens as black boards and visualization zones? What is the impact on the society, when invisible structures that underlie our daily life get visualised? What is the potential to create public awareness?[6]

However, the impact of visualization – its participatory potential to create awareness or lead to action, or even insight – is not straightforward. At closer inspection we can see how, as experimental project, *Deep City* questions the impact of visibility by addressing what it also exemplifies. Indeed, what is put on display is perhaps visible but not always legible, and hence actionable.[7] The algorithms that order, select and process the social and personal data below the surface trans-

6 http://www.connectingcities.net/city-vision/visible-city-2015.

7 Thanks to Karin van Es for suggesting the importance of this specification of "acting on" data, as well as some other helpful suggestions for improving this text.

late this data as input for its "visualization zone" at the surface. This process of translation is not necessarily aimed at comprehensibility. Perhaps more fundamentally, this façade as screen demonstrates the differences between input, output, observation and interpretation. As such, *Deep City* suggests not only the many layers of information that are hidden in cities, but also the many layers behind and beyond the surfaces of the interface.

6 Architectural Consoles

Like other projects developed for interactive displays and façades that have the ambition to allow for more democratic and dynamic access to what "lies beneath" or behind the screens that surround us in the city, *Deep City* aims to provide an interactive point of access – however visual and spectacular in form – to information. Rater than functioning as a flat surface of display, the façade as interface – extended with a small screen and a set of controllers – is an ensemble of screens and controllers that really functions as a console for different forms of input and output. We have explored how media architecture as a bracket for different architectural interfaces, via the model of the screen as point of connection and exchange, as site of display for data, brings to the fore the diverse forms and functions that we can recognize in how building façades work to mediate. As Hank Haeusler puts it in his contribution to this collection:

> When equipping building skins with screens and digital technologies one can argue that a building equals an autonomous system, able to sense and collect data, to process these data into information and lastly to communicate these information to other buildings or humans to generate new knowledge about the building itself or the urban context (Haeusler, this volume).

Digital and augmented, then, we can compare these interfacing "skins" of buildings with consoles. An object-concept in its own right, a console, as I have argued in relation to the digital, mobile screen, comprises multiple interfaces, or "skins" if you will. (Verhoeff 2012b) Like a game console that we use for very different games, making use of the technological affordances of the console in various ways, screens are also, by definition, objects that have a range of different uses. I have defined the digital screen as "a material site for interfacing, the screen can be multiplied by combining different interfaces." (Verhoeff 2012b, 292) Rather than an interface as singular object, the digital screen is a console for multiple interfacing objects: "Theoretically, it encourages the exploration of its possibilities as console, a polymorphous 'screenic' platform for a variety of applications and practices." (294) This notion of theoretical consoles puts a specific spin on my proposal to develop our thinking via the relations between object-concepts. Immediately appropriate for media architecture, the notion of "console" also opens up the status of the singular "object" itself. It demonstrates the versatility and multiplicity of interfaces as technological objects. Moreover, it underscores how, rather than focusing on the specificity of their singular use, it is in the cultural practices of *interfacing* – what we do with screens – that we get to their specificity. We can consider the console as the "extension" or "access-point" to the facade, allowing us to give input for their display – even if limited by algorithms and code.

To return to our point of departure, we can conclude that by exploring a comparative perspective on the interfacing potentials of media architecture as architectural screens – or perhaps, *architectural consoles* – we can find the diverse and often paradoxical specificities of media architecture precisely within the multiplicity of interfaces and interfacings that we can encounter on our streets.

Bibliography

Bolter, J.D.; Grusin, R. (2000): Remediation: Understanding New Media. Cambridge, MA: MIT Press.
Bolter, J.D; Gromala, D. (2003): Windows and Mirrors: Interaction Design, Digital Art, and the Myth of Transparency. Cambridge, MA: MIT Press.
Bruno, G. (2014): Surface: Matters of Aesthetics, Materiality, and Media. Chicago, IL: University of Chicago Press.
Crary, J. (1990): Techniques of the Observer: On Vision and Modernity in the Nineteenth Century. Cambridge, MA: MIT Press.
Crary, J. (1999): Suspensions of Perception: Attention, Spectacle, and Modern Culture. Cambridge, MA: MIT Press.
De Mul, J. (2009): "The Work of Art in The Age of Digital Recombination". In: M. van den Boomen et al. (eds.): Digital Material: Tracing New Media in Everyday Life and Technology. Amsterdam: Amsterdam University Press, 96–106.
De Vries, I.O. (2012): Tantalizingly Close: An Archaeology of Communication Desires in Discourses of Mobile Wireless Media. Amsterdam: Amsterdam University Press.
Friedberg, A. (2006): The Virtual Window: From Alberti to Microsoft. Cambridge, MA: MIT Press.
Galloway, A.R. (2012): The Internet Effect. Cambridge, UK: Polity Press.
Hesselberth, P. (2014): Cinematic Chronotopes: Here, Now, Me. London: Bloomsbury.
Hookway, B. (2014): Interface. Cambridge, MA: MIT Press.
Johnson, S. (1997): Interface Culture: How New Technology Transforms the Way We Create and Communicate. San Francisco, CA: Harper Edge.
Manovich, L. (2001): The Language of New Media. Cambridge, MA: MIT Press.
Mattern, S. (2014): "Interfacing Urban Intelligence." Places Journal, April. www.placesjournal.org/article/interfacing-urban-intelligence.

Modloch, K. (2010): Screens: Viewing Media Installation Art. Minneapolis, MN: University of Minnesota Press.
Papastergiadis, N. et al. (2013): "Mega Screens for Mega Cities". Theory, Culture & Society 30:(7–8), 325–341.
Teräväinen, H. (2014): "Introduction". In: M. di Marino; H. Teräväinen (eds.): Architecture as Human Interface 2012 (Aalto University Publication series, Art+Design+Architecture), 6–13. https://shop.aalto.fi/media/attachments/9e167/Architecture_as_human_interface.pdf.
Van den Boomen, M. (2009): "Interfacing by Material Metaphors: How Your Mailbox May Fool You". In: M. van den Boomen et al. (eds.): Digital Material: Tracing New Media in Everyday Life and Technology. Amsterdam: Amsterdam University Press, 253–266.
Verhoeff, N. (2012a): Mobile Screens: The Visual Regime of Navigation. Amsterdam: Amsterdam University Press.
Verhoeff, N. (2012b): "Theoretical Consoles: Concepts for Gadget Analysis". Journal of Visual Culture 8:3, 279–298.
Verhoeff, N. (2015): "Mobile Media Architecture: Between Infrastructure, Interface, and Intervention". Observatorio (OBS*) Journal. Special Issue "Media City: Spectacular, Ordinary and Contested Spaces", 73–84. http://obs.obercom.pt/index.php/obs/article/view/974/749.

Using Media as Construction Material: Prototypes and Case Studies

Glenda Amayo Caldwell and Marcus Foth

DIY / DIWO Media Architecture: The InstaBooth

1 Introduction

Architecture has embedded media into its surfaces for centuries where classic examples include hieroglyphics in Egyptian temples, stained glass windows in Gothic cathedrals, large murals such as the Sistine Chapel, and Baroque church facades. Building surfaces have been used to depict religious stories or information to city inhabitants however rarely has there been an opportunity for the citizens to create their own media on architectural surfaces. Technology has been argued to provide the means through which more people can gain control over their environment and contribute further to the information that can be accessed or displayed on or through the built environment. Building on previous discourse regarding the ability of media architecture to be more open and accessible for the purposes of community engagement (Caldwell/Foth 2014), this chapter explores a particular case study that was designed, constructed and implemented with the intention of allowing city users to participate in the development and creation of media architecture, the InstaBooth.

In this chapter, we first explore DIY (do it yourself) and DIWO (do it with others) phenomena to examine what motivates the DIY cultures, communities, and practices. It is critical to understand the driving forces behind these movements as they point towards a post-neoliberal trend where people actively occupy, shape and influence some of the spaces freed up by government deregulation. An example is participatory placemaking and urban planning that sees people become empowered over their surroundings and contribute to improving their local communities, relationships, and knowledge. It is in this context that we explore the concept of DIY / DIWO media architecture – as a shift of practice exclusive to media and architecture professionals, to one that promotes the interactions of laypeople for their own sake and purposes.

Secondly, in this chapter, we define and discuss our implementation of a DIY / DIWO media architecture example, the InstaBooth. The InstaBooth project provides an opportunity to question the effectiveness of a DIY driven media architecture artefact to see to what extent it impacts on the experience of its users and for what benefit. This case study highlights the challenges and limitations of such an approach in an attempt to provoke further iterations to continue to allow for city dwellers to not only participate but to lead change making in their communities.

DOI 10.1515/9783110453874-006

In terms of the thematic focus of this book, we argue that media architecture uses information and media as a construction material for the creation of citizen led communities of inquiry and practice that can shape city making.

The DIY phenomena is evident in the huge success of such commercial chains as Home Depot in the USA and several prime time reality TV shows such as The Block[1] (in Australia). Such media and commercial driven entities have capitalised on the fact that individuals are interested in improving, constructing, and designing their immediate living environments. These commercial entities and many more have made the DIY concept into a recognisable and almost brand of its own. However, if we look beyond the somewhat superficial branding of the DIY concept, we see that it is much deeper and meaningful.

The DIY movement reflects the value people place on craft and the skills required to create handmade and bespoke artefacts versus the skills of experts (Gauntlett 2007; Francisco 2007). Web 2.0, participatory culture, and ubiquitous mobile technologies have contributed to people's ability to do things themselves by allowing them to connect, communicate and share knowledge across the globe to do-it-with-others (DIWO) (Gauntlett 2007; Kolbitsch/Maurer 2006). The sharing and open sourcing of information goes beyond the DIY / DIWO creation of artefacts to include the creation of experiences, technologies, skills, cities, places, governance and urbanism (Caldwell/Foth 2014). We have previously discussed each of these different aspects of the DIY / DIWO movement and categorised them into three different domains (Caldwell/Foth 2014): 1. *DIY technical* which includes for example fablabs and hacker-spaces; 2. *DIY spatial* focusing on placemaking such as guerrilla gardening, yarn bombing and graffitti; 3. *DIY social* which includes the concept of DIY Citizenship (Ratto/Boler 2014) including such events as Park(ing) Day and DIY Urbanism (Iveson 2013).

We discuss the DIY social category in more depth as it allows us to interrogate the meaning and effects of the DIY phenomena in terms of the social and urban context. Ratto and Boler coined the term DIY citizenship as, *"a term intended to highlight the diversity of ways citizenship is enacted and performed"* (Ratto/Boler 2014 p. 4). It includes the diverse ways that people act as individuals or come together to creatively improve or change their communities for their own purposes. Similarly, DIY Urbanism leads to a bigger picture view of how small or local interventions in urban spaces, such as guerrilla gardening, create new opportunities, meanings, or functions that are linked to each other to transform the overall experience of a city (Iveson 2013).

1 https://en.wikipedia.org/wiki/The_Block_(Australian_TV_series)

2 DIY Media Architecture

We previously argued that applying the DIY approach to media architecture has led and could lead to a type of media architecture that allows for more laypeople to be a part of the creative process of media architecture initiatives in order to promote community engagement and foster genuine citizen empowerment (Caldwell/Foth 2014). Understanding the basis for DIY and DIWO cultures is a key aspect to the development of DIY media architecture. Examples of DIY media architecture not only aspire towards producing a bottom-up outcome, it is the process, the design, and development that entails a DIY approach and fundamentally seeks to provide a genuine voice or communication means for the local community or the public at large (Caldwell/Foth 2014).

We identified that one of the biggest challenges for DIY media architecture to become commonplace or part of everyday practices is technical knowledge. Other challenges include the design process and governance of media architecture projects, access to public spaces, frameworks, structures, buildings, and policies. We therefore proposed five strategies to help overcome these challenges (Caldwell/Foth 2014):

1. **Trans-disciplinary teams** with diverse expertise in areas of social, spatial, physical, and technical research and design;
2. **Participatory approaches and methodologies** – not just for the artefact at the end, but also the design process (e.g. Participatory Design, Co-design, Participatory Action Research);
3. **Open source** repositories of code and documentation;
4. **Creative commons** licensing;
5. **New design strategies** that allow for future tinkering, expansions, appropriations, remixes, and documentation.

So why is this important? In part one of this book, M. Hank Haeusler explains that neither content nor technology are the sole answer to successfully creating media architecture that is truly interactive with the public and goes beyond mere entertainment or advertising. He argues that the design process should acknowledge primarily the *content* of the media architecture, secondly, the *space* in which it is located, and thirdly, the *technology* used to create it. Could perhaps applying a DIY approach to the media architecture development be a possible solution?

In an attempt to explore and implement these strategies and answer these questions our team has devised a media architecture prototype: the InstaBooth.

3 The InstaBooth

The InstaBooth, as seen in Figure 1, has been defined as a pop-up, multimedia booth designed for the purpose of community engagement. *"The InstaBooth provides an engagement and discussion platform that leverages a number of bespoke display and interaction technologies in order to facilitate a dialogue of ideas and commentary. The InstaBooth blends multiple digital and analogue interaction modalities into a hybrid community engagement space"* (Johnstone et al. 2015). The InstaBooth is an example of media architecture allowing users to participate and interact with it and each other by writing a note, drawing a picture, hug a pillow, tweet, text, drop a pin, and more.

Fig. 1: Image of the InstaBooth at Queensland University of Technology, Gardens Point, Brisbane Australia. Photo Credit: Xavier Ho.

Based on our previous research and outcomes from conducting urban interventions around Brisbane, Australia, we were able to identify objectives, characteristics, and approaches for the InstaBooth project from the onset. Acknowledging the value of involving stakeholders in the creation and development of their cities is a valuable aspect of architecture and urban design. Through the interactive capacity of media architecture there is rich potential to involve more people in community engagement (Caldwell et al. 2012). Therefore, providing a voice for all people is the fundamental objective of the InstaBooth prototype. Applying a DIY and DIWO approach was critical to all aspects of the design, development, and implementation of the InstaBooth. Response to place through situated engagement (Schroeter et al. 2012; Schroeter 2012; Scheible 2010; Parra-Agudelo et al. 2012) guided the location of interventions. Building on the research of Dalsgaard, Dindler and Halskov (2011) and Kortbek (2008) we designed for engagement and interactivity by ensuring that the urban intervention should be: 1. accessible; 2. easy to use and understand; 3. relate to the context of the space.

In the following sections we will give an overview of our goals, our approach, and the outcomes we achieved.

3.1 The Design Process

In response to strategy number *1. Transdisciplinary teams*, the InstaBooth project was conceived by a group of academics from the Urban Informatics Research Lab, at the Queensland University of Technology (QUT), and comprised the disciplines of architecture, computer science, interaction design, interior design, urban planning, and business. An international partnership was also developed with academics from the California Polytechnic University (CalPoly) at San Luis Obispo in the U.S.. The initial concept of the InstaBooth as seen in Figure 2 takes the idea of a telephone booth further by implementing a range of interactions that are both physical and digital – originally intended to engage the community on urban design issues.

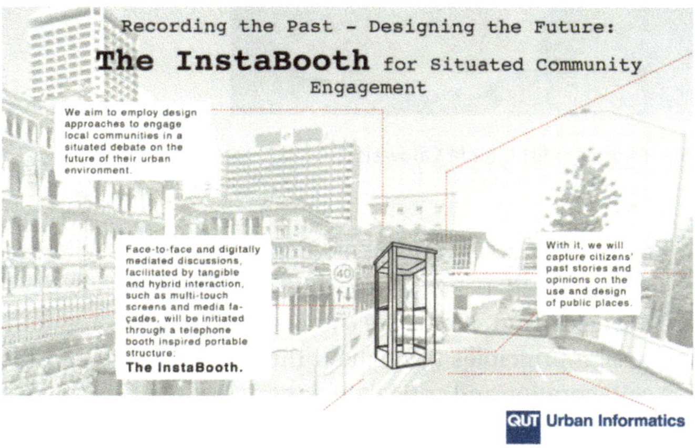

Fig. 2: The initial sketch of the InstaBooth concept. Photo Credit: Glenda Caldwell.

Implementing design strategy *2. Participatory approaches and methodologies*, we undertook a vigorous design approach in collaboration with industry and community partners that employed a series of co-design workshops to assist in the simultaneous evolution of both the architectural design of the structure and the interactive components within it (Caldwell et al. 2016). The co-design workshops, Figure 3, were hosted in the studios at the School of Design, QUT where practitioners, architects, interaction designers, academics, undergraduate and post graduate students were invited to attend. In parallel our colleagues from CalPoly were using a design brief we provided in their architectural design studio. From a set of six different designs produced by CalPoly students we chose one which suited our objectives best and continued to iterate the architectural design of the InstaBooth from there.

Fig. 3: Co-design workshop. Photo Credit: Glenda Caldwell.

During the co-design workshops at QUT a range of off the shelf materials including large sheets of corrugated cardboard, paper, string, tubes, etc. were used to physically prototype different aspects and interactive components of the InstaBooth. Applying participatory design principles throughout the workshops guided the participants promoting collaboration and critical thinking across the different disciplines that were represented (Caldwell et al. 2016). Using the large sheets of cardboard we made a 1:1 scaled model of the InstaBooth structure as seen in Figure 4, which allowed us to use experience prototyping (Buchenau/Suri 2000) to bodystorm the components with non-architects. The large scale model allowed us to use our bodies to get a physical feeling and sense of the space provided by the structure. Participants were able to act out the interactions created for the InstaBooth and test their initial ideas with others. The structure had to be large enough to allow up to three people inside it at once while providing access from multiple directions. The space had to accommodate a wheel chair and be fully accessible for the physically impaired and safe for use by small children. Documentation of the workshops included drawings and sketches, photographs, and videos.

Fig. 4: Cardboard scaled prototype of the InstaBooth. Photo Credits: Glenda Caldwell.

The design workshops allowed the team to make design decisions in an agile manner in line with the flexible and temporary nature of the InstaBooth design that would allow for it to respond to the local context in which it would be situated. The composition of the interactive modules would have to be tailored to suit each location and deployment, therefore the structure had to incorporate a swift exchange of interaction modules. It was critical to allow for a mix of both digital and tangible interactions to be accommodated to the InstaBooth structure with the intention to promote a range of users to interact with it despite their access or knowledge of digital technologies or ability to read or write (Caldwell et al. 2016).

As a result of the workshops, ideas for twenty one different interaction modules were established. Although all of the ideas are feasible and suitable to the InstaBooth, due to timing and funding constraints, only seven have been fully developed and implemented in the InstaBooth to date. The co-design workshops were successful mechanisms to generate interest from participants outside of the initial design team and their contributions have been valuable additions to the design development (Caldwell et al. 2016). The outcomes of the workshops also indicate that there are many possibilities for future development in terms of DIY / DIWO interaction design.

3.2 Constructing the InstaBooth

Once the design concept was finalised the final model and documentation for fabrication were created. With the intention to adhere to design strategies #3 and #4, we open sourced the design files of the InstaBooth to enable sharing it with anyone anywhere, and to encourage others to modify and 'remix' the design, such as is the case with our partners at CalPoly. We opted to utilise digital fabrication technology such as CNC machining for this purpose. Along with the need for flexibility and agility, a lightweight structure, and the ability to transport the InstaBooth easily, guided the design decisions for construction techniques and material selection. The InstaBooth is constructed using 17mm black Formply, it requires minimal fixtures as the flat pack structure clicks into place using scaled up furniture construction methods. Initially a laser cut scaled model, Figure 5, was created to test the construction system and evaluate the overall aesthetics of the system.

Fig. 5: Scaled laser cut model of the InstaBooth. Photo Credit: Glenda Caldwell.

The CNC files were created and machining of the InstaBooth commenced at the QUT School of Design digital fabrication workshop. The notching system used to assemble the structure required double-sided cutting of the plywood. This meant that the CNC operator had to be skilled and knowledgeable to be able to undertake the precision needed to do it properly. This also meant we needed extra time, materials, and resources due to the complex nature of the cutting. This in itself is a major challenge and although the design files can be open sourced it somewhat restricts the ability for reproduction. We acknowledge this as a design constraint of our first prototype and intend to simplify the design to allow for future iterations of the InstaBooth to be constructed anywhere with access to a CNC router in a less complex manner.

The structure, doors, and housing of technology can all be flatpacked and transported in the back of a pick-up truck or in a trailer. Assembly of the InstaBooth structure requires at least two people and can take approximately four hours[2]. More time may be necessary depending on the configuration of the interaction modules and the type of technology to be used.

4 Situating the InstaBooth

During 2015 the InstaBooth was deployed around South East Queensland, and situated into the urban fabric in seven different locations associated with public events for community engagement and consultation purposes. The amount of data collected throughout the different events is extensive and varied. Based on these experiences with the InstaBooth, the following section will respond to design strategy #5 – new design strategies allowing for future tinkering, expansions, appropriations, and remixes – and the question; *how can the DIY / DIWO approach be implemented in media architecture?*

As indicated previously the design process employed a participatory and co-design approach (Caldwell et al. 2016). Therefore we argue that the final design of the InstaBooth was the result of a range of stakeholders and participants from different disciplines and backgrounds. This was the first step towards a DIY / DIWO media architecture.

Recognising that the primary purpose of the InstaBooth is to ask questions of the local community by utilising a temporary and creative approach to solicit questions from a range of participants, we found that the focus has to be on:

2 https://vimeo.com/126311878

1. Who is asking the questions?
2. How are the questions being asked?
3. How are users interacting and responding to the questions?

4.1 Asking the questions

When we examine *who is asking the questions* we have to indicate that the deployment of the InstaBooth in each of the different locations was in close collaboration with local communities. The purpose of each deployment was unique to each location, the event, and the collaborators. A range of actors, including the researchers, university students, community leaders, government public servants, and policy makers, were asking the engagement questions. Although we worked in close collaboration with stakeholders and members of the local community, passers-by would usually find the InstaBooth pre-configured with questions posed by our research partners. Despite these preparations being conducted in a participatory manner, we are hoping to develop new interaction strategies that will allow community members themselves to be the ones asking questions. However, providing an 'empty canvas' and anticipating passers-by to take ownership is likely to fail. In our previous work we found that this is not solely a technical challenge, but requires careful consideration of the existing dynamics and power relationships within a local community ecology. We recommend an approach that involves participation, animation and design (Foth 2010). We are currently working towards tailoring this approach to the circumstances of the InstaBooth for a future deployment where people can ask questions they would like of each other.

4.2 How the questions are asked

How the questions are being asked has been the most challenging aspect of the InstaBooth as there are several factors that need to be considered. The design of; the question, the mechanism and material through which the question is asked, and the interaction the question solicits all have to be carefully thought through. This is where the use of technology and materials are controlled to be easy to use and easily understood by participants.

Interaction designers ranging from undergraduate students, post graduate students, and academics have contributed extensively to the design of the interaction modules that have been fitted into the InstaBooth. Existing social media platforms such as Twitter and Instagram have been used to allow people to easily use their mobile devices to respond to questions. Each of the interaction modules has been given a name of its own so that they can be recognised with their own identity and be used independently of the InstaBooth, however, we have found that through the InstaBooth the strength lies in the multiple ways of asking the questions simultaneously and in the same location. To understand the interaction modules a brief description of each is included here.

Discussions In Space

(DIS) is a situated interactive screen application for urban public places aiming to engage with local citizens about local civic issues (Schroeter et al. 2012). The screen forms part of the InstaBooth presenting a topic and a set of questions. Users are invited to directly provide their comments and feedback while being in front of the screen by either SMS texting or Tweeting. The comments collected are displayed through in a dynamic manner, allowing participants to see the ideas of others.

Print + Talk = Love

is a paper based version of DIS. Each paper has a question on it and people are invited to leave their response by writing on the paper with the pens provided (Parra Agudelo et al. 2013). The graphic design and name of this interaction can be adapted to the context or event associated with the deployment of the InstaBooth.

Drop Your Pin

asks “How do you feel about ...?” It was designed to allow for the topic to be changed when needed. People can respond to the question by dropping a pin in the circle, the closer to the smiley face the happier or closer in agreement they are to the question. Associating different colours to different pins can collect demographics, such as age group or gender.

Overhead + Overdrawn

asks people to respond to a question either through drawing a picture or leaving a note. An overhead projector records and displays the hands of the user as they draw their picture on the paper which is projected on to the outside of the InstaBooth.

Local Commons

is an application that runs on an iPad. The application displays photographs from an Instagram feed specific to a pre-defined hashtag and asks the user to vote for the photo which best responds to the question. As the photo gets more positive votes it grows larger in size. With negative votes it gets smaller. Participants are able to upload their own images by using the selected hashtag via Instagram.

Snuggle

is a tangible interaction, designed by undergraduate QUT Design students, that collects and counts hugs from participants. A balloon is fitted within a fluffy pillow and connected to a click counter. The quantity of hugs received each day is displayed on a computer monitor.

Interactive Maps

have been fitted into the InstaBooth through physical and digital interactions. In most deployments a Google Map was displayed via an iPad asking participants to indicate where in the world they would like to place the InstaBooth. A physical map was created by a QUT Masters of Design student that uses a pin board and a range of materials from pipe cleaners to play dough to investigate the playful tangible interaction of participants. Users were asked to place the materials onto the map to indicate areas that needed more love or their favourite places.

4.3 Interacting with the questions

How are users interacting and responding to the questions?

As previously mentioned the interaction modules of the InstaBooth are digital, physical and tangible, or a mixture of both. The purpose for this is to attract responses from a range of participants regardless of their knowledge of, or access to technology, or ability to read or write (Parra Agudelo et al. 2013). The people responding to the questions are the ones who create the content of the media that is displayed in the InstaBooth, they do it themselves and with each other. Because the content is created by the users, the content is indeterminate, we may prompt the response but we – the project team or the InstaBooth itself – have little control over what the content will look like, what it will say, or how people will respond to it. The project team have shared the responsibility of moderating the comments with the actual users, as they tend to be aware of and remove inappropriate comments. The indeterminate nature of the InstaBooth content provides a unique characteristic, where it is surprising and continually evolving. We have found that people do return to see how it changes over time, from one day to the next.

In each deployment the general public have been curious about the InstaBooth and many people used it. It is helpful to have someone associated with the project or event at the InstaBooth to invite users into it and help answer questions about the booth, how to use it, or the project. From our observations and interviews with participants we can conclude that people generally respond to the questions with genuine interest. The open yet anonymous ability for users to comment seems to provoke honest responses. Many participants have indicated that the overall design of the InstaBooth, the fact that it is open on all four sides and can be seen through it, gives it an overall inviting feeling of openness. The pop-up nature of the InstaBooth appears to surprise and attract people into it.

When asking participants why they used the InstaBooth there are three major trends. There were many people who had something they wanted to say, a particular issue or concern they have pertaining to the place in question, and found the InstaBooth a useful opportunity and platform to share their voice. Secondly some people spent a lot of time going through each interaction and reading other people's comments and responses. They were interested about what other people had to say and wanted to learn from others. Lastly the third trend is that users were playful and curious. They were attracted by the technology and pop-up personality of the InstaBooth and were interested in experimenting with the different interactions. The majority of users wanted to know what the InstaBooth was about, why it was there and who was going to read the responses. They would engage with the InstaBooth once they realised that their comments were going to be read and assist in creating some change in some way.

As can be expected there were different levels of engagement with the InstaBooth where some people would use all the interactions and do all the questions, some would only do one or two, some would come back to do it later. Some people would simply watch others use it and a few would seek it out and follow it from different locations. There were many people who walked past and would not use it at all. These findings concur with previous experiences of deployments situated in urban public space (Dalsgaard et al. 2011).

Referring back to Haeusler's discussion (in this book) of the difference between participation and interaction, we acknowledge that the InstaBooth provides a range of opportunities for people to express themselves, and it is through these expressions that an exchange of dialogue often occurs. People have commented on each other's ideas directly or next to their piece of paper. Figure 6 is an example showing two different sets of handwriting in different colours depicting someone's comments on another's response. The dialogue often extended beyond the physical location of the InstaBooth through social media channels and through word of mouth. People congregated around the InstaBooth would start to talk about local issues inspired by the questions being asked and in some instances a sense of community building could be felt.

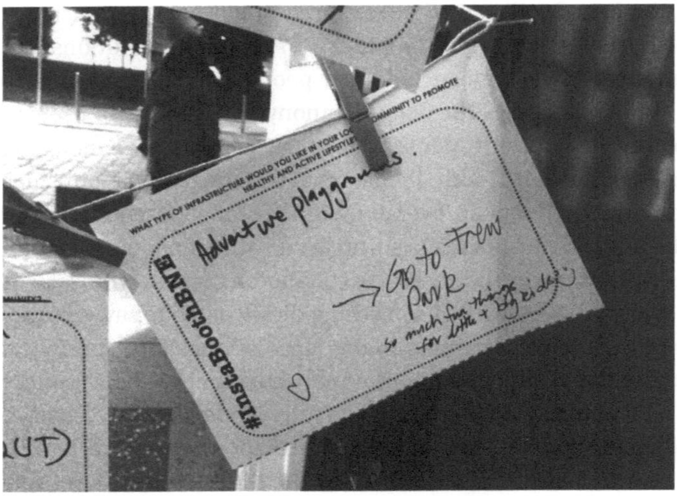

Fig. 6: Piece of paper showing the dialogue created between participants. Photo Credit: Glenda Caldwell.

In other instances, it was observed that people would appropriate the interaction module for their own purpose. Instead of responding to the question being asked they would use the paper to ask their own question of others. During one of the deployments in the Queensland regional town of Pomona, the local yarn bombers, welcomed the InstaBooth into their town centre by decorating it with colourful knitted pompoms and animals, see Figure 7.

The adaptation of the interaction modules also occurred where participants would use the interaction in unexpected ways such as combining one module with another or using the tangible materials in unforeseen combinations or with different intentions. An example of this can be seen in Figure 8 where participants used papers from *Print + Talk = Love* on the *Drop Your Pin* interaction, because they felt the need to elaborate and explain their response, which was not an option through simply dropping a pin.

The moderation and control of the content to our surprise has not been an issue. The public have respected the InstaBooth, and it has received minimal van-

Fig. 7: The InstaBooth decorated with yarn pompoms thanks to the Pomona Pixies. Photo Credit: Glenda Amayo Caldwell.

dalism. Negative or inappropriate responses have also been small in comparison to the largely positive comments. During its opening hours the InstaBooth has mainly been supervised or accompanied by someone, and it is their role to moderate the responses. However, we have observed that there have been instances where participants have done the moderation themselves. They have seen inappropriate responses and taken them down so that others would not be offended by the comment. This is an important finding as it indicates to us that the users have taken some ownership of the InstaBooth where they display respect for it, its intention and each other.

5 Conclusions

Taking a DIY / DIWO approach to the design, fabrication, and implementation of the InstaBooth has been a useful methodology in creating a media architecture that attracts the attention of users and promotes interaction amongst them. The InstaBooth is largely perceived as a platform for sharing ideas. The strength of the

Fig. 8: Paper from Print + Talk = Love used in Drop Your Pin which shows how participants adapted the module to suit their needs. Photo Credit: Glenda Amayo Caldwell.

InstaBooth lies in its design and combination of interactions that allow for users to combine different media inside and on the structure. Therefore we have been successful in achieving our main objective of prompting a larger cross-section of the community to respond. Although we have accomplished our primary goal there were challenges that go beyond the usual challenges associated with logistics such as time, funding, and space.

When initially conceiving a DIY media architecture prototype we envisioned the community members coming together to construct or create the interactive components of the actual InstaBooth structure. To this date we have not been able to reach that extent of the imagined DIY media architecture and it is here we must address the challenges associated with creating physical structures in public space. We acknowledge that there is a possible need for curatorial control, and general safety of the public. Also we begin to question the definition of public space, due to the fact that all of our deployments required permission to be granted by city council or property owners. There has not been an instance yet where the general citizens have deployed the InstaBooth when they wanted to, for their own purposes or asked their own questions. Although we can aspire to reach this level of citizen control over a media architecture such as the InstaBooth, the reality is that such physical and technical interventions require certain levels of management, knowledge and interest. The InstaBooth has limitations in that it requires access to an electricity and wifi source, and is not completely weather proofed impacting on the locations in which it can be placed.

There are many lessons that have been learned through each deployment from our collaborators and users. The InstaBooth asks questions of the people, and we have found that asking questions in a positive manner has helped promote positive responses. Also acknowledging that the information collected through the InstaBooth will inform some element of change. The InstaBooth works best in public space versus inside buildings. Signage and descriptions are required to inform participants of the expectations, the purpose of the InstaBooth and each interaction module, and inviting them to use it. The principal finding is that the communities we engaged with are seeking alternative avenues to have their say on a wide variety of issues ranging from the future of their city to gender equity. People are interested in learning from one another, sharing their ideas, and having a voice in creative ways.

The findings from evaluating our deployments of the InstaBooth show that the potential of media architecture goes beyond just combining information, media and physical infrastructure as a new form of construction material. Aristotle's famous saying applies: "The whole is greater than the sum of its parts." In the so-called 'Age of Access,' we still face many challenges and boundaries not just to accessability but also to usability, usefulness and impact. Quantity of data does not imply quality, and thus with more sources of content, spread via more digital media channels, to more people, we face the problem of information overload. Foth et al. (2015) point out that corporations such as Facebook and Google have deployed sophisticated filters and recommendation systems designed to help us navigate the otherwise bloated social mediascape. The content displayed on Facebook's news feed is selected based on a user's profile, their location, interests, habits, online transactions – what they post, share, recommend, and "like." The popularity of social media stems from its power to create personalised spaces, walled gardens, which are tailored to individual preferences and favour content relevant to each user. Corporate algorithms proprietary to each social media site determine what is deemed relevant: With the absence of a journalistic or editorial code of ethics, these algorithms determine the make-up of the Facebook news feed, Google's top search results, and the recommendations on whom to follow on Twitter and what to buy on Amazon. They are optimised to prioritise content that will generate more traffic. Yet, Lotan (2014) warns that, *"We're not seeing different viewpoints, but rather more of the same. A healthy democracy is contingent on having a healthy media ecosystem. As builders of these online networked spaces, how do we make sure we are optimizing not only for traffic and engagement, but also an informed public? ... The underlying algorithmics powering this recommendation engine help reinforce our values and bake more of the same voices into our information streams."*

The compounding aspects of this polarisation of opinions in social media have been studied in political science and media and communication studies, e.g., *echo chambers* and *filter bubbles* (Pariser 2011). These issues in social media risk a political polarisation. Yet, there is an opportunity in media architecture where pretty lights and colourful LED façades are increasingly making way for situated installations, civic interventions and DIY / DIWO deployments fostering community engagement and citizen empowerment.

In our work, we found that the values and potential of media architecture is embedded in its capacity to provide an innovative avenue for fostering depolarisation, diversity of discourse, and a functioning public sphere.

In the next chapter of this book, Martin Tomitsch presents the notion of the city as an operating system and the development of city apps that plug into the data streams that are collected and shared through smart city initiatives. Although the InstaBooth does not display digital real time data like the IBM control centre in Brazil it does allow for the collection of data in various digital and analogue formats. Different to an API the InstaBooth's data does not require a computer or smart phone to make the data visible and accessible to others allowing for future commentaries and the sharing of opinions. It is in this way that the InstaBooth can be seen to act as a city app. When comparing the success of the different interaction modules within the InstaBooth the paper based and tangible interactions consistently collect more responses than the purely digital interactions. This supports previous findings that handwritten responses tend to stimulate more meaningful responses from participants (Parra Agudelo et al. 2013) but also highlights the importance of the human factor in the data that is collected. The handwritten notes, the drawings, the playdough, these tangible and analogue data sets reflect the people who have created them, thus revealing the human quality and personal nature of the comments and ideas that are shared through the InstaBooth. We believe that it is this DIY human quality which helps to attract the interest of others and assists in stimulating engagement from more people.

When considering the future directions of this research there is further potential in exploring how the InstaBooth could improve its connection into the city's data streams to assist in making such information more visible and accessible to all people. The InstaBooth could act as a physical porthole into the city's data by leveraging its technological aspects to assist in visualizing the information but also allow for direct analysis, comprehension and discussion to be stimulated through its different interactive components. In the first section of this book

Patrick Fischer and Eva Hornecker introduce urban HCI focusing on the creation of space to promote shared encounters. The InstaBooth creates a semi private series of spaces within the broader context of public urban space and through its interactive modules shared encounters are encouraged. Exploring these elements of the InstaBooth further could contribute to the growing dialogue connecting media architecture and urban HCI.

6 Acknowledgements

We are grateful for research funding that the InstaBooth project has received from a 2014 QUT Engagement Innovation grant and a QUT Women in Research grant. We thank the InstaBooth project team, partners, collaborators and contributors for their support, interest, and continued enthusiasm.

Bibliography

Buchenau, M.; Suri, J.F. (2000): "Experience prototyping". In: Proceedings of the 3rd conference on Designing interactive systems: processes, practices, methods, and techniques. Brooklyn, NY: ACM, 424–433. doi: 10.1145/347642.347802.

Caldwell, G.; Bilandzic, M.; Foth, M. (2012): "Towards visualising people's ecology of hybrid personal learning environments". In: M. Brynskov (ed.): Proceedings of the 4th Media Architecture Biennale: Participation. Aarhus, Denmark: ACM, 13–22. doi: 10.1145/2421076.2421080.

Caldwell, G.; Foth, M. (2014): "DIY media architecture: Open and participatory approaches to community engagement". In: P. Dalsgaard; A. Fatah gen Schieck (eds.): Proceedings of the 2nd Media Architecture Biennale Conference: World Cities. Aarhus, Denmark: ACM, 1–10. doi: 10.1145/2682884.2682893.

Caldwell, G.; Guaralda, M.; Donovan, J.; Rittenbruch, M. (2016): "The InstaBooth: Making common ground for media architectural design". In: P. Dalsgaard; A. Fatah gen Schieck (eds.): Proceedings of the 2016 Media Architecture Biennale. Sydney, Australia: ACM (In Press).

Dalsgaard, P.; Dindler, C.; Halskov, K. (2011): "Understanding the dynamics of engaging interaction in public spaces". In: Proceedings of the 13th IFIP TC13 International Conference on Human-Computer Interaction, INTERACT 2011, Part II. Lisbon, Portugal: Springer Berlin Heidelberg, 212–229. doi: 10.1007/978-3-642-23771-3.

Foth, M. (2010): "Participation, animation, design: a tripartite approach to urban community networking". AI & Society: the journal of human-centered systems and machine intelligence 25:3, 335–343. doi: 10.1007/s00146-009-0263-9.

Foth, M.; Choi, J.H.; Satchell, C. (2011): "Urban Informatics". In: Proceedings of the ACM 2011 Conference on Computer Supported Cooperative Work. New York, NY: ACM, 1–8. doi: 10.1145/1958824.1958826.

Foth, M.; Fischer, F.; Satchell, C. (2013): "From Movie Screens to Moving Screens: Mapping Qualities of New Urban Interactions". In: J. Geiger; O. Khan; M. Shepard (eds.): Proceedings of the 4th MediaCities conference. Buffalo, NY: University at Buffalo, 194–204.

Foth, M.; Tomitsch, M.; Satchell, C.; Haeusler, M.H. (2015): "From users to citizens: Some thoughts on designing for polity and civics". In: OzCHI '15 Proceedings of the Annual Meeting of the Australian Special Interest Group for Computer Human Interaction. Melbourne, Australia: ACM, 623–633. doi: 10.1145/2838739.2838769.

Francisco, S. (2007): "The Way We Do Things Around Here: Specification Versus Craft Culture in the History of Building". American Behavioral Scientist 50:7, 970–988. doi: 10.1177/0002764206298322.

Gauntlett, D. (2011): Making is Connecting. Cambridge, UK: Polity.

Iveson, K. (2013): "Cities within the City: Do-It-Yourself Urbanism and the Right to the City". International Journal of Urban and Regional Research 37:3, 941–956. doi: 10.1111/1468-2427.12053.

Johnstone, S.; Caldwell, G.; Rittenbruch, M. (2015): "Defining the InstaBooth: Facilitating debate and content creation from situated users". In: MediaCity 5 International Conference and Exhibition, Plymouth, UK: Plymouth University, 187–206.

Kolbitsch, J.; Maurer, H. (2006): "The Transformation of the Web: How Emerging Communities Shape the Information we Consume". Journal of Universal Computer Science 12:2, 187–213. doi: 10.3217/jucs-012-02-0187.

Kortbek, K.J. (2008): "Interaction Design for Public Spaces". In: MM '08 Proceedings of the 16th ACM International Conference on Multimedia. Vancouver, Canada: ACM, 1031–1034. doi: 10.1145/1459359.1459566.

Lotan, G. (2014): Israel, Gaza, War & Data: Social networks and the art of personalizing propaganda. Retrieved from https://medium.com/i-data/israel-gaza-war-data-a54969aeb23e (Feb 15, 2015).

Pariser, E. (2011): The filter bubble: What the Internet is hiding from you. New York, NY: Penguin Press.

Parra Agudelo, L.; Caldwell, G.; Schroeter, R. (2013): "Write vs. type: tangible and situated media for situated engagement". In: K. Sugiyama (ed.): Consilience and Innovation in Design: Proceedings and Program: 5th IASDR 2013. Tokyo, Japan: Shibaura Institute of Technology, 4818–4829.

Ratto, M.; Boler, M. (eds.) (2014): DIY Citizenship: Critical Making and Social Media. Cambridge, MA: MITP.

Scheible, J. (2010): Empowering Mobile Art Practice: A Recontextualization of Mobile and Ubiquitous Computing. Doctoral Dissertation, Aalto University, Helsinki, Finland. Retrieved from http://urn.fi/URN:ISBN:978-952-60-3650-2 (Aug 30, 2016).

Schroeter, R. (2012): "Engaging new digital locals with interactive urban screens to collaboratively improve the city". In: Proceedings of the ACM 2012 Conference on Computer Supported Cooperative Work. Seattle, WA: ACM, 227–236. doi: 10.1145/2145204.2145239.

Schroeter, R.; Foth, M.; Satchell, C. (2012): "People, content, location: sweet spotting urban screens for situated engagement". In: Proceedings of DIS12 Designing Interactive Systems. Newcastle Upon Tyne, UK: ACM, 146–155. doi: 10.1145/2317956.2317980.

Martin Tomitsch

City Apps as Urban Interfaces

1 Introduction

Media architecture is an umbrella term to describe the integration of digital media and the built environment. In early studies of media architecture this approach was seen as a way of creating an 'architecture of images', which at the time was also referred to as 'mediatecture' (Fahmi, 2001). This integration of physical and digital media creates a hybrid interface, where the physical world is augmented with digital media, typically in the form of images or videos, displayed on digital screens. Media architecture is therefore often used as synonym for building-scale displays integrated into the built architecture in the form of media facades.

This chapter, along with M. Hank Haeusler's chapter in this book and other scholars, argues for a more refined distinction between media architecture and media facades. In a 2011 paper presented at a CHI workshop on "large displays in urban life" my colleague Gernot Tscherteu and I offered definitions for urban screens, media facades and media architecture (Tscherteu and Tomitsch, 2011). In this paper, we described urban screens as mid- to large-scale screens that can either be freestanding or attached to a building façade. Media façades in comparison feature a closer integration of the screen and the building layers, if not a complete integration into a new hybrid structure. Media architecture includes media installations that work with the depth of space, in which case it is no longer possible to speak of a screen or a façade. This implies that media architecture interfaces are not necessarily limited to screens. Brynskov et al. (2013) expand this definition by describing media architecture as an "overarching concept that covers the design of physical spaces at architectural scale incorporating materials with dynamic properties that allow for dynamic, reactive or interactive behavior".

While early protagonists of media architecture in the form of media facades might easily be dismissed as pastel-colored light embellishments, media architecture as an overarching concept provides rich opportunities for city and place making (Caldwell and Foth, 2014; Wouters et al., 2015; Fredericks et al., 2016). In particular of relevance in today's age of access, is the deployment of media architecture installations for visualizing situated data, which can increase awareness about contextually relevant topics (Claes and Vande Moere, 2013; Colangelo, 2014; Valkanova et al., 2015) and ultimately improve aspects associated with livability (Tomitsch, 2014). It is because of this extended view of media architecture as a framework that the field has started to draw interest from smart city initiatives and advocates. Both, media architecture and smart city initiatives, build on the

DOI 10.1515/9783110453874-007

premise of advanced sensing technologies being distributed across the city. In the case of smart city initiatives, the data streams generated from these sensor networks are consolidated and visualized in smart city data centers (Kitchin, 2014). This 'smart-city-in-a-box' approach (Hemment and Townsend, 2013) has seen criticism in regards to the way data is being managed and only made accessible to a selective group of government organizations.

In the case of media architecture installations, the data collected through city-scale sensors is displayed in a highly public and accessible way on hybrid interfaces, for example in the form of media facades or urban screens. This chapter expands the traditional view of media architecture installations taking the form of building-scale displays. It proposes that media architecture installations can take on a range of scales from palm-sized devices to building facades. The chapter draws on media architecture as a framework to guide the design and deployment of hybrid interfaces. More specifically, it describes a citizen-centered design approach to provide situated access to real-time data in the city. To that end, the chapter puts forward the concept of the city as an operating system, consisting of a series of input channels and using media architecture as city-scale output devices.

The remainder of the chapter discusses the evolution of signage and the opportunities enabled by new computing paradigms, such as ubiquitous computing and ambient displays, for communicating real-time information in the city. It then describes the vision of the real-time city and reviews current trends and practices from cities and governments for implementing this vision. Based on this discussion, the chapter proposes the notion of 'city apps' as urban real-time interfaces, grounded in an analysis of existing real-time interfaces and proposing ways for advancing city apps through the lens of media architecture. This discussion includes approaches for designing and deploying city apps. The chapter concludes by reflecting on potential synergies between media architecture and smart city initiatives and the role of city apps for addressing some of the challenges that cities face due to mass urbanization and population growth.

2 Digital displays in the city

The idea of embedding information into the built environment is not new. Media in the form of signage has been used in cities for as long as the written language has existed. Weiser (1991), who coined the notion of ubiquitous computing, even suggested that the written language could be considered the first form of information technology. Whether signs indicate traffic regulations, depict sites, or advertise shops and their offerings, they communicate some form of message to the public. Drawing analogies to ubiquitous computing, Weiser described written signage as a perfect example of calm technology, as it is readily available to provide information when needed, without being in the way. Because signage is so ubiquitous, we don't notice it, unless we need to access the information conveyed by it. In comparison, today's personal computing devices require the user's full attention when accessing information and use visual and audio signals to compete for the user's attention, for example to announce incoming messages or an application waiting for user input.

2.1 Ambient digital displays

Concepts of ubiquitous or calm computing inspired decades of research determined to implement Weiser's vision of calm technology. One of the notions that emerged from these efforts is the ambient display of real-time information (Mankoff et al., 2003). At the core of this concept is the idea of communicating information at the periphery of the user's vision, using a range of modalities, such as visuals or sound (Tomitsch et al., 2007). The premise is that ambient information displays allow people to access information while being engaged in a primary activity.

For example, the *Ambient Orb*[1] was a consumer product that implemented this idea by translating real-time information into shades of color. Users were able to choose from a range of data sources, such as weather data, surf conditions, or stock markets, which would then be mapped to a color scale. Apart from allowing people to receive information without having to turn on one of their personal computing devices, the Ambient Orb was also designed to match the character of a home environment. Similarly, other ambient information displays were proposed, such as the *informative art* series (Holmquist and Skog, 2003), which communicated information, such as weather data and the arrival of new email messages, through visuals implementing the style of well-known artists. Using this approach, information could be consumed through artwork hung on the wall, or embedded into wallpaper (Skog, 2004), again matching the character of home environments, rather than forcing humans to enter the computing environment (Weiser, 1991).

1 http://ambientdevices.com/about/consumer-devices

2.2 Pervasive urban displays

Although computers today are ubiquitous, this is far from Weiser's original vision of computers receding in the background, being there to support people in their day-to-day experiences without being in their face (Aylett and Quigly, 2015). How this vision can achieved is therefore still a matter of discussion (Rogers, 2006; Bell and Dourish, 2007), however the enabling technologies continue to evolve, leading to new forms of digital interfaces and paradigms. Of particular relevance in the context of this chapter is the advancement of digital display technologies as an interface between people and the digital world. Public displays in the form of LED or plasma screens are now pervasive in the built environment. However, their primary focus in many cases is to compete for people's attention – which follows the same single-attention approach implemented by personal computing devices. The advancement of display technologies in the built environment, it seems, has led to a 'signage on steroids' approach. Displays are flashing at passers-by to announce early bird parking rates (Figure 1), and advertising content is given significantly more attention and display space than the information that actually matters to people, demonstrated for example in airport environments (Aylett and Quigly, 2015).

Fig. 1: LED display at a car park in Melbourne, Australia, advertising special rates for car parking using an animated, flashing label.

This trend is contrasted by the rollout of media facades as building-scale low-resolution displays, which use LEDs to complement or support the physical topology of buildings. In many ways, media facades were enabled by similar technological advancements that led to the vision and realization of ubiquitous computing. However, it was mostly architects and artists who drove their implementation rather than computer scientists and they have seen little to no attention in the human-computer interaction (HCI) community until Dalsgaard and Halskov's (2010) paper on challenges for designing urban media facades. On the one hand, architects argue that media should be treated as building material with the aim to support the character and appearance of the architecture (Haeusler et al., 2012). On the other hand, the HCI community has mostly focused on strategies for enabling passers-by to engage and interact with large displays (Hespanhol et al., 2012; Memarovic et al., 2012; Ackad et al., 2013) and media facades (Wiethoff and Gehring, 2012) and studying people's behavior around them (Fischer and Hornecker, 2012; Tomitsch et al., 2014). We can currently see a convergence of media facades and public display research, manifested through shared discourse venues, such as the International Symposium on Pervasive Displays and the Media Architecture Biennale, which bring together academics and practitioners working across the disciplines of HCI, architecture, design and visual art.

This chapter therefore takes an inclusive approach and proposes the use of media architecture as an umbrella term for a holistic design approach to multi-scale urban displays, from small embedded interfaces to large media facades. To that end, the chapter also attempts to integrate concepts from HCI and architecture with the aim to advance approaches for real-time data access in the city.

2.3 Ambient architectural displays

Ultimately, media architecture installations can offer similar characteristics to ambient information displays (Mankoff et al., 2003; Tomitsch et al., 2007). A key element of this approach is that the media layer is appropriately integrated into the built environment. Media facades achieve this integration by using media as architectural building component (Haeusler, 2009). However, in most cases to date the media takes the form of ambient patterns rather than communicating information (Haeusler et al., 2012; Tomitsch et al., 2015).

More recently, advancements in sensing technologies and networked devices, have led to the conception of media façade installations, that communicate information. For example, Colangelo (2014) described an application for the existing media façade on the Ryerson Image Centre in Toronto, Canada, which displays two types of real-time information: first, the wind speed and direction is visualized as a blue wave on the building, and second, occurrences of the hash-tag

#homelessness on Twitter trigger a red pulse (Figure 2). Another example of a building-scale media façade that communicates information is the National Football Stadium in Lima, Peru. The media façade installation uses distributed microphones to capture the noise levels within the stadium during games to visualize the mood of the spectator audience through light patterns on the building façade (Haeusler et al., 2012; page 134).

Fig. 2: Media façade installation at the Ryerson School of Image and the Ryerson Image Centre visualizing wind patterns and social media activity.

Similarly, media architecture installations of smaller scale integrate real-time data as media input and physical form to convey information in an ambient way. For example, the *Hybrid Media Display* project[2], described in more detail by Alexander Wiethoff and Marius Hoggenmüller in their chapter, visualizes the arrival time of underground services using a combination of text-based information and low-resolution ambient visualization drawing on the metaphor of an hourglass.

3 The real-time city

The examples of media architecture installations described thus far are highly-site specific. Their description typically includes a discussion of the immediate context as this has an effect on the design of the intervention (Wouters and Vande Moere, 2011). However, there is not much literature that looks at the systemic nature, implications and opportunities of media architecture installations. In con-

2 http://www.dielight.com/portfolio/ambient-display/

trast, smart city initiatives often start from a system-centered approach, partly due to the fact that such initiatives are top-down implementations of standardized software solutions (Townsend, 2013). While this top-down approach has rightly received much criticism (Greenfield, 2013; Hill, 2013), there are some considerations emerging from smart city initiatives that can inform the development of media architecture. This section identifies these considerations through a discussion of the vision of the real-time city, which forms the foundation for the concept of the city as operating system and city apps.

3.1 The vision of the real-time city

Urban digital media are transforming the city landscape not only on its surface, evidenced through large public screens and media facades, but also through an invisible network of digital service infrastructures, which are continuously collecting and generating data throughout the city. For example, sensors collect information about vehicle traffic, electricity usage, the city's public transport network, its water network for leakage detection, etc.

In the real-time city, this data is transmitted to some form of control interface and visualized in real-time. There is a trend towards establishing centralized control rooms, in which these data streams are brought together and displayed on large arrays of digital screens for analysis and to inform decision-making. For example, the 'Centro De Operacoes Prefeitura Do Rio' in Rio de Janeiro, Brazil, collects data from 30 different government agencies, to monitor the life in the city in real-time 24 hours a day (Ferguson, 2013). The aggregated data, which ranges from traffic to the social mood in the city to weather conditions, is visualized on a giant control interface. The aim of this centralized real-time control and data analytics center is to enable sustainable development and economic growth.

While these data centers offer promising opportunities for making cities more livable, they have seen some criticism, mostly associated with the top-down approach in which they are implemented (e.g. Townsend, 2013; Hill, 2013). In line with this criticism, Kitchin (2014) describes three concerns about the real-time city, being technocratic governance, "corporatization" of city government and panoptic cities. Kitchin links these concerns to the observation that smart city proposals are based on an approach that is narrow in scope, the fact that smart city agendas are heavily promoted by large ICT and service companies, and the risks associated with recording data about all aspects of city life in a central database that is processed through corporate systems.

Following this criticism, there have been arguments that data generated by citizens should remain freely and openly accessible to all citizens. How this data can best be used to the advantage of citizens is still unclear (Townsend et al., 2010). An approach, implemented by an increasing number of cities around the world is to provide open application programming interfaces (APIs) that make it possible for people to implement their own applications using civic data. To date, most of the applications that have emerged through these initiatives are in the form of websites or mobile apps. However, with data about public transport, traffic conditions and other civic services becoming openly available, there are opportunities to connect this movement with the principles of media architecture in order to create new situated urban interfaces that connect citizens with the digital real-time layer of the city.

3.2 Accessing the digital layer of cities

The rise of the internet has led to opportunities for innovating the way cities are being managed and run. The term 'digital city' is generally used to describe any aspects of city making and governance that involve digital ingredients. For example, one of Sydney's suburbs was said to be the first digital city in Australia in a media announcement in 2010[3]. The statement listed digital strategies, such as providing free public wifi and mobile apps for parking and other municipal services. Although free public wifi is still heralded as innovation in smart city master plans, the more interesting aspect in the context of this chapter, are the apps made possible through the provision of data. For cities, this is an important shift from not only collecting the data but also making it available to developers and designers in a standardized format. Governments around the world are joining the open data movement, releasing access to civic data, ranging from real-time transport data to garbage collection schedules. This movement is an important first step to release data from the smart city control centers and making it available to citizens.

An increasing number of cities around the world, such as Chicago, further decided not to attempt creating apps themselves but to rather encourage the community to decide how to use this data and to develop their own applications. The city of Chicago even promotes these emerging "civic data apps" through the Chicago Digital initiative and platform[4]. This move may indicate an acknowledgment of the creativity of citizens, who use civic data to solve problems they observe within their own communities. At the same time, it might be seen as indication that cities lack the technical competence and resources to conceive and deploy civic data

3 http://www.news.com.au/technology/parramatta-to-be-australias-first-digital-city/story-e6frfro0-1225936913058

4 http://digital.cityofchicago.org/index.php/open-data-applications/

apps themselves. An approach that has been adopted by cities and organizations around the world to spark civic data app development are hackathons, in which designers and developers come together to compete for prizes awarded for innovative ideas. Despite their popularity, this raises the question whether the people, who invent such apps are indeed the ones experiencing the issues that the apps aim to address. Nonetheless, these trends depict an important shift in how governmental institutions understand their responsibilities. Rather than safeguarding the data generated by the city and its citizens, they are seeing their role as an interface between the city and the citizens.

A variation of hackathons are so-called "hothouse" events, which involve the mentoring and support of winning participants beyond the event. For example, Transport for NSW, the transport authority for the state of New South Wales, Australia, ran a hothouse in Sydney in 2013, which successfully pushed the development of real-time transport apps (Tompson, 2015).

On a more conceptual level, such civic data apps provide portals into the digital layer of the city. They grant access to data that was previously hidden and not available. Through advanced sensing and mobile technologies, it is now possible to know at what time the next train arrives, to see around the corner for finding parking spots, or to take a virtual glimpse into buildings to find the nearest bathroom facilities with access for people with disabilities. Civic data apps can be seen as protagonists of true bottom-up solutions that enable smarter living in today's cities. However, to date they are mostly confined to websites and mobile devices, requiring people to a) possess a personal computer or mobile device, b) understand how to use these devices, and c) know about the apps and how to access them.

Media architecture, as described by Brynskov et al. (2013) and in other chapters of this book (e.g. M. Hank Haeusler's chapter on designing content) provides a framework to transgress the boundaries of personal computers and mobile devices, weaving civic data into the built environment and providing in-situ access when and where it matters. To achieve this, the next section proposes the concept of the city as operating system.

3.3 The city as operating system

Smart city solutions offered by large ICT providers are typically sold much like a proprietary operating system that consists of sensors and IT infrastructures, essentially locking governments into that particular provider (Townsend, 2013). Where this approach fails is that these top-down systems consist of standardized modules and restrict any adaptions to be carried out by the provider. In many ways, this is similar to the outdated model used for operating systems on desktop computers in the 1970s and early operating systems for smartphones. Even the first version of Apple's operating system developed for the original iPhone was originally a closed system that confined the development of new apps to Apple. In 2008 by opening up their mobile operating system, Apple made it possible for anyone with the appropriate tools and skills to develop an app that would be available to every iPhone (and later iPad) user.

As described earlier, many cities are already moving towards offering and managing access to civic data through standardized APIs. As such, the city offers similarities to personal computing devices in that it consists of a series of input and output channels. The term 'operating system' here is used in a much more conceptual sense compared to how it is used in the context of desktop computers and smartphones. But essentially the city is providing the infrastructure on top of which 'user interfaces' are built along with pre-existing input and output mechanisms. Input channels include urban activities, such as traffic or pedestrian flow, and environmental conditions, such as air quality, temperature, light, etc. Output channels include surfaces, such as the street or building façades, and urban furniture, such benches, street lamps, etc.

Of course, the city is a messy operating system and it is difficult to impossible to develop a clearly defined, universal API. But conceptually this metaphor adds to the emphasis that the citizen is given not only as user but also by enabling bottom-up solutions to emerge, opening up new opportunities for DIY media architecture as described by Glenda Amayo Caldwell and Marcus Foth in their chapter. Similar to desktop and smartphone operating systems, providing access to the city's input channels, allows anyone who has the tools and skills to build user interfaces. Using the concept of the city as operating system moves possibilities beyond the development of mobile apps. Much more, this concept through the lens of media architecture makes it possible to think about city apps as access points sitting on top of the city's infrastructure.

The next section will take a closer look at these forms of 'city apps' and how they can contribute to making cities more livable.

4 City apps

City apps can take any form of digital interface that people use in the public space of the urban environment. Examples for city apps include, digital information screens, digital wayfinding signs, and applications running on urban screens or media façades. Even smartphone applications can be considered city apps when they are designed to be explicitly used in the public space of urban environments, such as apps for finding parking spots or to receive information about public transport services.

4.1 Real-time data access through city apps

The presence of digital technology in the definition of city apps plays an important role to distinguish the design of city apps from traditional urban design. In that sense a park bench is not a city app, while a traffic light push button for pedestrians is a city app. This is essential, as digital technology a) enables people to interact with the city's infrastructure through the city app or for city apps to respond reactively to the behavior of people, and b) provides the means for mapping digital information into a form that can be accessed by passers-by.

Fig. 3: Digital display used in Vienna, Austria, to visualize the arrival times of upcoming tram and bus services.

From the perspective of the real-time city, public screens represent a promising platform to reveal digital information in a physical context, with the capability to update their content in real-time. An example for this type of use of public screens that has already found its way into many cities is the use of digital screens at transport hubs to display upcoming services (Figure 3). One might argue that it is much more economic to rely on smartphones to disseminate this information, however

Fig. 4: A traffic light in Seoul, displaying a countdown of the remaining time left for crossing the road.

such an approach would exclude people who do not own or know how to operate a smartphone. Having access to information in-situ has also been reported to be the preferred method compared to smartphone applications (Rahman, 2012).

Fig. 5: StreetPong allows people to kill time while waiting for the traffic light to turn green by playing pong with someone waiting at the other side of the road. (Image from: http://www.streetpong.info, copyright: Amelie Kuenzler and Sandro Engel / http://urban-invention.com).

Traffic lights can maybe considered to be the first examples of city apps. The first electric traffic light was installed in Cleveland, Ohio, and featured a green and red light to control the flow of traffic at a busy intersection. Traffic lights are an interface into the city's infrastructure. They use simple lights as output channel to dynamically visualize road conditions to drivers and pedestrians. Traffic lights may even be described as early forms of media architecture, although they only offer a two or three pixel resolution. More advanced implementations of traffic lights now feature numerical displays that show a countdown of the red or green phases (Figure 4). An example for a traffic light that uses digital technologies to add even further value to pedestrians is *StreetPong*[5] (known as 'ActiWait' in its next iteration), which turns the traffic light's push button device into a high-resolution interface. The interface allows people to play pong while waiting for the light to turn green. To encourage social encounters, the game is played with another person waiting on the other side of the road. As outlined by Patrick Tobias Fischer and Eva Hornecker in their chapter, designing shared encounters through media architecture can enrich everyday life in cities. The *StreetPong* interface also provides a visualization of the remaining waiting time through an animated, declining bar in the background of the game (Figure 5).

Fig. 6: Low resolution media displays used to provide feedback about domestic electricity usage in a neighbourhood setting.

City apps can also take the form of situated data visualizations (Vande Moere and Hill, 2012) or street info graphics (Claes and Vande Moere, 2013). Such interventions typically use more complex and larger datasets than the simple information associated with traffic lights or the arrival time of public transport services. For example, in a project investigating the concept of urban neighborhood displays, we used mechanical low-resolution displays to visualize the electricity consumption of households (Figure 6). The displays also offered passers-by a way of interact-

5 http://www.streetpong.info/

ing with the display through a simple push button, which triggered an animation based on the electricity consumption patterns of all participating households. In another study we used large analogue displays to visualize patterns of domestic electricity consumption along with a neighborhood ranking (Vande Moere et al., 2011). We found that real-time data was perceived to be useful even when it was updated on a very low cycle (once a day in the case of our study). Indeed, the low update rate added a concrete value to how study participants experienced the intervention, as the daily updates became an important recurring part of their lives during the 7-week period of the study. Urban interventions that display complex datasets can increase social awareness and discourse, however their design needs to be carefully informed to ensure people can easily understand the information provided (Valkanova et al., 2015).

4.2 The human scale of city apps

Using the notion of city apps places an emphasis on citizens as users of the intervention. This approach complements the focus of media architecture and smart city solutions, which is typically on the architecture, the cities and their governance. Similar to how some scholars in urban planning and architecture have put forward arguments for considering the human scale of cities (Gehl, 2013; Burke, 2016), city apps introduce a human scale to media architecture. Just as the success of mobile apps is heavily dependent on the employment of a human-centered design approach, city apps rely on the citizen being at the core of the design process for their successful deployment.

The experience of cities is even more complex compared to how people experience products, since people compose their own city. As de Waal (2014) describes, "they use a network of cities that is spread over the whole city", meaning that people live in one place, work in a different suburb across town, shop in their favorite shopping center or sometimes in the city center, and spend their spare time in recreational places, such as an indoor pool or a nearby park. People compose the city as a network of places that meet their particular requirements.

The way people experience the urban environment is therefore not so much a result of strategic urban planning, but rather "driven by the individual planning of the inhabitants of the city" (de Waal, 2014). It is difficult to design for a specific urban experience, similarly to how it is impossible to design the user experience of a digital product. As designers we can only design the conditions for a great experience to unfold (Zmijewski, 2008). On a higher level the design of city apps should therefore employ design frameworks established from other domains, such as participatory design (Floyd et al., 1989) and action research (Lewin, 1946).

On a more concrete application level, it is important to understand the citizens' needs in a particular environment or situation, and to identify opportunities for city apps to empower citizens. A useful approach is to think about city apps as tools that provide citizens with superpowers. For example, real-time data displays at bus stops allow people to "see" the whereabouts of their service before it arrives at the stop; and digital countdown displays at traffic lights enable drivers and pedestrians to exactly know how much longer they have to wait for the light to turn green.

Ultimately, city apps that are designed around citizens and their needs can help to improve the livability in cities, for example by improving the experience of public transport services, but also lead to more sustainable use of resources, by making the actions of people visible.

4.3 The physical context of city apps

City apps are always used in a particular physical context. Many city apps further consist of a physical as well as a digital user interface. A traffic light push button with feedback light, for example, has a physical input component (the push button) and a digital output (the light signal). The *TetraBIN* project (Bai and Tomisch, 2015) consists of a higher resolution output channel compared to a traffic light push button. It uses an LED screen wrapped around a city bin to turn the act of disposing rubbish into a playful experience. In this example, physical input is in the form of trash being disposed into the bin, which is translated into digital output mapped onto the LED screen (Figure 7).

Media architecture provides a framework for the physical design of city apps, as it specifically described the integration of media and the built environment. Seen through the lens of city apps, media façades exemplify a perfect integration of the digital and the physical user interface. The screen element of a media façade is closely integrated with the building layers, if not a complete integration into a new hybrid structure (Haeusler, 2009). Although from a technical perspective the image production still takes place on certain parts of the façade, the visual imagery is designed to be perceived as part of the built architecture (Tscherteu and Tomitsch, 2011). This is fundamentally different to media displays that are installed without close connection to the underlying building layers, described earlier as urban screens. If an urban screen is attached to a building, the screen and the building façade remain two separated layers both in terms of the technical installation as well as in the way the two elements communicate their function. If urban screens appear as freestanding, independent architectonic elements, they tend to take on the single purpose to communicate media content (McQuire et al.,

2009). The same principle can be translated to the integration of digital displays of any scale, from 30-inch plasma screens to small, embedded displays.

In traditional screen-based interaction design, the software usually outlives the device platform. For example, mobile apps are continuously developed, and remain available and functional for new smartphone models. It's relatively easy to update software and push out a new version if any adaptions are necessary to ensure it runs on the new model. The physical user interface of city apps is much more complex, or in some cases impossible, to replace. Replacing the physical user interface is associated with high costs and time-consuming. Unlike with software updates, updates to the physical user interface cannot be rolled out at the push of a button.

Fig. 7: LED screen used on city bins to gamify the act of disposing rubbish. While providing an interactive game experience, the display also visualizes data about garbage collection in the city.

It is therefore crucial to consider the life span of city apps in their design. How long a city app will be deployed for determines not only the implementation but also the design of the city app. If it is meant to be deployed for several years or even decades, it may be necessary to allow any necessary updates or replacements through the design of the physical user interface, similar to Brand's (1994) notion of 'shearing layers' in architecture. A potential solution is to separate the digital user interface from the underlying physical structure, or designing them in a way so that they can be easily replaced. Technology is evolving at such a rapid pace, that it is necessary to allow for specific components to be upgraded or replaced, without having to completely redeploy the display, including fixtures, cabling, etc.

5 Conclusion

This chapter introduced the notion of the city as operating system as a conceptual framework for designing access to dynamic information in cities. It further described the concept of city apps as human-scale interfaces that are built on top of the city as operating system. Using this approach to media architecture thinking, almost any object in the public space of the urban environment, be it a swing, a traffic light, a bench, or a trash bin, can be turned into a city app. Based on the examples discussed throughout the chapter, city apps offer the following characteristics:
- Designed to be used by citizens;
- Designed to be primarily used in an urban environment;
- Improve the urban experience for citizens;
- Make use of digital technology for sensing and/or displaying data;
- Can be interactive, reactive, or dynamic;
- Can be mobile or situated.

As exemplified through the examples discussed in this chapter, city apps are not limited in or defined according to their physical size. They can be completely embedded, the size of a smartphone, or the scale of a high-rise skyscraper. Although the notion of city apps is derived from the nowadays pervasive concept of smartphone apps, it requires some rethinking of what constitutes an 'app'. On a smartphone, an app is a software program that can be downloaded from an application store. It is primarily designed to run on smartphones or other mobile devices. City apps are designed to use the city as operating system. Here the operating system is not a software package with pre-defined application interfaces, window managers, etc. Instead the city as operating system is a complex construct that consists of the urban fabric, people passing through the space, other services, and so on. Every space of the city is different in regards to all these aspects that form the operating system. In that sense the operating system, or the part of the operating system, on which the city app is implemented is highly dependent on the specific location and its physical, social and cultural context.

All the examples discussed in this chapter were designed for a specific site. Even though it may seem that city apps, such as *StreetPong* and *TetraBIN*, could easily be transferred to any other crossing, street, precinct or city, their deployment within a different site would require adjustments. For example, for *TetraBIN* we augmented bins that were identical in their physical form to the ones that were already used in the site, which determined the fabrication of the digital media layer. We further considered viewpoints, the paths of people walking past, and the type of audience passing through the site. Such site-specific adjustments may be subtle but are essential to ensure the city app will fit into the existing built environment and its fabric. It is important here to also distinguish between abstractions that need to be made to the software versus the physical components of the city app, as each component might require different approaches and different levels of adjustments.

The chapter extends ways of designing for today's age of access by encouraging bringing urban data out of control rooms and into the streets and public spaces of the city. The examples discussed in this chapter illustrate how data that is already being sensed and processed, such as traffic light cycles and data about garbage collection, can be made accessible to citizens through urban interfaces. However, there are still challenges around accessing civic data, posing barriers to the application of the ideas described in this chapter in practice. For example, some city institutions are still reluctant to make their data publicly available due to political, ethical or legal concerns. Even in cases, where data is being made available, it is sometimes not possible to get access to real-time data and the processing of data is complex, leading to inaccurate or incomplete datasets.

By taking on a holistic approach and using media and information as building components, city apps have the potential to increase aspects associated with the livability of cities. Rather than following the trend of ICT-focused smart city solutions to standardize all aspects of the digital city, the notion of city apps allows for the design of brittle and unique solutions that can co-exist with the messy state of cities that has been described as an important factor for creating and maintaining livable environments.

Bibliography

Ackad, C.; Wasinger, R.; Gluga, R.; Kay, J.; Tomitsch, M. (2013, November): "Measuring interactivity at an interactive public information display". In: Proceedings of the 25th Australian Computer-Human Interaction Conference: Augmentation, Application, Innovation, Collaboration. New York, NY: ACM, 329–332.

Aylett, M.P.; Quigley, A.J. (2015): "The Broken Dream of Pervasive Sentient Ambient Calm Invisible Ubiquitous Computing". In: Proceedings of the 33rd Annual ACM Conference Extended Abstracts on Human Factors in Computing Systems. New York, NY: ACM, 425–435.

Bai, S.; Tomitsch M. (2015): "Playful Urban Interfaces: Transforming Public Space Through Game Thinking". In: Proceedings of Mediacity 5 – Reflecting on Social Smart Cities. Plymouth University, Plymouth, UK, 130–149.

Bell, G.; Dourish, P. (2007): "Yesterday's tomorrows: notes on ubiquitous computing's dominant vision". Personal and Ubiquitous Computing 11:2, 133–143.

Brand, S. (1994): How Buildings Learn: What Happens After They're Built. New York: Viking.

Brynskov, M.; Dalsgaard, P.; Halskov, K. (2013): Understanding Media Architecture (Better): One Space, Three Cases. Presented at the CHI'13 Workshop on Interactive City Lighting, Paris, France.

Burke, S. (2016): Placemaking and the human scale city. Projects for Public Spaces, January 12, 2016, accessed April 5, 2016. http://www.pps.org/blog/placemaking-and-the-human-scale-city/.

Caldwell, G.A.; Foth, M. (2014): "DIY media architecture: open and participatory approaches to community engagement". In: Proceedings of the 2nd Media Architecture Biennale Conference: World Cities. New York, NY: ACM, 1–10.

Claes, S.; Vande Moere, A. (2013, June): "Street infographics: raising awareness of local issues through a situated urban visualization". In: Proceedings of the 2nd ACM International Symposium on Pervasive Displays. New York, NY: ACM, 133–138.

Colangelo, D. (2014): "The empire state building and the roles of low-resolution media façades in a data society". In: Proceedings of the 2nd Media Architecture Biennale Conference: World Cities. New York, NY: ACM, 11–20.

Dalsgaard, P.; Halskov, K. (2010): "Designing urban media façades: cases and challenges". In: Proceedings of the SIGCHI Conference on Human Factors in Computing Systems. New York, NY: ACM, 2277–2286.

de Waal, M. (2014): The City as Interface: How New Media Are Changing the City (reflect #10). Rotterdam, The Netherlands: Nai10 publishers.

Fahmi, W.S. (2001): "Reading of post modern public spaces as layers of virtual images and real events". In: The 37th international planning congress, session three: Cyberspace and the loss of concentration. Planning in the Information Age. The Hague, The Netherlands: ISOCARP, 17 pages.

Ferguson, R. (2013): Smart Cities and Economic Development: What to Consider. Big Idea: Data & Analytics, MIT Sloan Management Review, accessed April 5, 2016. http://sloanreview.mit.edu/article/smart-cities-and-economic-development-what-to-consider/.

Fischer, P.T.; Hornecker, E. (2012): "Urban HCI: spatial aspects in the design of shared encounters for media facades". In: Proceedings of the SIGCHI Conference on Human Factors in Computing Systems. New York, NY: ACM, 307–316.

Floyd, C.; Mehl, W.M.; Reisin, F.M.; Schmidt, G.; Wolf, G. (1989): "Out of Scandinavia: Alternative approaches to software design and system development". Human-Computer Interaction 4:4, 253–350.

Fredericks, J.; Hespanhol, L.; Tomitsch, M. (2016): "Not Just Pretty Lights: Using Digital Technologies to Inform City Making". In: Proceedings of the Media Architecture Biennale (MAB'16). New York, NY: ACM, 9 pages.

Gehl, J. (2013): Cities for people. Washington, DC: Island press.

Greenfield, A. (2013): Against the smart city. New York: Do Publications.

Haeusler, M.H. (2009): Media Façades: History, Technology, Content. Stuttgart, Germany: Avedition.

Haeusler, M.H.; Tomitsch, M.; Tscherteu, G. (2012): New Media Facades: A Global Survey. Stuttgart, Germany: Avedition.
Hemment, D.; Townsend, A. (2013): "Here Come The Smart Citizens". In: D. Hemment; A. Townsend (eds.): Smart citizens. Vol. 4. Manchester, UK: FutureEverything Publications.
Hespanhol, L.; Tomitsch, M.; Grace, K.; Collins, A.; Kay, J. (2012): "Investigating intuitiveness and effectiveness of gestures for free spatial interaction with large displays". In: Proceedings of the 2012 International Symposium on Pervasive Displays. New York, NY: ACM, 6 pages.
Hill, D. (2013): On the smart city: Or, a 'manifesto' for smart citizens instead. City of Sound, February 1, 2013, accessed April 5, 2016. http://www.cityofsound.com/blog/2013/02/on-the-smart-city-a-call-for-smart-citizens-instead.html.
Holmquist, L.E.; Skog, T. (2003): "Informative art: information visualization in everyday environments". In: Proceedings of the 1st international conference on Computer graphics and interactive techniques in Australasia and South East Asia. New York, NY: ACM, 229–235.
Kitchin, R. (2014): "The real-time city? Big data and smart urbanism". GeoJournal 79:1, 1–14.
Lewin, K. (1946): "Action research and minority problems". Journal of social issues 2:4, 34–46.
Mankoff, J.; Dey, A.K.; Hsieh, G.; Kientz, J.; Lederer, S.; Ames, M. (2003): "Heuristic evaluation of ambient displays". In: Proceedings of the SIGCHI conference on Human factors in computing systems. New York, NY: ACM, 169–176.
McQuire, S.; Martin, M.; Niederer, S. (2009): Urban screens reader (INC reader #5). Amsterdam, The Netherlands: Institute of Network Cultures.
Rahman, M; Wirasinghe, S.C.; Kattan, L. (2012): "Users' views on current and future real-time bus information systems". Journal of Advanced Transportation 47, 336–354.
Rogers, Y. (2006): "Moving on from weiser's vision of calm computing: Engaging ubicomp experiences". In: UbiComp 2006: Ubiquitous Computing. Berlin u.a.: Springer, 404–421.
Skog, T. (2004): "Activity wallpaper: ambient visualization of activity information". In: Proceedings of the 5th conference on Designing interactive systems: processes, practices, methods, and techniques. New York, NY: ACM, 325–328.
Tomitsch, M.; Kappel, K.; Lehner, A.; Grechenig, T. (2007): "Towards a taxonomy for ambient information systems". In: Proceedings of the 1st International Workshop on Ambient Information Systems, Colocated at Pervasive 2007. Aachen, Germany: CEUR Workshop Proceedings, 42–47.
Tomitsch, M. (2014): "Towards the real-time city: An investigation of public displays for behaviour change and sustainable living". In: Proceedings of the 7th Making Cities Liveable Conference, PANDORA Archive, Canberra, Australia: National Library of Australia, 19 pages.
Tomitsch, M.; Ackad, C.; Dawson, O.; Hespanhol, L.; Kay, J. (2014): "Who cares about the content? An analysis of playful behaviour at a public display". In: Proceedings of The International Symposium on Pervasive Displays. New York, NY: ACM, 6 pages.
Tomitsch, M.; Haeusler, M.H.; McArthur, I.; Foth, M. (2015): "The Role of Digital Screens in Urban Life: New Opportunities for Placemaking". In: M. Foth; M. Brynskov; T. Ojala (eds.): Citizen's Right to the Digital City: Urban Interfaces, Activism, and Placemaking. Singapore: Springer, 37–54.
Tompson, T. (2015): "Development of Real-time transport applications in Sydney – A hybrid model". In: State of Australian Cities Conference (SOAC'15), Gold Coast, Australia: Urban Research Program at Griffith University on behalf of the Australian Cities Research Network, 11 pages.

Townsend, A.; Maguire, R.; Liebhold, M.; Crawford, M. (2010): 2020 Forecast: The Future of Cities, Information and Inclusion. Technical report, Rockefeller Foundation, Institute for the Future.

Townsend, A. (2013): Smart cities: big data, civic hackers, and the quest for a new utopia. New York, NY: WW Norton & Company.

Tscherteu, G.; Tomitsch, M. (2011): Designing Urban Media Environments as Cultural Spaces. Presented at the CHI'11 Workshop on Large Urban Displays in Public Life, May 2011, Vancouver, Canada.

Weiser, M. (1991): "The computer for the 21st century". Scientific American 265:3, 94–104.

Valkanova, N.; Jorda, S.; Vande Moere, A. (2015): "Public visualization displays of citizen data: design, impact and implications". International Journal of Human-Computer Studies 81, 4–16.

Vande Moere, A.; Tomitsch, M.; Hoinkis, M.; Trefz, E.; Johansen, S.; Jones, A. (2011): "Comparative feedback in the street: exposing residential energy consumption on house façades". In: Human-Computer Interaction – INTERACT 2011. Berlin u.a.: Springer, 470–488.

Vande Moere, A.; Hill, D. (2012): "Designing for the situated and public visualization of urban data". Journal of Urban Technology 19:2, 25–46.

Vande Moere, A.; Wouters, N. (2012): "The role of context in media architecture". In: Proceedings of the 2012 International Symposium on Pervasive Displays. New York, NY: ACM, 6 pages.

Weiser, M. (1991): "The computer for the 21st century". Scientific American 265:3, 94–104.

Wiethoff, A.; Gehring, S. (2012): "Designing interaction with media façades: a case study". In: Proceedings of the Designing Interactive Systems Conference. New York, NY: ACM, 308–317.

Wouters, N.; Claes, S.; Vande Moere, A. (2015): "Investigating the Role of Situated Public Displays and Hyperlocal Content on Place-Making". Interaction Design and Architecture (s) 25, 60–72.

Zmijewski, B. (2008): User Experience Design Does Not Exist. ZURB Blog, December 3, 2008, accessed April 5, 2016. http://zurb.com/article/155/user-experience-design-does-not-exist.

Alexander Wiethoff and Marius Hoggenmueller

Experiences Deploying Hybrid Media Architecture in Public Environments

1 Introduction

As exemplified by Tomitsch and Verhoeff previously, the idea of augmenting public spaces with digital media, commonly referred to as *Media Architecture*, is no longer a future vision. We are now entering a time where actuators in the form of computer-controlled lighting and display elements are being deployed at large scales in our cities. At the same time, the coverage of high-speed internet allows manifold interaction opportunities between open data and citizens, thereby enabling the Internet of things in the public domain. In a previous chapter of this book, Tomitsch argued to shift away from the traditional view of media architecture taking the form of large-scale media façades. He introduced the notion of 'city-apps' that can take the form of any digital interface that provides real-time data or enables people to interact with the city's infrastructure. With 'DIY / DIWO Media Architecture', Caldwell and Foth explored a bottom-up approach that is more open and accessible for laypeople with the purpose of fostering community engagement. Complementing the aforementioned research, in this chapter we focus on the question how situated data should be integrated and visualized in the urban environment. We share our practical experiences from exposing a display prototype to public places. The development of the prototype builds on a recently discussed do-it-yourself (DIY) toolkit for *hybrid* media surfaces combining low-resolution and high-resolution display techniques. Making our approach available to others, we aim to reduce the technical burdens that currently hinder the wider dissemination of alternative solutions to current city developments.

Urban interfaces in the form of instrumented buildings and public displays can provide additional communication channels that are not addressed to individuals but rather to the public with in-situ access. In current implementations, the mainstream approach is retrofitting the urban environment with giant-sized television (TV)-like screens to display ubiquitous advertising and to serve as large-scale billboards where content and information can be exchanged at a fast pace. Apart from a questionable aesthetic appearance and integration into the environment, these high-resolution screens demand constant foreground visual attention, as multiple information streams compete for attention, and they fail to take advantage of humans' background processing capabilities. Ambient information as an overarching concept for more integrated, non-intrusive and responsive com-

DOI 10.1515/9783110453874-008

puting can be one alternative way of using media architecture by learning about people and their identities: their *habits, preferences, behavioral patterns, etc., and how to apply such knowledge in varying contexts* (Ishii et al., 1998). Following this design philosophy, however, poses several challenges; one includes the task of aesthetically integrating media architecture into physical surroundings and structures, which demands careful considerations of content, context, and users to create meaningful experiences within the built environment (Dalsgaard and Halskov, 2010). We consider it advantageous that media architecture is not just perceived as an information layer-on-top filled with advertising. Instead, in our everyday lives, media architecture can provide mutual benefits: Citizens can, for example, gain more awareness of their surroundings and become more informed about what is happening around them, which, in turn, can provoke the better use of common resources. Examples in this field range from citizens' reported infrastructure issues (Korsgaard and Brynskov, 2014), empowering sharing economies among neighborhoods (Pop, 2014), or real-time data visualization in urban contexts (Calabrese and Ratti, 2006). However, one dominant question persists: In which way should such digital information be integrated and visualized in the built environment? In order to prevent increased distraction in cities due to information overload, the need exists to rethink information visualization in conjunction with media architectural displays, as "clutter and confusion are failures of design, not attributes of information." (Tufte, 1992) In this vein, ambient information provides the benefit of a more seamless integration into the environment than do large-scale TV-like screens. Moreover, aesthetic animations can add further value, activating citizens' peripheral attention. One way of making ambient information comprehensible to people is to utilize strong metaphors (Ishii et al., 1998). However, their range of options is unimaginably large. Therefore, former investigations dealt with finding the right target dimensions for ambient displays in the public domain (Wiethoff and Gehring, 2012).

In this chapter we share our experiences investigating the integration of media architecture. Our chapter includes our experiences exposing an ambient display to different locations (i.e., indoor vs. outdoor) and contexts (i.e., work vs. leisure). In doing so, we aimed to understand people's perceptions and reactions of such a display type in the public domain.

1.1 Integration of Media Architecture

For media architecture to be successfully integrated into physical surroundings and structures, it has to function on different levels (Wiethoff, 2013). Based on our previous research from conducting various media architectural interventions in the past years and building on research findings in the emerging media architecture community, we identified the following key aspects: (1) Media architecture has, on its most basic level, to deliver aesthetic architectural experiences in order to gain widespread acceptance (Hoggenmueller and Wiethoff, 2014) even if users are not in favor of or interested in the displayed information. The ambient nature of the content can be perceived as an *added aesthetic value* (Hoggenmueller and Wiethoff, 2015). (2) The encoding of digital information must not be of a high cognitive load (McCullough, 2013) so as to support the easy perception of digital information through the built environment (Dalsgaard and Halskov, 2010). (3) If content can be manipulated via interactivity, the interface should be barrier free and must not require additional alternative means to enable control. This matter is especially demanding in order to include all users and age groups present in the public domain (Wiethoff et al., 2014).

Fig. 1: The Allianz Arena in Munich, Germany, is capable of displaying ambient low-resolution information on the outer shell of the building (Alm et al., 2012). Photo credits: © Richard Bartz.

Fig. 2: Urban Pixels is an example how to integrate display technology more seamlessly into the urban environment, breaking with the regular grid of a screen. Photo credits © Susanne Seitinger.

Fig. 3: Big Vortex is a conceptualized installation by realities:united indicating CO2 emissions from a waste-to-energy plant using smoke rings. Photo credits: © realities:united.

1.2 Visualizations for the masses

Appropriate visualizations of datasets can allow professionals to better understand overall situations in critical events (such as in emergency or crisis management roundtables) or trends, projections, future evolutions of processes, and decision-makings (Tufte, 1992). However, visualizations in this context are highly specialized interpretations of data and are often not easy for the average citizen to understand. Therefore, it is a challenge to develop a framework that allows everyone to create, select, and understand publicly available data and visualizations about data within the urban landscape, and new correlations and usages between data that can be derived from them.

1.3 Ambient information

"A persistent layer of messages for somebody else ..." (McCullough, 2013)

Ambient information systems take advantage of humans' background processing capabilities. Ishii et al. first described the vision of an architectural space that serves as an interface for displaying information in the periphery of the user's attention (Ishii et al., 1998). Inspired by natural phenomena, such as wind, sunlight, or temperature, ambient media displays were embedded into the physical environment using subtle changes to process information. Using similar metaphors, the Power-Aware-Cord, a re-design of a common-electrical power strip, encodes the current energy consumption using light intensity as a visual variable (Gustafsson and Gyllenswärd, 2005). In general, ambient displays feature high aesthetic qualities and support the monitoring of non-critical information. However, some systems also provide alerts to inform the user about important changes. Pousman et al. (2006) described the degree at which an ambient information system forces users to interrupt their primary tasks on a *notification level.*

Applying "ambient media" to urban contexts has been recently discussed by various researchers (Chatzitsakyris et al., 2004; Colangelo, 2014; Sade, 2014; Seitinger et al., 2009). They stress that predominant high-resolution public displays are competing for the user's undivided attention and cannot be integrated in an architecturally friendly way. Seitinger et al. (2009) therefore proposed a network of wireless, solar-powered lighting units, called *Urban pixels*, which can be flexibly arranged on any surface (see Figure 2). These new approaches explore the transition among urban displays, ambient information systems, and street lighting. They are also inspired by already-realized cases of media architecture. One prominent example is the Allianz Arena in Munich (see Figure 1), of which the outer shell can be transformed into an ambient display to monitor what is going on inside: using color and patterns as ambient media information. One limitation coming with the low-resolution nature of ambient media is the encoding of information in a way that large audiences can understand: While locals and soccer fans can decode the meaning here, it might be more difficult for visitors to understand the information. In this vein, Offenhuber and Seitinger (2014) stress the arbitrariness of visual encoding when communicating information via low-resolution media architecture. Claiming that "content follows resolution," they discuss five visual variables, including *color, movement, text, images*, and the intrinsic *shape of the building*, to encode information depending on the infrastructure. In order to convey explicit information via low-resolution displays, they investigate the use of a mobile interface as an additional layer for annotations, which does not, however, enable barrier-free use. Another example of ambient information visualization in the urban realm is a conceptualized art installation from realities:united that demonstrates the wide range of media architectural expression: Big Vortex transforms the emissions of a waste-to-energy plant into smoke rings to indicate and make people aware of the city's carbon dioxide (CO2) emissions (see Figure 3). McCoullough (2013) states that "this is not just data visualization but also data formation," referring to *embodied information*, which leads to Offenhuber and Seitingers' (2014) conclusion that the medium – in the case of media architecture, the building – is never neutral to the viewer's interpretation.

Fig. 4: Our Hybrid Media Display at the location in the Olympic Village at dusk during a week-long field investigation addressing the question of how real-time data can be visualized and integrated into the built environment.

2 Case Study: A Hybrid Media Display

In our recent work, we developed our *Hybrid Media Display* to address the integration of media architecture and the presentation of real-time data in the public domain (see Figure 4). Our Hybrid Media Display combines low- and high-resolution display techniques: the low-resolution screen uses light-emitting diodes (LEDs) and is capable of displaying ambient information with high aesthetic qualities. In a different mode, high-resolution information is projected on top of the LED surface to provide more detailed information about the data acting as an additional layer of annotations. We exposed the study prototype in two cases, both investigating the ambient visualization of real-time data but applied to different contexts in terms of location and content. The first case study explores the monitoring of environmental information, such as temperature and air quality, in a semi-public room. In the second case, we exposed the display to the main plaza of a residential complex, displaying the departure times of a nearby subway station.

2.1 Architectural Design

As aforementioned, the communication of information through media architecture does not solely rely on dynamic visual content by means of flexible programmed pixels; information can also be encoded in the architectural shape of a display or a building (Offenhuber and Seitinger, 2014). Since the low-resolution LED layer of our prototype Hybrid Media Display restricts visual and textual representations, we considered the architectural design from both an aesthetic and a functional point of view.

Using existing square panels with a matrix of 4x4 LEDs as the basic element, a geometrical design composed of rectangular shapes was already predetermined. In correlation with the Gestalt Laws, a symmetrical design was chosen in order to fetch the viewer's attention and effectively communicate information in short-time frames. The shape of our Hybrid Media Display is composed of four diamond-shaped squares, two with 3x3 panels and two with 2x2 panels. This results in two equal-sized surfaces, each containing 144 LEDs, and one slightly smaller surface that is partitioned on two squares with a total of 128 LEDs (see Figure 4). The two larger squares are arranged symmetrically on the horizontal axis, and the two smaller squares are arranged symmetrically on the vertical axis.

In total, our Hybrid Media Display measures a maximum height of 2.55 meters and a maximum width of 1.70 meters. From the perspective of information design, the individual surfaces are well suited to display various data simultaneously. Considering that the surfaces have a similar size, it is appropriate to use that area to visualize numeric data values and, if desired, to enable coherence and comparability between the datasets. The symmetrical design allows for the flexible use of our Hybrid Media Display because the congruent surfaces are capable of representing *one* variable by simply mirroring the visualization or *two* variables using the surfaces separately from each other. This enables high flexibility during the design process and the opportunity to apply the display to different contexts, as changes can be applied on the software side.

2.2 Display Modes

We presented information on our Hybrid Media Display via LEDs only in low resolution; we referred to this as **LED Mode.** Using front-projected content was carried out in **Projection Mode** by having the high-resolution visual information projected onto the HDF panels and the LEDs switched off. Using both ambient LED representations and front-projected imagery was realized in **Hybrid Mode.** We paid attention to the circumstance that one mode might outperform the other modes because of a higher lighting output, as in the case of the high-power outdoor LEDs vs. a standard data projector.

The LEDs were therefore dimmed appropriately to match the lighting output accordingly. Measuring the different modes, we gained 516 Lux in the LED and Hybrid modes, while the Projection Mode performed at a comparable 496 Lux.

2.3 Cases

In order to investigate the concept of public information visualization that combines low-resolution ambient LED presentation and additional high-resolution content, we applied our display prototype in two different contexts. We have chosen two distinct scenarios for which we have developed visual content and exposed these data to an urban setting. Van de Moere and Hill (2012) state that urban visualization is properly *situated* if embedded in a physical environment. We therefore chose the appropriate study location and developed the final design in close alignment with the local context. The first case was situated in a working environment in a public institution, whereas the second case took place in a leisure environment in an urban prime location. For both cases, we represented the data in the three abovementioned conditions, including (1) pure ambient LED low-res representations (2) explicit text- and image-based information via projections and (3) a combination of both, which we refer to as a hybrid.

2.4 Case 1: Indoor climate

Indoor climate constantly displays real-time data on the indoor air quality with the aim of making people aware of their surrounding environments in relation to the health, comfort, and capacity for mental work of the building occupants. In the case of bad environmental conditions, people were notified through the system and encouraged to open their windows for air exchange. The determination of the indoor air quality was based on several measurement values, namely temperature, relative humidity, and carbon dioxide (CO2). These measurement values were selected because they are crucial for good air quality, most people are familiar with their meaning, and they can be measured using affordable off-the-shelf measurement hardware[1].

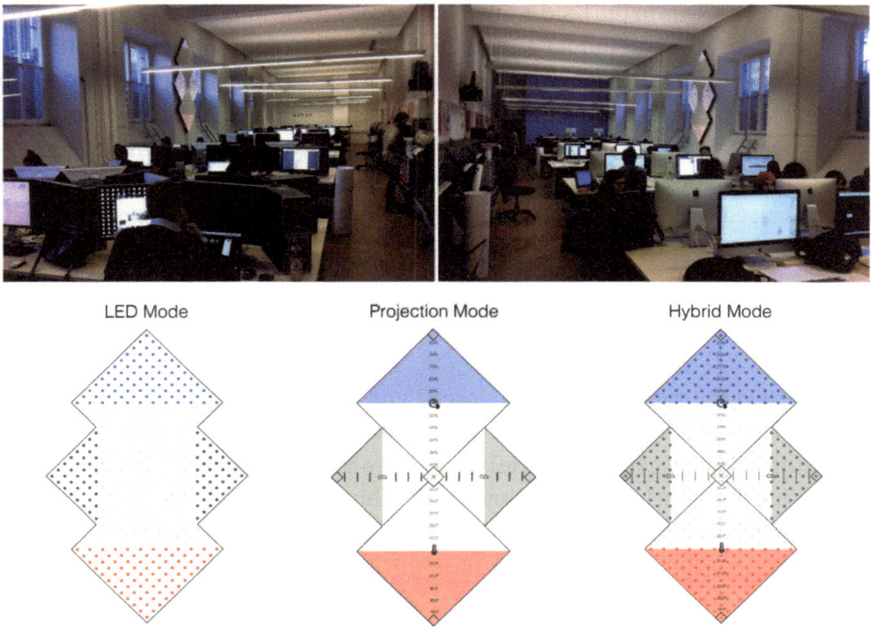

Fig. 5: The co-working space viewed from both room ends, and the display located in the center of the room (top). The different content representations in the first setting displaying temperature + humidity and CO2 levels (bottom). Photo credits: Korbinian Steiger.

2.4.1 Location One

For the indoor climate case, the study prototype was exposed in a work room at a large university building (see Figure 5). The room was situated in the basement of the building. Thus, artificial lighting was required because not enough natural light could enter the room through the windows, leading to a homogeneous illumination irrespective of the time of day. The room was mainly used by architecture students, containing 40 work stations, each equipped with high-performance

1 http://www.ic-meter.com/

computers. Our Hybrid Media Display was placed in the middle of the window side, midway between the floor and ceiling, thus visible from all work stations (see Figure 5, top). The study location was considered promising for various reasons: The working place has high fluctuation, with many individuals visiting the area throughout the day. Thus, the ambient visualizations in the room would reach a large audience. Due to the hard-to-reach window handles and the waste heat from the computers, the bad indoor air quality in the particular room was already well known to its users. The large number of students – in particular, at the end of the term when we conducted our field investigation – intensified these problems. Thus, our application had a direct reference to the local context addressing an existing problem for which Van de Moere and Hill (2012) stress that processing "data that is sensed, measured, or acquired within the physical environment immediately surrounding the display," is crucial for reasonable public visualizations.

2.4.2 Visual Content

We designed the visual content in close alignment with the architectural design. For the pure ambient representation, three measurement values (temperature, relative humidity, and carbon dioxide) were assigned to three screens. Because of the correlation between temperature and relative humidity, it was considered reasonable to assign those values to the large, opposing faces (see Figure 5), with relative humidity on top and temperature at the bottom; therefore, the carbon dioxide was assigned to the horizontal split screen. Due to the restricted resolution, the choice of an image or text-based visualization was excluded from the onset. Therefore, we encoded the physical quantities via color: Blue represented relative humidity, red stood for temperature, and white stood for carbon dioxide levels. The measured values were encoded via area visualizations with the square screens as *physical containers* for the filling level. The illuminating areas represented a numeric value in *data lumen* representing temperature in degrees, relative humidity in percent, and carbon dioxide in parts per million. The filling level was *growing* toward the center of the display with increasing values functioning as a metaphor for the displacement of fresh air. In the case of temperature and relative humidity, the measured values were additionally encoded via saturation.

In order to provide more detailed information, we designed a high-resolution visualization that was projected on top of the surface. In this vein, the basic design concept for the ambient visualization was extended by symbol- and text-based explanations, scales, and divides (see Figure 5). In high-resolution mode, the filling levels with the given color encodings were adopted from the ambient visualization design. For the Hybrid Mode, using both low-resolution and high-resolution display technology, the data were presented by the LED-based *filling levels* and the additional supporting information, e.g., explanations and scales, projected on top as a layer of annotations.

Besides providing unobtrusive information about the surrounding environment condition, we added an *alarm mode* with higher notification level (Pousmann and Stasko, 2006) to address the contextual problem of fresh air supply at the study location: If a carbon dioxide limit was reached, a *visual alarm* notified the users to open the windows for ventilation. After sufficient air renewal, a second visual alarm notified the users to close the windows in order to avoid low temperatures. While in the normal mode, data changes were represented subtly and slowly, we utilized fast transitions in the notification mode referring to the taxonomy for ambient displays discussed by Tomitsch et al. (2007). This setting was realized by flashing arrow-like movements on the entire display surface.

2.5 Case 2: Public transport

The second case was situated in the urban realm, focusing on the ambient visualization of public transport information. The processed information was based on real-time departure times provided by the local transport company via a Web service[2]. The study prototype was exposed to a prominent urban site near a subway station.

2.5.1 Location Two

For displaying real-time public transport data, it was necessary to find a study location in close proximity to a station. Thus, we aimed to place our prototype at a busy spot in order to provide usefulness for large audiences. We decided to conduct the second case at the Olympic Village in Munich, Germany. This popular residential district was built for the 1972 Olympic games and has 6,000 inhabitants today with a very high population density (Chalkley and Essex, 1999). The entire residential area is completely car free. We exposed our Hybrid Media Display at the main plaza of a residential complex that is primary inhabited by students. Figure 6, top shows the location of the Hybrid Media Display, the surrounding housing units, and the nearby subway station. The location of the display was approximately 3–4 minutes' walking distance away from the subway station. The display was placed under a concrete roof construction and fastened to a central

2 http://www.mvg-live.de/

pillar (see Figure 4). Located immediately behind the covered area was a temporary used kiosk that is run and operated by students. This position was selected for several reasons: First, the covered plaza is situated in the center of the surrounding housing units and serves as a meeting point for social activities, such as celebrations or flea markets. Furthermore, the display's position is visible from multiple spots, even from large distances. Thus, the display can be seen from a large area in front of the covered square, from the balcony of a dozen of the surrounding two-storied bungalows, and from more than 100 apartments of a high-rise flat. These zones relate to the *"display spaces"* – the areas from which a display can be seen – discussed by Fischer and Hornecker (2012) in their analysis of the spatial setup of media architectural interventions. In this vein, our visualization also strongly differs from existing public transport displays that are usually directly placed on the platform, not designed for long-range visibility in a city. Finally, the position of the display was also motivated by practical reasons, such as the roof construction, which protected the display prototype against rain, and the hardware, for which was possible to get power by a high-voltage system provided via the nearby infrastructure.

Overall, the public transport visualization was exposed to the Olympic Village inhabitants over a period of seven days in midsummer. Because of the strong sunlight, the projection was only visible from dusk onward; the LED Mode was apparent throughout the day. However, both reflected and emitted light sources became highly visible during the early evening up to the early morning. To protect the hardware from theft, we removed the computer and the data projector overnight after the last subway train had passed, at about 1:30 am.

2.5.2 Visual Content

To obtain a better understanding *what* and *how* presented information could be useful for inhabitants and visitors in the chosen district, we conducted initial observations: While observing people who entered the subway station and talking to inhabitants of the nearby residential district where the display was placed, it became obvious that most of them mainly use the subway line in the direction toward the city center. Furthermore, it became apparent that passers-by around the plaza would consider live information about the next departure time as being the most important piece of information, as people could estimate if there is enough time left to reach the subway.

Contrary to the first use case with the high-resolution presentation strongly oriented at the low-resolution presentation, serving as a layer of annotation, in this case, the two layers were clearly separated from each other using distinct visual elements for encoding. For the projected layer, the visualization was purely text based, conveying explicit information. The presentation was derived from common passenger information displays. The line number was projected on the left side of the horizontal split screen; the remaining time in minutes with the unit symbol “min” was projected on the right side of the horizontal split screen (see Figures 4 and 6). Because the decision was made to monitor only one direction, the destination was not displayed in order to reduce the information density, focusing on a *pass-by-and-use* scenario (Fischer and Hornecker, 2012). For the ambient representation (see Figures 4 and 6), the remaining time was depicted as an hourglass serving as a metaphor for time. Here, the architectural design enhances the overall visual appearance, as the two horizontal screens look like the bulbs of an hourglass, encoding information in the shape of the display (Offenhuber and Seitinger, 2014). The filling levels of the hourglass were aligned with the remaining time. The filling levels were colored orange according to the color coding of the local transport system in order to recognize the subway lines. To strengthen the pictorial representation, the ambient visualization was supplemented by an animated

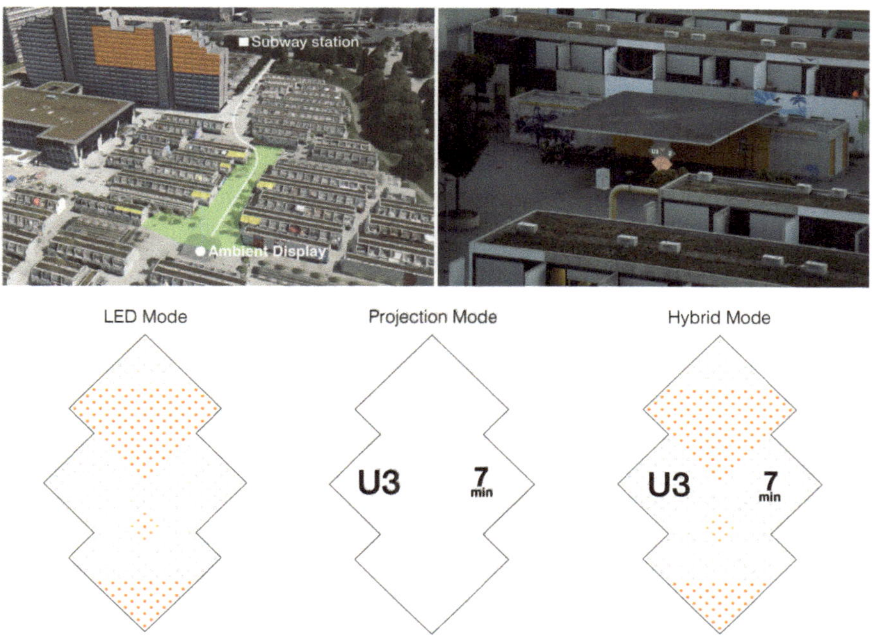

Fig. 6: The study location in the heart of the Olympic Village with common pathways to the next subway stop about three minutes’ walking distance away (top). The different content representations in the second case displaying the time remaining via an hourglass and text (bottom).

sequence: A drop fell from the upper bulb that represented the remaining time to the lower bulb that represented the elapsed time, thus connecting both *physical containers*. The movement was similar to that of a water drop, which made the filling levels look like *luminous liquids*. Through the irregular pixel grid, the diagonal alignment of the LED panels, these slow visual animations created an additional aesthetic effect, contributing to a clear, unbounded display design. For the Hybrid Mode, using both low-resolution and high-resolution display technologies, the transport information was represented by the conjunction of the metaphoric visualization in the form of an hourglass and the previously described text-based information.

3 Observations

Looking back after observing both settings for several weeks we learned that experiences of the people were very different from case to case. In the first case, at the computer room of a university, our Hybrid Media Display got ignored by most of the users of the space. This was contradicting our assumption that such an display that is a) highly visible and b) supplied with localized and situated information would provoke rich discussions and raise attention by the people populating the space. To compensate the lack of interest we tried to raise more awareness for the display by, for example talking to people in the space directly and handing out flyers which were advertising the display and its capabilities or making the animations brighter. Interestingly also these strategies did not make hardly any difference in order to raise more awareness among the students in the space. The majority of the people observed during the time the display was located there were, when entering the space, just scanning the room for a free seat and computer, carried out their work highly concentrated and left the space as soon they were done without noticing the display or asking questions about it. Conducting semi-structured interviews, we have learned that the students were simply too concerned with the work they had to deliver for exams so that they did not at all care about their surroundings or the air quality they were breathing. One student expressed that he thought the display was some kind of decoration to improve the appearance of the space and even enjoyed the animations when the display was communicating severe CO2 levels.

In the second case our installation left a very different impression as many passersby were stopping and viewing the display for longer time-spans. Because the setting in the Olympic Village was deployed during a very warm summertime week, many other people and residents were populating the square. Even during the setup of the Hybrid Media Display in this location we were constantly involved in discussions with residents and visitors. Informal conversations with architects who were involved in the design and re-design process of the Olympic Village proved to be a highlight during this setup, as the architects expressed their enthusiasm about our work: transforming their original design using mediated architecture. One resident confirmed the decorative function of the display, providing an added value for the built environment by "coloring the grey concrete buildings" and, thus, providing added value for the residential complex. Regarding the functional benefit, one occupant of the nearby high-rise mentioned that he coordinated his timely arrival at the subway station by means of the display which was visible from his apartment on the twelfth floor. Statements such as these caused us to presume that still after several days the display was perceived as an integral part of the location and the residents we have interviewed were positive about the hypothetical scenario of a permanent deployment.

Concerning the preferred display mode, interviewees perceived our Hybrid Media Display using only the LED Mode as difficult to encode the presented information. They referred to the LED Mode as being aesthetic and considered the animations as successful artistic intervention: "I found the pure LED version most aesthetic, but the most sense for the average user would make the Hybrid Mode." In the Hybrid Mode, people were more positive and enthusiastic, considering the other modes in direct comparison: "...because I perceive the glowing LEDs being very beautiful, but more information is communicated via the Hybrid Mode compared to the LED Mode."

The majority of the interviewed people raised further the issue of demanding more explicit information when Hybrid Media Display was in pure LED Mode. This is a common issue with ambient information systems that focus on peripheral interaction and background processing capabilities. Our chosen use cases (Case 1: indoor climate and Case 2: public transport information) demanded more precise information on time and thresholds than the low-resolution LED visualizations were capable of delivering. We consider therefore a hybrid setting using both ambient information and explicit data as an appropriate way to overcome this issue.

In the second case Hybrid Media Display served its purpose of presenting real-time data to different audiences compared to case one. Hence, one prominent insight derived from this field investigation was that the context of where media architectural installations are integrated in existing structures and surroundings play a large role. Our chosen locations were extremely different form one another in two aspects such as indoor vs. outdoor, work vs. leisure. The observation that the display received much more attention and feedback in the second case leaves us with the impression that the selection of the location and the occupancy of people in this location are factors that will have an impact on the general acceptance of any media architectural installation deployed and should therefore demand careful considerations. Hence, the busyness of people around media architectural installations affects their recognition in public environments. While work environments and highly transitory spaces as exemplified in case one might not lead to high attention when it comes to communicating ambient information, leisure environments where people can also remain for longer periods of time will likely lead to more attention and acceptance as experienced in our here discussed case study. Our findings also complement and confirm similar research in this domain as, for example, described in the chapter by Caldwell and Foth.

4 Conclusion

In this chapter we presented the experience of our efforts of outsourcing information in the public domain from the focal to the peripheral attention area of people and investigated the integration of a hybrid media architecture into physical surroundings and structures.

While carrying out our preliminary observations, we could notice that our Hybrid Media Display was being perceived after several days of operation as an integral part of the study location. Considering the challenge of how media architecture displays can be integrated more seamlessly into their surroundings, we acknowledge that this can be realized rather through visual aesthetics represented by an appropriate interpretation of data that also reflects the surrounding architectural structures. Through the perception of the display as a decorative element, we have added a pleasant additional value and propose one solution of fitting ambient real-time information into the built environment.

We have also noticed that low-resolution ambient information in the public domain still requires additional explanation via *pockets of explicit information*. We therefore consider hybrid media architecture to be a promising means of communicating these data via ambient displays. We would like to point out that the combination of low-resolution LEDs with high-resolution frontal projection is thereby just one possible solution to overcome the issue of conveying information through ambient media architecture. Our initial insights might encourage further research, for example, on a more integrated and embedded version via dedicated areas with a higher density of LEDs or additional information layers realized using augmented reality applications to add explicit content. The latter might be an interesting solution, as people can learn and adapt to ambient data in an early stage of deployment using alternative means that can help them to grasp ambient data more easily. Proposing the aesthetic integration of data visualizations through ambient media architecture, we aim to provide an alternative solution to current city developments, and hope to enable and inspire the future work on this topic.

Bibliography

Alm, J.; Tofft-Jørgensen, L.; Brandt, H.; Bang, S. (2012): World Stadium Index: Stadiums built for major sporting events-bright future or future burden. Danish Institute for Sports Studies/Play the Game, Copenhagen, Vol. 53.

Behrens, M.; Valkanova, N.; Brumby, D.P. (2014): "Smart Citizen Sentiment Dashboard: A Case Study Into Media Architectural Interfaces". In: Proceedings of The International Symposium on Pervasive Displays, PerDis'14, ACM Press, New York, 2014, p.19.

Calabrese, F.; Ratti, C. (2006): "Real time rome". Networks and Communications Studies, 20(3–4): 247–258.

Chalkley, B.; Essex, S. (1999): "Urban development through hosting international events: a history of the Olympic Games". Planning perspectives, 4(14): 369–394.

Chatzitsakyris, P.; Ducla-Soares, G.; Zulas, A. (2004): "IN-Visible: Perceiving Invisible Urban Information Through Ambient Media". In: Proceedings of Extended Abstracts on Human Factors in Computing Systems, CHI EA'04, ACM Press, New York, 1348–1350.

Coelho, M.; Zigelbaum, J.; Kopin, J. (2011): "Six-forty by Four-eighty: The Post-industrial Design of Computational Materials". In: Proceedings of the Fifth International Conference on Tangible, Embedded, and Embodied Interaction, TEI'11, ACM Press, New York, 253–256.

Colangelo, D. (2014): "The Empire State Building and the Roles of Low-resolution Media Façades in a Data Society". In: Proceedings of the 2nd Media Architecture Biennale Conference: World Cities, MAB'14, ACM Press, New York, 11–20.

Dalsgaard, P.; Halskov, K. (2010): "Designing Urban Media Façades: Cases and Challenges". In: Proceedings of the SIGCHI Conference on Human Factors in Computing Systems, CHI'10, ACM Press, New York, 2277–2286.

Fischer, P.T.; Hornecker, E. (2012): "Urban HCI: Spatial Aspects in the Design of Shared Encounters for Media Façades". In: Proceedings of the SIGCHI Conference on Human Factors in Computing Systems, CHI'12, ACM Press, New York, 307–316.

Gustafsson, A.; Gyllenswärd, M. (2005): "The Power-aware Cord: Energy Awareness Through Ambient Information Display". In: Proceedings of CHI'05 Extended Abstracts on Human Factors in Computing Systems, CHI EA'05, ACM Press, New York, 1423–1426.

Hazlewood, W.R.; Stolterman, E.; Connelly, K. (2011): "Issues in Evaluating Ambient Displays in the Wild: Two Case Studies". In: Proceedings of the SIGCHI Conference on Human Factors in Computing Systems, CHI'11, ACM Press, New York, 877–886.

Hoggenmueller, M.; Wiethoff, A. (2014): "LightSet: enabling urban prototyping of interactive media façades". In: Proceedings of the SIGCHI Conference on Designing Interactive Systems, DIS'14, ACM Press, New York, 925–934.

Hoggenmueller, M.; Wiethoff, A. (2015): "Blinking Lights and Other Revelations – Experiences Designing Hybrid Media Facades". In: Proceedings of the SIGCHI Conference on Pervasive Displays, PerDis'15, ACM Press, New York, 77–82.

Ishii, H.; Wisneski, C.; Brave, S.; Dahley, A.; Gorbet, M.; Ullmer, B.; Yarin, P. (1998): "ambientROOM: Integrating Ambient Media with Architectural Space". In: Proceedings of the SIGCHI Conference on Human Factors in Computing Systems, CHI'98, ACM Press, New York, 173–174.
Korsgaard, H.; Brynskov, M. (2014): "City bug report: urban prototyping as participatory process and practice". In: Proceedings of the 2nd Media Architecture Biennale Conference: World Cities, MAB '14, ACM Press, New York, 21–29.
McCullough, M. (2013): Ambient Commons: Attention in the Age of Embodied Information. MIT Press, Cambridge.
Offenhuber, D.; Seitinger, S. (2014): "Over the rainbow; information design for low-resolution urban displays". In: Proceedings of the 2nd Media Architecture Biennale Conference: World Cities, MAB '14, ACM Press, New York, 40–47.
Pop, S. (2014): Connecting Cities Network. Retrieved April 05, 2016. http://www.connectingcities.net/.
Pousman, Z.; Stasko, J. (2006): "A Taxonomy of Ambient Information Systems: Four Patterns of Design". In: Proceedings of the Working Conference on Advanced Visual Interfaces, AVI'06, ACM Press, New York, 67–74.
Sade, G. (2014): "Aesthetics of Urban Media Façades". In: Proceedings of the 2nd Media Architecture Biennale Conference: World Cities, MAB '14, ACM Press, New York, 59–68.
Seitinger, S.; Perry, D.S.; Mitchell, W.J. (2009): "Urban Pixels: Painting the City with Light". In: Proceedings of the SIGCHI Conference on Human Factors in Computing Systems, CHI'09, ACM Press, New York, 839–884.
Strauss, A.; Corbin, J.M. (1990): Basics of qualitative research. Vol. 15. Newbury Park, CA: Sage.
Tomitsch, M.; Kappel, K.; Lehner, A.; Grechenig, T. (2007): "Towards a Taxonomy for Ambient Information Systems". In: Pervasive 2007 Workshop 9 Ambient Information Systems, May 13th, Toronto, Canada.
Tscherteu, G. (2012): Media Façades Online Catalogue 2012. http://mediaarchitecture.org. Retrieved September 12th, 2016.
Tufte, E. (1992): The Visual Display of Quantitative Information. Vol. 2, No. 7, Cheshire CT, Graphics Press.
Vande Moere, A.; Hill, D. (2012): "Designing for the Situated and Public Visualization of Urban Data". Journal of Urban Technology, Vol. 19, No. 2, 25–46.
Vande Moere, A.; Wouters, N. (2012): "The Role of Context in Media Architecture". In: Proceedings of the International Symposium on Pervasive Displays, PerDis'12, ACM Press, New York, p. 12.
Wiethoff, A.; Butz, A. (2010): "ColourVision Controlling Light Patterns through Postures". In: Proceedings of the International Symposium on Smart Graphics, Springer, Heidelberg, 281–284.
Wiethoff, A.; Bloeckner, M. (2011): "Lightbox – Exploring Interaction Modalities with Colored Light". In: Proceedings of the Fifth International Conference on Tangible, Embedded, and Embodied Interaction, TEI'11, ACM Press, New York, 399–400.
Wiethoff, A.; Gehring, S. (2012): "Designing interaction with media façades: A case study". In: Proceedings of the SIGCHI Conference on Designing Interactive Systems, DIS'12, ACM Press, New York, 308–317.
Wiethoff, A. (2013): "Designing Media Architecture: A Research Agenda for Urban Interfaces". Workshop Proceedings: Symposium on Digital Cities, No. 8, Munich.

Wiethoff, A.; Hoggenmueller, M.; Hornecker, E. (2014): "Orkhēstra: on the design of interactive media architecture for public environments". In: Proceedings of the Nordic Conference on Human-Computer Interaction, NordiCHI'14, ACM Press, New York, 1077–1080.

Designing Media Architecture: Technology, Tools and Processes

Peter Dalsgaard and Kim Halskov

Designing Media Architecture: Methods and Tools

1 Introduction

In this chapter, we offer an overview of the methods and tools for designing media architecture. In our conception, design spans from initial discussions with stakeholders about the purpose and vision of the architectural outcome through concept development on to the final development stages. Media architecture represents a very clear and physical manifestation of the "information society" trope, in that it materialises information and merges it with the built environment, there for all to see. However, if it is to be accessible and meaningful, careful thought must be put into not only the technical implementation, but also the initial examination of the context in which media architecture will be placed and the potential effect on the people who will encounter it.

Given the large scope of media architecture design, the methods and tools involved are diverse. Some address the 'softer' sides of the process, e.g. aligning stakeholder interests and generating ideas and concepts, whereas others address technical challenges, such as creating prototypes with novel digital technologies. In order to bring structure to this diversity of methods and tools, we therefore organize our presentation into three phases of media architecture design: 1) preliminary research into context and use situations, 2) development of concept, and 3) mock-ups and prototyping. The methods and tools presented here represent the accumulated results of seven years of research and development of media architecture in our research lab, CAVI (Halskov 2011). In order to ground them in practice, we will show examples from three specific cases, in which we worked with a range of collaborators and stakeholders to create novel media architecture installations: Aarhus by Light, Odenplan, and the Expo Pavilion. We will first briefly introduce these cases, and then move on to the methods and tools employed in each of the five phases, before concluding the chapter with a summary and discussion of key issues.

DOI 10.1515/9783110453874-009

2 Three examples of media architecture design

To exemplify how methods and tools can be employed in media architecture design processes, we have selected three cases, in which our research and development lab has worked with external partners in real-life projects: Aarhus by Light, Odenplan, and the Expo Pavilion. The three cases are similar in terms of being large-scale installations in public settings, but also differ on a number of counts, for instance in terms of setting, purpose, and technologies, and thus represent some of the diversity that characterises media architecture. They also represent the development and refinement of the methods and tools employed in the field. Aarhus by Light was in many respects a pioneering project, which also means that many methods and tools were employed for the first time. Since then, they have been refined and developed, as represented by Odenplan, in which particular attention was paid to develop and tune the process, and in the Expo Pavilion case, in which a series of novel tools specifically for media architecture design were developed.

2.1 Aarhus By Light

Aarhus by Light was an interactive media façade that engaged local citizens in new kinds of public behavior, in order to explore new possibilities of digital media in urban life, (Brynskov et al. 2007; Dalsgaard/Halskov 2010). The 700 m^2 glass façade of the Musikhuset, the city concert hall of Aarhus, was fitted with 180

Fig. 1: Aarhus By Light installed on the concert hall façade.

square meters of semi-transparent LED screen, which was distributed in a non-rectangular pattern behind the surface of the Musikhuset, facing an adjacent public park. Visitors to the park were met with a view of animated creatures crawling around the structure of the glass façade, along with a constantly moving outline of the Aarhus skyline, see Figure 1. Visitors interacting with Aarhus by Light. When visitors walked through the park, they passed through three interactive zones marked with coloured carpets. Once someone walked onto a carpet, a camera, together with custom designed software, identified the outline of the person's body, thereby creating a silhouette on the screen. This silhouette encouraged a curious and playful investigation of the façade among the users, while enabling them to interact with the creatures, by pushing, lifting, and dropping them. The motivation behind Aarhus by Light was driven by research interests and curiosity, but was also supported by the concert hall management's interest in challenging its own rather conservative image. They did not, however, in any way wish to influence the actual design.

2.2 Odenplan

Odenplan is a projected metro station in Stockholm, Sweden. The building was designed by 3XN Architects for the Odenplan plaza in Vasastan, in the centre of Stockholm, Figure 2. For the exterior stairs of the metro, the proposal was to integrate bands of LEDs along each step. During the design process, three design concepts were created: Contours, Playhead, and Traces (Korsgaard et al. 2012).

Fig. 2: Odenplan.

Contours emphasizes the contours of stairs by drawing lines along their edges, followed by each step being lit slowly upward, together with other simple visual effects. Playhead and Traces relied on camera technology enabling identifying the position and movements of people on stairs. Playhead turns the stairs into a musical score sheet. Each step represents a stave, and the position of a person sitting on the stairs represents a note, which is played when a virtual playhead moves across the stairs. Traces creates visual traces of the people sitting or moving about on the stairs, (Dalsgaard/Halskov 2010; Korsgaard et al. 2012).

2.3 The EXPO Pavilion

The Danish Pavilion at Expo 2010, designed by BIG Architects, was part of the huge 2010 world EXPO exhibition in Shanghai visited in total by more than 73 million people of which more than 5 million people visited the Danish Pavilion. According to The Danish Enterprise and Construction Authority "the aim of the Danish pavilion was to create an opportunity for visitors to experience first hand the feel of a Danish city". The façade had a double-loop shape, and from some angles appears as two bands, one above the other. When unfolded, the facade of the pavilion yielded a 300-metre-long, 12-metre-high structure, with a wavy shape due to the helical form of the building with 3,600 holes of various sizes and configuration. These holes were equipped with light fixtures hidden behind PVC tubes, diffusing light uniformly. In daylight, the façade displayed flickering white animations consisting of white surfaces broken by lines, fades, or silhouettes of people

Fig. 3: The EXPO Pavillion.

walking or bicycling along the façade. In the evening, animations included shimmering, abstract graphics, sweeps, fades, and animations along the entire length of the façade. Colours were mostly restricted to white and red (Halskov/Ebsen 2013) Figure 3.

After this introduction to the three cases, we now turn our focus to the methods and tools involved in designing media architecture.

3 Methods and Tools

Since the design of media architecture can span from initial explorations of potential project ideas to final implementation and integration of digital technologies into buildings and spaces, the methods and tools involved are highly diverse. In the following, we focus on three phases 1) preliminary research into context and use situations, 2) development of concept, and 3) prototyping in order to give an overview of central media architecture methods and tools. We have selected these both on the basis of our own work as well as extensive surveys of the field of media architecture in general and exemplify them using the three cases described above.

For each phase, we first describe the main characteristics and challenges of the phase. We then present tools and methods suited to support designers at each phase of the process and offer examples of how this has been accomplished in specific projects.

3.1 Preliminary research of context and use situations

Although media architecture is often considered a highly technical discipline, the foundational work for designing new media architecture often begins long before specific technological considerations. Just as is the case with traditional architecture, the preliminary examinations of the context and potential use situations of a new installation are essential in setting the direction for the design process. It is often said that every design process is unique, and this certainly seems to hold for media architecture, since it is a field in rapid development, where the development of new technologies go hand in hand with the development of concepts and ideas for how to use them. Core activities in the preliminary phase involve 1) exploration of the location, 2) examination of potential use situations, 3) integration into new or existing architecture, and 4) negotiations and alignment among stakeholders.

3.1.1 Exploration of location

One of the ways in which media architecture differs from other types of IT development is that the end product is typically tied to a specific location, which influences many of the subsequent design choices. For this reason, a good starting point for designers will often be to explore salient features of the location. This entails geographic concerns that might influence the project, such as weather and lighting conditions, the built environment, such as existing buildings, and sociocultural features, such as current uses of a space.

In practice, there is a range of design activities that can support designers in exploring a location. In the Odenplan case, the design team carried out a *Site Tour* in the early phases of the project. A Site Tour lets the workshop participants go to the site they are designing for or to a site with similar characteristics as the design site – either in physical shape or in the actions or situations taking place. The objective of a Site Tour is to sensitise participants to site-specific elements through an embodied experience of the site. While this can seem somewhat strange from the technical perspective that is often predominant in media architecture, research underlines how our physical bodies play a central role in shaping human *experience* in the world, *understanding* of the world and *interactions* in the world (Dourish 2004; Klemmer et al. 2006).

In the Odenplan case, the main architectural feature was a large public staircase akin to the Spanish steps in Rome. The design team therefore sought out a similar public staircase for the Site Tour to observe how this type of architecture affected social life, and to get a first-person understanding and experience of the place. The Site Tour thus focused on the qualities and constraints connected to a

Fig. 4: Bthere.

stairway area and its use as sitting area. It made the participants reflect on architectural elements such as points of view, physical positioning, etc.

In addition to Site Tours, design methods such as *Bthere* (Eriksson et al. 2006), see Figure 4, and *Design Space Schemas* (Biskjaer et al. 2014) can support on-location explorations of the location and context. In addition to facilitating specific ways of examining the site, these methods also offer designers concrete means of mapping and documenting these insights, by capturing it either on physical maps or in a schematic form.

3.1.2 Examination of potential use situations

Thoughtful media architecture is based on an understanding of the use situation that unfold in the space in which it is introduced. While there are instances in which media architecture is placed in settings in which few and stable situations unfold, it will in many cases be deployed in urban settings with a diverse range of situations and rhythms. For instance, a public plaza may be a market in the morning, a transit area in the afternoon, and a place for gathering and socialising in the evening. The design of media architecture for such a setting must take all of these into account, for it is likely to alter them, either by reinforcing, transforming, or hindering them – or perhaps by fostering entirely new situations into the existing setting.

Aarhus by Light is a prominent example of an installation specifically developed to alter existing situations. Prior to the deployment of the installation, the park in front of the concert hall was primarily a transit space. A key objective of the installation was to transform this experience and use of the park. The installation was therefore designed to envelop the concert hall so as to be visible from the side, as well as from the front, and the zones in which users could interact were spread out so both people directly in front of the building, as well as people passing through main transit lanes would see and be able to interact with the installation.

Thus, the interactive façade, in combination with the Concert Hall and the park area, became a stage for new situations. These consisted both of intended use, for instance when passers-by used the installation as foreseen by the designers, as well as unforeseen and unintended use-patterns. A key design consideration prompted by the intention to transform the use situations in the park was to design for situational interaction flexibility, meaning that people could ease in and out of use: they could start by observing how other people interacted and how the façade responded, and then gradually enter and take over interaction if they wanted to. In effect, the use and experience of the park area and the identity of the Concert Hall changed. The park went from being a place of transition to a more diverse place where people still pass by, but with additional explicit hotspots in the interaction zones and the nearby areas. This indicates that the interactive zones have fostered new situations within the park. As a starting point for exploring the complexities of diverse and overlapping situations in the urban domain, McCullough (2004) has defined a number of 'situational types' and their implications for interaction design. In addition, part of Alexander's pattern language for architecture provides a rich language for urban situations (Alexander 1997).

3.1.3 Integration into new or existing architecture

A third core design activity in the preliminary phase is to examine how technological components can be integrated into the planned architectural structures. In some cases, it entails integration into new structures, as in the cases of Odenplan and the Expo pavilion; in other cases, such as Aarhus by Light, it is a question of finding suitable ways of integrating the technological components with pre-existing architecture, be it buildings and/or physical surroundings. Media architecture can be a dramatic intervention, and this prompts designers to consider

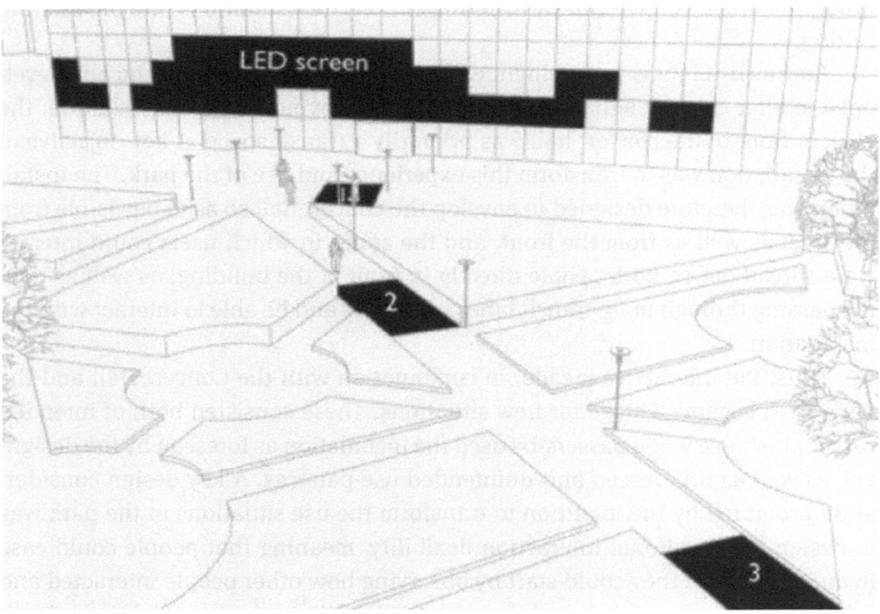

Fig. 5: Working sketch for integrating displays into the concert façade.

how it will impact not only the architecture of an individual building but also neighbouring structures, including plazas and streets. A further consideration is that the rapid pace of technological development on the one hand affords media architecture with a wealth of opportunities. On the other hand, it requires very careful consideration in order to avoid installations that quickly appear out-dated.

In the case of Aarhus by Light, the installation had to be integrated into an iconic concert hall, for which reason we had to very carefully consider how to create an end-product that both respected the existing building and added something new and worthwhile. One of the key design decisions was to avoid a huge rectangular display and instead make the display an integrated part of the façade. This was achieved by fitting semi-transparent LED panels into the existing steel framing of the building, and configuring the panels in an elongated, irregular shape. The integration of the display was also supported by having the content adhere to the existing concert hall architecture. For instance, the luminous creatures would be programmed to crawl up and down the steel framing. Furthermore, the positioning and semi-transparent appearance of the LEDs meant that the installation was visible both from the park outside the building, and from the foyer, thus offering something both for passers-by and concert hall visitors.

In the case of the Expo pavilion, the objective was to integrate the installation into a new building. As designers, we entered the process when the building shape had been developed by the principal architects, BIG, but the construction had not yet been undertaken. While this meant that we could not affect the fundamental architectural form, it did enable us to entirely integrate the installation into the building skin by using the 3600 holes that perforated it as fixtures for LED tubes that could function as individual pixels. On the technical side, it also enabled us to embed light sensors into each of the holes so the light of each pixel could be adjusted to the external lighting conditions. In terms of content, it also afforded us a thorough process of developing visuals that suited the very unique character of the building.

3.1.4 Negotiations and alignment among stakeholders

Media architecture often affects a wide range of stakeholders. This entails both the developers, e.g. architects and interaction designers, as well as paying clients and the various groups of people who will in one way or the other be affected by the introduction of a piece of media architecture, e.g. traffic authorities, local businesses and shop owners, cultural institutions, and of course a variety of citizens and citizen groups who inhabit and make use of urban spaces. Development of media architecture will often take place as collaboration between architects and interaction designers. One of the recurring challenges for these cross-disciplinary teams is to align the architectural visions for a project with the technological potentials and visions. In some cases, alignment is reached both through negotiation, where members of the different involved professions develop mutual understandings and concepts of the end product; in other cases, it is reached in a more asymmetrical way, for instance when interaction designers are hired as sub-contractors to deliver a component of a larger piece of work developed by architects.

In the Odenplan case, the media architecture installation was to be a permanent part of a highly visible public transportation hub at a square in the centre of Stockholm. Firstly, this meant that there were a range of constraints in terms of rules and regulations to abide by, e.g. the building had to be permanently lit, which eliminated the option of using projections as part of the installation. Furthermore, it meant that many interests had to be negotiated and aligned in order to reach an end-product that would be acceptable. While there were key discussions between the architects and our research group in terms of developing an installation that would augment the architectural vision, there was also a constant alignment of the developed concepts with the identified needs and wishes of the public, e.g. metro travellers and residents living near the metro station. In the Aarhus by Light case, there were similar concerns for the local residents, in addition to initial negotiations between representatives of the concert hall, our research lab, the city architect's office, and the lighting manufacturer. The concert hall had a natural interest in promoting their activities, the city architect in keeping a consistent architectural experience, the researchers in pushing the envelope and experimenting with novel forms of interaction, and the lighting manufacturers in getting a good showcase for their new LED products. All of these agendas had to be negotiated and aligned in order for the installation to be implemented successfully.

3.2 Development of concept

Development of the basic design concept is at the core of all design projects. Media architecture is a distinctive field of design, since it is in rapid development with a constant drive to create novel products. Therefore, creative ideation and concept development is an essential part of media architecture. Media architecture designers not only use standard concept development methods but also ones that are customized for the media architecture field. A repertoire of such concepts development methods are 1) ideation, 2) sketching, 3) 3D modelling, 4) virtual video prototyping, and 5) 3D projection mapping.

3.2.1 Ideation

Development of the basic idea or concepts is a fundamental aspect of all design projects and one of the widely applied methods for this particular activity is the inspiration card workshop methods (Halskov/Dalsgaard 2006; Halskov/Dalsgaard 2007). An inspiration card workshop is in its general format a collaborative design event in which domain and technology insights are combined to create design concepts. The technique is intended for the early stages of the design process, in which designers and stakeholders develop concepts for future products and systems by combining so-called Technology Cards and Domain Cards. The workshop is organized in three parts: *introduction*, *combination* and *co-creation*, and presentation of concepts; furthermore there is an initial preparation phase and a subsequent processing phase.

Fig. 6: Ideation workshop in the Odenplan project.

The inspiration card method was applied in a modified form during the main ideation activity for the development of the early ideas for the Odenplan media architecture. As preparation for the workshop a number of domain cards visualizing and representing the staircase structure of the outer part of the metro station was prepared. Likewise, a number of technology cards were produced, which visualized a diversity of display formats and interaction forms. Moreover, some of the technology cards showed examples of technologies that relied on emergent and open-ended interaction, which was one of the self-imposed constraints for the design process. In the standard way of setting up Inspiration Card Workshops, the two collections of cards would have been applied to generate the specific design concepts but for this particular workshop the presentation and discussion of cards only served as inspiration for the subsequent sketching activity, see below.

3.2.2 Sketching

Sketching is in almost all design disciplines a well-established approach to developing and visualizing design ideas (Buxton 2007). Sketches are commonly created using pen and paper, but may also be remedied through the use of smart-boards and multi-touch surfaces. Another option is to combine traditional sketching with technologies such as projection, e.g. by projecting a background image onto a whiteboard and sketch on top of it. As a sketching approach, the benefits of projection are that it is cheap, easy, fast, and fairly easy for a wide range of participants to engage in. The drawbacks are that the output will typically need to be refined and transformed into other formats in the subsequent phases of the process.

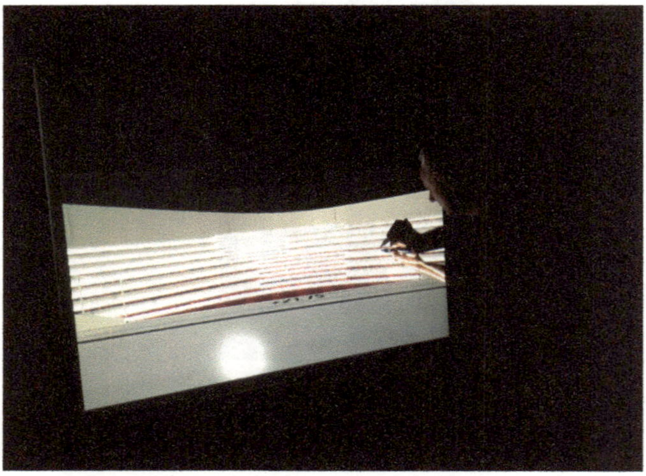

Fig. 7: Odenplan sketching.

In the Odenplan project, sketching was used in combination with projection of a basic 3D model of the metro station onto a whiteboard, Figure 7. A second projection on an adjacent wall enabled designers to display and browse inspirational material, see the above section. The participants in the concept-sketching phase could change both the inspirational sources in the background and the viewing angle and position of the 3D rendering of the model. By alternately sketching on the whiteboard and taking a snapshot with a still camera the designers created a storyboard, which served as a platform for subsequent visualization in the shape of video prototypes, see below.

3.2.3 3D Modelling

3D modelling is a key part of many architectural practices, and media architecture is no exception. There are a variety of software options available for designers, and the choice is often dependent on the specific subjects that designers wish to examine.

In the Aarhus by Light design process, we employed a variety of sketching methods, especially to examine how the façade would appear from different viewpoints, and to scaffold in-team discussions about the potential interaction zones and the layout of the display stretched across the building façade. An essential part of this process was a straightforward 3D sketching tool, Sketchup, which in comparison to most traditional 3D modelling software is very accessible and easy to start using, and therefore well-suited to quick explorations and joint concept development, see Figure 8. As stated, one of the important aspects of Media Architecture is the integration of display technology into physical structures, which are fundamentally three-dimensional. Except for a minor section of the LED modules, which was wrapped around the left corner of Musikhuset, the media architecture of this particular building was two-dimensional, whereas both the

Fig. 8: Sketchup model of Aarhus By Light.

Expo 2010 building and the Odenplan architecture were both complex geometrical structures.

The 3D modelling tool 3DS Max was applied in several ways during the design of the Expo pavilion and the Odenplan metro station. In the Odenplan case, the interaction designers created a 3D model of the out-door staircase-structure of the Odenplan station. The model consisted of two parts, the building structure itself and the LED-strips integrated into the edge of each of the stairs. Animating the light of the LED-strips enabled the production of short videos, which visualized the dynamics of the three proposed media architecture solutions. One of them only visualized the dynamics of the light whereas the other two also included animated figures siting on or moving around the staircase-structure. Such visualization are particular suitable for addressing interactive aspects of the media architecture installation.

For one of the main workshops during the Odenplan design process, the basic 3D model of the Odenplan building was available on a large 3D stereo display providing designers an opportunity to interactively explore the metro station itself as well as the city-square and surrounding buildings. Here, the 3D model was thus used as a means of exploring the already developed building model and understand how it would be perceived, and through this get a better foundation for making design decisions about the media architectural components.

3.2.4 Virtual video prototypes

3D modelling tools may not only be employed as stand-alone tools but also as platforms for more complex design approaches such as virtual video prototyping and 3D projection mapping. Virtual video prototypes are videos produced using virtual studio technology that makes it possible to combine videos of physical objects, including people, with video images generated in real time from digital 3D models.

Halskov and Nielsen (2006) explain the basic principle of virtual studio productions in the following way. Physical objects, including people, are filmed in a blue studio while the positions of the cameras and the focus and zoom adjustments are registered. These data are used to render a corresponding virtual camera view in a 3D model The two pictures, one taken by the real camera and the other by the virtual camera, meet in a keyer, where the background colour in the picture from the monochrome TV studio is removed and replaced by the computer-generated picture, see Figure 9. Using real people, as opposed to animated models of people, enables the creation of more realistic visualizations of interactive

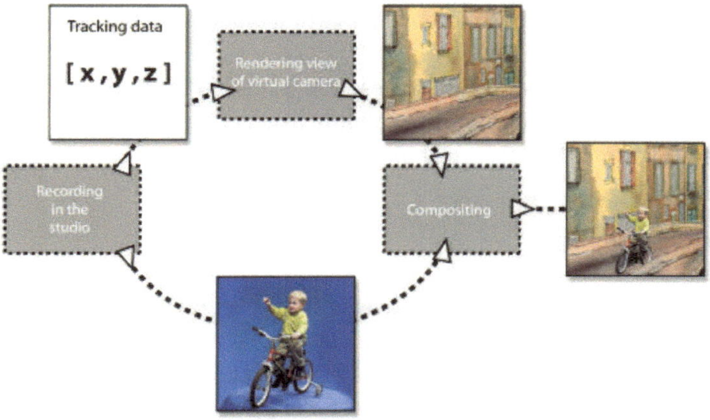

Fig. 9: Virtual video prototyping principles.

Fig. 10: Virtual video prototyping of Traces.

elements of the media architecture. Moreover, a virtual video prototype is a very concrete form of visualization.

One of the three *Odenplan* concepts, Traces, was visualized as a virtual video prototype, providing a visualization of how people interacting with installation would appear, see Figure 10 (Dalsgaard et al. 2016).

3.2.5 3D projection mapping

Another sophisticated application of 3D models is 3D projection mapping, which provides an additional opportunity to visualize the integration of a unique interface into the building. 3D projection mapping is based on having an accurate 3D model of the physical part of the installation, see Figure 11 (Dalsgaard/Halskov 2012). In the digital 3D world, we can produce digital content corresponding to the shape of a physical object, which may be subsequently projected onto the physical model of the installation, thereby augmenting the physical object.

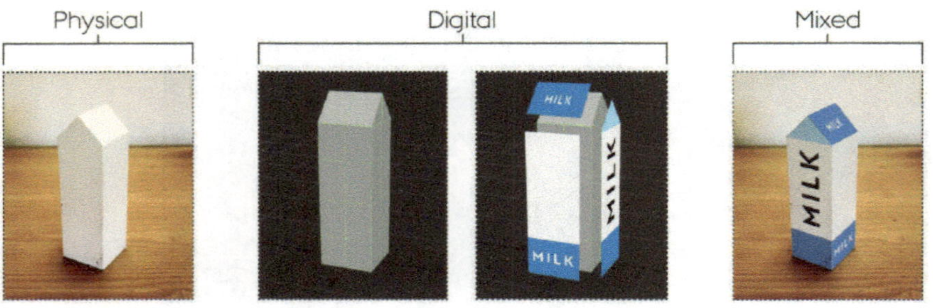

Fig. 11: 3D projection mapping principles.

Projection mapping has been used for implementing media architecture installation in a number of cases, for instance the City Hall in Sugar Land (Pop 2012; Falck/Halskov 2013). In the case of the Expo Pavilion, 3D projection mapping was applied in the design process by projecting the exact pixel configuration of the Expo Pavilion onto 1:100 scale physical model. Using virtual 3D technology, the model showed the holes as they would be illuminated on the pavilion and simulated the sunlight and cast shadows, Figure 12 (Halskov/Ebsen 2013). This 3D Mixed Reality tool was based on technology recently developed by our research laboratory, in order to match physical objects with their virtual 3D counterparts, and thereby add visual content to precise locations on the object, (Dalsgaard/Halskov 2012).

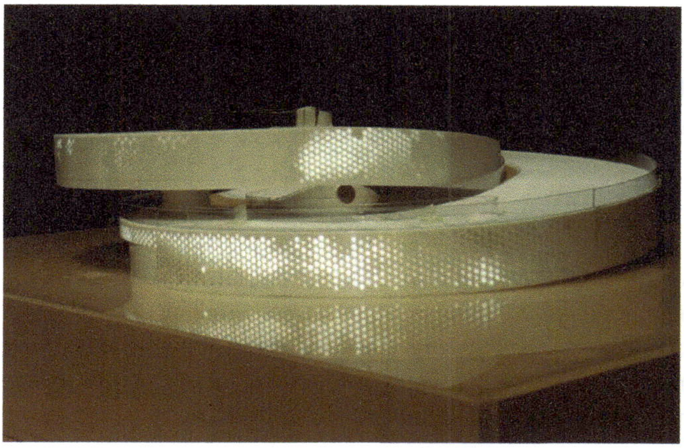

Fig. 12: 3D projection mapping – the Expo Pavilion.

The physicality of the mixed reality model made for a valuable visualization for discussion among the members of the design team, and also made it possible to visualize the display in relation to the building in its totality, which turned out to be a powerful way to explain ideas to the collaborating architects. The main projector was mounted in the ceiling, and designers could walk around the table on which the model was placed, and share their views on the design.

Gehring et al. (2013) has developed power full a media façade toolkit consisting of separate modules for interaction, application, 3D model and rendering, which in one of the test cases has been applied for visualizing a media façade by projecting on miniature model similar to the 3D projection mapping in the Expo case. The media façade toolkit has also been applied for the development of prototypes.

3.3 Prototyping and mock-ups

For the phase following development of the basic design concept, a media architecture project takes on a more technology oriented focus in order to identify how the design concept may be implemented. One of the main challenges for media architecture designers is that interfaces are non-standard in particular with respect to the display itself. As discussed in detail by Halskov and Ebsen (2013) media architecture extends into three-dimensional space and may have any shape and often with pixels part of the visual expression of the media architecture. Moreover the pixels of conventional displays are organized in a grid or matrix structure whereas there is no standardized way of organizing pixels when it comes to media facades. Another challenge is the physical integration of the technology into the building itself. Both of these aspects may be addressed by two of the most prominent design approaches, 1) mock-ups and 2) hardware prototyping.

3.3.1 Mock-ups

Mock-ups are low-tech design artefacts that simulate future technology by using physical materials such as cardboard, paper, wood, and slide projectors (Ehn/Kyng 1991), but may be created by combing such physical material together with electronic components. Since Media Architecture consists of innovative combinations of display technology and other kinds of physical components, the use of Mock-ups is a very productive way to facilitate testing of the integration of the interface into the built structure.

Fig. 13: Full scale mock-up of part of the Expo building.

In the early phases of the Expo Pavilion case, the designers created a full-scale mock-up of a section of the building, in order to experiment with how to turn the holes in the façade into pixels by mounting light fixtures behind PVC tubes, Figure 13 (Halskov/Ebsen 2013). A number of experiments led to a conclusion with respect to which combination of light fixtures and PVC tubes produced the most uniform light distribution. Moreover the experiments revealed that the shape of the individual pixels depended on the viewing angle, that is, from a very acute angle a pixel would appear as a circle whereas from a less acute angle as a crescent.

A smaller section of the mock-up was used for testing the idea that the building would react to the amount of natural light, which was explored by integrating a light sensor reacting to a shadow cast on the surface of the building.

3.3.2 Prototyping

A prototype is a software implementation of part of a system, for instance selected aspects of the interface or a particular part of the functionality (Floyd 1984). In the later phase of the design process, the prototyping activities typically focus on testing and exploring the hardware technologies. In the case of Aarhus by Light, the designers and the engineers tested the effect of mounting different diffusers in front of the LED modules in order to explore how various kinds of PVC material affected the appearance and light quality of the individual pixels and the image formation. Similar tests were conducted during the EXPO project using a full-scale mock-up of part of the building, see below.

The Odenplan project also required a detailed investigation of the LED technologies, which potentially could be applied for the implementation of light sources mounted along each of the stairs of the outdoor part of the metro station building. The software engineers tested various solution to the problem of controlling the individual pixels of LED strips as well as mapping conventional matrix-organized pixels on to a set of curved LED strips.

Fig. 14: Prototyping LED panels for Aarhus By Light.

A more conventional prototyping approach was applied during the design of the Aarhus By Light installation. Aarhus by Light was the design team's very first large media architecture project and in order to explore the visual aspects (the perceptual qualities and resolution) of the LED panels a single module of the panels was mounted in one of the windows of the façade of the design lab, see Figure 14. Such a very basic prototype enabled the exploration of various content and provided the opportunity to test the resolution of the LED modules in full scale. During the Aarhus By Light prototyping process custom developed software enables the designers to map a video signal onto the irregular configuration of low-resolution LED modules.

Within media architecture the development of specialized prototyping tools is widespread. One example is the Lightbox developed by Wiethoff and Bloeckner (2011), see also (Wiethoff/Gehring 2012), which is a collection of hardware components providing people with limited technical skills the opportunity to create simple prototypes of elements of the media architecture.

4 Summary

The methods and tools described here represent the core components of our approach to media architecture as developed through seven years of carrying out projects in a range of settings. Table 1 offers an overview of these tools and methods in the three overarching design phases.

Tab. 1: Methods and tools for the three design phases.

Phase	Tools and processes
Preliminary research	Exploration of location Examination of potential use situations Integration into new or existing architecture Negotiations and alignment among stakeholders
Development of concept	Ideation Sketching 3D modelling Virtual video prototyping 3D projection mapping
Prototyping and mock-ups	Mock-ups Hardware prototyping

In our experience, media architecture design processes often unfold in an iterative way, and designers gain new insights along the way that cause them to revisit and revise aspects they had previously worked on. For instance, prototyping may reveal that ideas about how to integrate technologies into a building may not hold up in practice, prompting the need for new concept development workshops to reorient the design process. Similarly, the development of virtual video prototypes may support negotiations and alignment with stakeholders because they clarify and concretise aspects of interaction that can be hard to communicate.

The approaches have been inspired and informed by other practitioners in media architecture and related fields, e.g. urban planning and interaction design. They offer a starting point for practitioners venturing into media architecture to develop meaningful installations. However, the field is still new, so existing tools and methods are continuously being refined, and new ones being developed. This is likely to continue, in part because media architecture spreads into new domains, in part because the available technologies develop at a rapid pace. In continuation, we do not consider these methods and tools to offer a fixed approach to design processes. Rather, they can be seen as a collection from which designers can select the methods and tools that are best suited for a given design process.

Bibliography

Alexander, C. (1997): A Pattern Language: Towns, Buildings, Construction. Oxford: Oxford University Press.

Brynskov, M.; Dalsgaard, P.; Ebsen, T.; Fritsch, J.; Halskov, K.; Nielsen, R. (2009): "Staging Urban Interactions with Media Facades". In: Proceedings of Interact 2019. Berlin: Springer Verlag, 154–167.

Brynskov, M.; Dalsgaard, P.; Halskov, K. (2015): "Media Architecture: Engaging Urban Experiences in Public Space". In: J. Lossau; Q. Stevens (eds.): The Uses of Art in Public Space. New York, NY: Routledge, 51–66.

Buxton, B. (2007): Sketching User Experiences: Getting the Design Right and the Right Design. Burlington: Morgan Kaufmann.

Dalsgaard, P.; Halskov, K. (2010): "Designing Urban Media Façades: Cases and Challenges". In: Proceedings of CHI 2010. New York, NY: ACM, 2277–2286.

Dalsgaard, P.; Halskov, K. (2012): "3D Projection on Physical Objects: Design Considerations and Challenges". In: Proceedings of NordiCHI 2012. New York, NY: ACM, 109–118.

Dalsgaard, P.; Halskov, K.; Nielsen, R. (2008): "A Design Space Explorer for Media Facades". In: Proceedings of OzCHI 2008. New York, NY: ACM, 219–226.

Dalsgaard, P.; Halskov, K.; Wiethoff, A. (2016): "Designing Media Architecture: Tools and Approaches for Addressing the Main Design Challenges". In: Proceedings of CHI 2016. New York, NY: ACM, 2562–2572.

Dourish, P. (2004): Where the action is: the foundation of embodied interaction. Cambridge: MIT Press Cambridge.
Ehn, P.; Kyng, M. (1991): "Cardboard Computers: Mocking-it-up and hands-on the future". In: J. Greenbaum; M. Kyng (eds.): Design at Work: Cooperative Design of Computer Systems. Hillsdale, NJ: Lawrence Erlbaum Associates, 169–195.
Eriksson, E. (2006): "Bthere or be Square: A Method for Extreme Contextualizing of Design". In: Proceedings of Wonderground International Conference 2006. Lisbon, Portugal: CEIADE, 1–11.
Falck, H.W.; Halskov, K. (2013): "Towards a Framework for Projection Installations". In: Proceedings of PerDis 2013. New York, NY: ACM, 67–72.
Floyd, C. (1984): "A Systematic look at Prototyping". In: R. Budde; K. Kuhlenkamp; L. Matthiassen; H. Zu¨llighoven (eds.): Approaches to Prototyping. Berlin: Springer Verlag, 1–16.
Gehring, S.; Hartz, E.; Löchtefeld, M.; Krüger, A. (2013): "The media façade toolkit: prototyping and simulating interaction with media façades". In: Proceedings of the UbiComp 2013. New York, NY: ACM, 763–772.
Halskov, K. (2011): CAVI – An interaction design research lab. Interactions 18:4, 92–95.
Halskov, K.; Dalsgaard, P. (2006): "Inspiration Card Workshops". In: Proceedings of DIS 2006. New York, NY: ACM, 2–11.
Halskov, K.; Dalsgaard, P. (2007): "The Emergence of Ideas: The interplay between sources of inspiration and emerging design concepts". Journal of CoDesign 3:4, 185–211.
Halskov, K.; Ebsen, T. (2013): "A framework for designing complex media facades". Design Studies 34:5, 663–679.
Halskov, K.; Nielsen, R. (2006): "Virtual video prototyping". Human-Computer Interaction Journal 21, 199–233.
Klemmer, S.R.; Hartmann, B.; Takayama, L. (2006): "How bodies matter: Five themes for interaction design". In: Proceedings of DIS 2006. New York, NY: ACM, 140–149.
Korsgaard, H.; Hansen, N.B.; Basballe, D.; Dalsgaard, P.; Halskov, K. (2012): "Odenplan – a media façade design process". In: Proceedings of MAB 2012. New York, NY: ACM, 23–32.
McCullough, M. (2004): Digital Ground. Cambridge, MA: MIT Press Cambridge.
Pop, S.; Tscherteu, G.; Stalder, U.; Struppek, M. (2012): Urban Media Cultures. Ludwigsburg: avedition GmbH.
Wiethoff, A.; Bloeckner, M. (2011): "Lightbox – Exploring Interaction Modalities with Colored Light". In: Proceedings of TEI'11. New York, NY: ACM, 399–400.
Wiethoff, A.; Gehring, G. (2012): "Designing interaction with media façades: a case study". In: Proceedings of DIS 2012. New York, NY: ACM, 308–317.

Sven Gehring

Interacting with Media Architecture

1 Introduction

Over the last years, urban environments and public places emerged as prime locations for deploying digital technologies. Besides large scale digital displays, an increasing number of media facades (see Figure 1) are embedded into the urban landscape (Bouchard 2007; Seitinger 2008; Winogard 2001), thus becoming more and more ubiquitous (Weiser 1991). In a common sense, the term media facade describes the idea of turning the facade of a building into a huge public screen. This is achieved by either equipping its outer shell with interactive, light-emitting elements or by projecting digital content onto the building (Bullivant 2006; Haeusler 2009; Schoch 2006). The display might appear as a secondary skin of the building. Media facades can be classified based on different characteristics and properties. Among others, these might include their technical composition, as well as the main principles of how media content can be displayed. With the increasing number of media facades, urban environments are on their way to being turned into dynamic and programmable surfaces (Greenfield/Shepard 2007). Media facades provide a new way for accessing information at a large scale in urban spaces. Due to their technical requirements, their size and resolution, they can make information of different granularity accessible for a large audience. Passersby can not visually access information but often also interact with it with the help of various interaction techniques, that will be described in this chapter. The visualized information can range from low resolution ambient visualization of data such as energy consumption or traffic to high resolution content such as dynamic videos and text. In the remaining part of this chapter, we will analyze interactive media facade settings with respect to their technical requirements and their potential for providing access to information of different granularity. Besides media facades, the manifold use of light and light-emitting elements in urban environments plays an important role in the architecture of such spaces.

Haeusler (Haeusler 2009) identified three different uses of light in urban spaces: *light architecture*, *media architecture*, and *media facades*. He distinguishes these terms as follows: *Light architecture* subsumes the illumination of a building using both daylight and artificial light to underline parts of the building and to create a certain atmosphere. *Media architecture* uses a similar approach, but also includes all aspects of dynamically displaying media, such as dynamic graphics, dynamic text and spatial movement, but with a strong focus on *dynamic* content. *Media facades* build on this by including media to transform the building facade

DOI 10.1515/9783110453874-010

into a communicative element, that is embedded into the architecture of the building. Note that there is a fluent transition between these three terms.

Fig. 1: Media facades of different sizes, shapes and resolutions.

The definition of architecture as a whole includes both the design of the entire environment around media facades and its effect on a given urban space (Haeusler 2009). Thus, whereas media facades embed communication into a facade in the form of digital media, media architecture describes the cultural, social and economic implications of these facades for the immediate environment (Haeusler 2009). It is noteworthy that Haeusler's notions of media facades are created from a architectural perspective. Since we are dealing with media facades as large-scale digital screens from a human-computer interaction perspective, we do not explicitly address the architectural implications of media facades and we therefore do not distinguish between light architecture and media architecture. Thus, we define the term media facade as follows:

> **Media facades** are digital public screens with arbitrary form factors and of varying resolution, which are created by either equipping the outer surface of an architectural building with controllable, uniformly shaped, light emitting elements or by projecting digital content

onto it. Media facades are embedded into the architectural structure of the underlying building and transform the building into a communicative element.

Unlike designing the actual media facade (i.e., the underlying hardware) for a particular building, designing interactive media facade installations today is far from being standardized. There is neither a common ground for which technologies and which interaction techniques work in a particular situation, nor is there any categorization that puts the components of media facade installations into context. Existing installations usually are *one-of-a-kind* deployments that (1) are specifically designed from scratch for the particular building, and (2) only to a limited extent exploit the spatial context of the setting as well as the building's surrounding. The design is usually driven by trying to make an idea somehow fit into a given location, rather than analyzing the location and context of the media facade in question to design an installation that specifically addresses the properties of the facade's environment.

In this chapter we analyze the technical opportunities of interactive media facade installations regarding the properties that frame the installation, its spatial context as well as the applied interaction techniques and utilized input devices. Based on our analysis, we derive a taxonomy for describing interactive media facade installations, which provides insights about the appropriateness of different technologies in particular situations. The taxonomy considers (1) the technical and spatial properties of a media facade and its surroundings, as well as (2) different input modalities. The goal is to inform the design of interactive installations for media facades in such a way that designers can choose a suitable interaction technique based on the facade's particular setting addressing technical opportunities, as well as limitations. Within this scope, we investigate different ways of participating in a media facade installation, and we analyze properties of media facades and their deployment environments in terms of their impact on interaction.

2 Related Work

While many installations are *one-of-a-kind* deployments, researchers have begun to analyze systematically interactive media facade installations. It is important to consider the unique technical properties and requirements of this whole domain in order to create successful and enjoyable installations.

Dalsgaard et al. presented one of the first systematic analyses of the design of interactivity for media facades (Dalsgaard et al. 2008). Using their *Design Space Explorer*, they present a framework for managing multiple sources of information and domain concerns for the design of collaborative design process, which combines these aspects in scenarios for design concepts (Dalsgaard et al. 2008). The *Design Space Explorer* captures and gives an overview of design materials and forms, domain locations and situations, interaction styles, and content types. It is a tool to gain an overview of the design space, to conceptualize key aspects of interaction design, as well as to support communication and discussions among designers, clients and partners. Furthermore, it provides a platform for designers to combine these aspects into scenarios for design concepts (Dalsgaard et al. 2008). Dalsgaard and Halskov further expanded this work (Dalsgaard/Halskov 2010), identifying eight key challenges that need to be addressed when designing for media facades in an urban context. In this chapter we are mainly addressing the challenges (1) new interface, (2) integration into physical structures and surroundings and (4) developing content to suit the medium. Halskov and Ebsen provide a conceptual framework for addressing how content for a media facade may be designed taking into account the specific qualities of the display of media facade interfaces: scale, shape, pixel configuration, pixel shape, and light quality (Halskov/Ebsen 2013)). Van de Moere and Hill analyze the concept of research through design in the context of teaching urban computing (Moere/Hill 2009). They further point out the importance of the context of an urban installation for its design process (Moere/Wouters 2012). Reeves et al. provided a taxonomy to classify public interfaces according to the extent to which the interactions of a user and the resulting effects are hidden, revealed or amplified for spectators (Reeves et al. 2005). Korsgaard et al. approached the question of how to design for media facades by discussing how they structure their design processes to address specific sets of challenges raised in the literature (Korsgaard et al. 2012).

Fischer and Hornecker analyzed the spatial aspects in the design of shared encounters for interactive media facades (Fischer/Hornecker 2012). They reflected on various urban technology interventions by analyzing their spatial configuration in relation to the structuring of interaction. They introduce the term *Urban HCI*, which focuses on urban settings where context is not only a location point but also an activity carried out – it emphasizes situations composed of the built environment, the interfaces and the social context. Understanding the spatial configuration of the spaces around a media facade is an important factor for the design and development of successful interactive media facade installations. When creating such systems, the spatial configuration of the media facade's environment further influences the appropriateness of certain content and it further restricts the applicability of different interaction techniques.

The aforementioned works aim at formalizing specific aspects of interactive media facade installations. Yet they focus on specific aspects and are thus not suitable for holistically describing the overall installation – including its technical specification – in order to categorize and compare it. It is noteworthy that there is work on multi-person-display ecosystems (Terrenghi et al. 2009). However, their taxonomy is not applicable to interactive media facade installations. Due to their physical characteristics, the outdoor urban environment, and the various available input modalities and interaction styles, a taxonomy characterizing interactive media facade installations needs to address those particular characteristics as well as the technical parameters of the setting. In the following, we therefore review existing interactive media facade installations and identify characteristic (and sometimes unique) properties and technical capabilities to ultimately create a taxonomy.

3 Interactive Media Facade Installations

Researchers, artists and designers have been exploring media facade installations in a variety of ways: (1) they experimented with different input modalities and interaction techniques in a playful and artistic manner; and (2) they shared their valuable experiences and lessons learned as a solid ground for developing novel, universal interaction approaches. The following review of existing installations will serve as the basis to extract characteristic properties that frame and shape interactive installations.

3.1 Whole Body Interaction

With the design intervention *Aarhus by Light*, Brynskov et al. created an interactive installation for a concert hall (Brynskov et al. 2009). It was installed on the glass facade of the building, which was fitted with $180m^2$ of media facade consisting of semi-transparent LED screens (see Figure 2). The goal of this installation was to engage local citizens into new kinds of public behavior to explore the potential of digital media in urban life. Within three interactivity areas in front of the facade (marked with colored carpets), the silhouettes of people standing on the carpet were tracked. Their movements were mapped to playful creatures on the media facade to encourage a curious and playful investigation of the expression among the users. The movement of the virtual characters further served as visual feedback on the users' movements. Brynskov et al. (Brynskov et al. 2009) further revealed valuable insights around the themes of people's *interaction patterns*, *initiation*, as well as their *engagement* with the installation and their *interaction style*. This led to an overview of social interaction patterns. Dalsgaard et al.

further investigated the ability of this design intervention to *support* engagement (Dalsgaard et al. 2011). They describe how the presence of territorial issues (people's social encounters) lead to social activities around the installation.

Fig. 2: Interactive media façade installations. From left to right: Aarhus by Light, (Brynskov et al. 2009), Laser Tag (Klanten et al. 2011), Lummoblocks (Guitiérrez et al. 2009).

Fritsch and Dalsgaard utilized the whole body interaction approach from the Aarhus by Light installation in an interactive design intervention (Fritsch/Dalsgaard 2008). Their *Climate Wall* was an installation at an historical building in Aarhus, where it was running during the climate conference *Beyond Kyoto*[1]. It displayed generated, fragmented climate statements, giving passersby the opportunity to take part in the ongoing climate debate. People could grab and move around words by body movement to form new climate statements. During interaction, users received visual feedback on their input through the motion of controlled word. As key aspects from the Climate Wall and Aarhus by Light installations, the authors revealed their insights into how people interact with such novel urban interfaces and how they can be engaged to interact. They utilized media facades to create engagement, where the particular interaction technique supported the playful character of the installation.

Gutiérez et al. showed how whole body interaction can enhance the experience of a user during interaction by taking the interaction to a spatial level. With Lummoblocks (Gutiérrez et al. 2009), they created an interactive Tetris game, running on the media facade of the Medialab Prado[2] in Madrid (see Figure 2). The aim of the installation is to provide a playful, interactive, space-located experience and engaging social interaction between users and spectators. The facade showed the game itself, combined with a live video feed displaying a bird's eye view of the users in front of the facade. The installation mapped rotating and moving actions (the two dominant interactions in Tetris) to two separate interaction spaces, thus

1 http://klima.au.dk/dk/forside/konferencebeyondkyotoconferen/
2 http://medialab-prado.es

forcing the two players to collaborate: one had to rotate a Tetris block, while the second player moved it to the right spot. Players had to do so by running around within the boundaries of their particular interaction space.

With the installation *12m4s*, the LAb[au] group created an interactive installation that generated a real-time visualization of passersby based on their average walking speed (Klanten et al. 2011). The movements are tracked in real-time with cameras and ultra-sound sensors to generate a visual (3D particles) and auditory (granular synthesis) scape on the facade. The visualization is based on the position, orientation and speed of passersby. It is projected on a 12m long Mylar[3] screen (an electro insulating film made of PETP), combining projection and reflection of the passerby's body, while creating an interactive space in between the digital and the body space. The characteristics of the Mylar screen amplify the visual effects. The screen remains a mirror on non-enlightened zones, but turns transparent on enlightened zones.

The *Night Lights* installation by YesYesNo combines three different interaction techniques (Klanten et al. 2011) to display interactive silhouettes and animations on a projected media facade with 3D projection mapping: tracking movements of people standing on a platform, hand gestures above a light-table and waving of mobile phones. The installation turned a building into an interactive playground. The goal of the installation was to adapt the concept of *shadow puppets* to allow any passersby to become a performer. There are dedicated interaction zones for the particular interaction techniques, which are designed as small stages, where people can walk up and interact with the projection. The movements of people within these interaction zones are tracked and amplified by an approximately 15m tall projection on the building.

The building of *La Vitrine Culturelle* in Montreal, Canada, is equipped with a small, low-resolution media facade of approximately $23m^2$ consisting of 35000 RGB LEDs that change their color as a reaction to the movements of passersby (Haeusler et al. 2013), thus providing various animations and media content. When walking past the facade, the walking direction is mapped to animated arrows. When people stop and stand in front of the facade, they can create further animations through body gestures. These animations range from snowflakes around the user's silhouette to movable light spots. Although designed as temporary installation for Montreal's city of lights festival in 2009, it was the first interactive media facade in North America to be turned into a permanent installation due to its huge popularity.

---

3 http://www.mueller-ahlhorn.com/en/mylar/

The aforementioned installations illustrate the importance and suitability of body-movement as input modality as it usually has a playful character combined with performance elements and enables people to interact without a dedicated interaction device. However, its applicability as general interaction technique to interact with complex content on distant screens is limited as it requires extensive instrumentation of the space.

3.2 Pointing

A common interaction technique utilized in various interactive installations is pointing. With *Spread.gun*, Fischer et al. present an interactive shared encounter for media facades, inspired by established forms of graffiti culture (Fischer et al. 2010). The installation took place within the scope of the 2008 Media Facade Festival in Berlin, Germany with the aim of creating a digitally augmented forum in public space. The tangibility of the interaction is mentioned as the most important part of the design work. The stationary interaction device – called *Spread:gun* – is a model of an ancient cannon that a user rotates to aim at a particular point on the facade. A user can enter a text message through a digital touch screen. While aiming at the facade, a virtual crosshair is displayed as visual feedback. The position of the crosshair is calculated with data from two potentiometers that are integrated in the cannon-like interface for the horizontal and vertical axis. By shooting the cannon, a color bag is virtually shot onto the projected facade. The color spots on the facade are displayed enclosing the text messages of the particular user. One disadvantage of this installation is that the interaction device is highly tailored to the purpose of the installation and environment around the particular facade. They point out the effect of the social and spatial setting and describe how the location and the surroundings may drastically alter the context of the installation.

As a conceptual enhancement of Spread:gun, Fischer et al. presented the *SMSlingshot* (Fischer et al. 2010). Instead of a stationary input device, they provided a mobile, custom built input device, based on the metaphor of a wooden slingshot. The aim of the installation was allowing people to shoot information onto public screens. The slingshot device is equipped with a small LCD display and a mobile phone keyboard, allowing a user to enter text messages. By aiming and shooting at a particular point on the media facade with the slingshot, a user can shoot his entered message on the facade together with a virtual color bag, analog to the Spread.gun approach. Additionally, the entered text messages are twittered in real-time. In comparison to Spread:gun, SMSlingshot has the advantage of providing a portable and flexible interaction technique. With *TXTual Healing*, Notzold followed an approach very similar to SMSlingshot, applying the same interaction metaphor and feedback mechanisms utilizing the model of an assault rifle to fire text-based messages onto a projected media facade (Klanten et al. 2011).

For the described approaches, a user only points at the media facade to transfer locally created content onto the facade. In contrast, the installation *Laser Tag* by the Graffiti Research Lab allows for continuous pointing interaction to create content directly on the media facade (Klanten et al. 2011). As depicted in Figure 2, users can paint and write onto the media facade by pointing at it with a laser pointer. The scope of this installation was to create a playful approach for allowing people to digitally write on buildings in public spaces. In an attempt to provide a universal interaction technique for media facades, Gehring and Lander introduced the GPS Lens (Gehring/Lander 2013), a technique to control a pointer on a large-scale distant screen by pointing at the screen with the mobile device. The position of the pointer is calculated based on GPS, accelerometer and compass data from the mobile device's built-in sensors.

Most of these installations have in common that they utilize a pointing approach where a laser is tracked by cameras. Although this is a trivial, from a technical perspective easy to realize approach providing immediate visual feedback on the pointing, it's applicability as a general interaction technique for permanent media facades that are not permanently monitored is rather limited. From the technical side, the tracking does not work with standard, free to use laser pointers. The utilized lasers require special permissions to be used in public. From an interaction perspective, it is hardly possible to distinguish between users, or limit the interaction to particular users, as there is no association between user and laser pointer. Such a system only detects a certain number of laser dots, yet it is not aware of the absolute number of lasers used.

3.3 Touch & Gestures

Both direct touch and gestures with mobile devices have been explored with different media facade installations. Within the scope of the Illuminating York Festival[4], in conjunction with the GaiaNova Productions Ltd., the OMA International group presented the *Wall of Light* installation (Klanten et al. 2011), an artistic installation to paint in real-time on a projected media facade. Using the *Tag Tool* – a digital graphics tablet for painting – as the input device, people were able to paint onto the facade by drawing on the Tag Tool with a digital pen. The installation was

4 http://www.illuminatingyork.org

intended as a canvas for daily performances of artists, but they also allowed visitors to use the installation to express themselves. According to the creators, the performance of the inexperienced visitors shows that the installation is intuitive and easy to use.

The urban media installation *Touch* by the LAb[au] group allows passersby to interact with the Dexia Tower in Brussels, Belgium (Klanten et al. 2011). They installed a stationary multi-touch screen at the base of the building to allow people to individually or collectively manipulate the color of the approximately 4200 windows of the 145 m high tower in real time. This window animation facade allows for both dynamic and static inputs. People can create basic geometric forms on the tower as well as change its color. The concept of this installation tries not to treat the facade as a plain 2D surface. The goal is to integrate characteristics of the building, such as orientation, scale or volume, to create an interactive experience. The stationary screen displays a virtual representation of the buildings surface, on which the users get immediate visual feedback on their interactions.

With *MobiSpray* (Scheible/Ojala 2009), Scheible and Ojala presented a digital graffiti tool utilizing a mobile phone as a virtual spray can. Users can spray digital dabs onto a projected media facade. The movement of the spraying nozzle is based on the orientation of the mobile phone, determined by continuous data from the built in accelerometer. A dedicated drawing client application on the mobile phone provides controls to adjust the properties of the virtual spray can such as blob size, colors or intensity. A user can draw onto a facade by performing spray gestures with the mobile phone, similar to a real spray can. Since there is no absolute mapping between the spray canvas and the facade, the advantage of this approach is that it does not require any calibration when used in a different location for a different building. Shamma et al. utilized and adapted MobiSpray to create a collaborative space for the voice of a local community to make statements about the world around them (Shamma et al. 2009). Participants and spectators can observe how digital graffiti is created while they receive feedback provided by dancers interacting with the virtual projected content and physical space. To create graffiti, people can use MobiSpray and they can additionally upload text messages as well as images from the mobile phone to the media facade.

With the installation iRiS, Boring et al. presented an approach utilizing the interaction through live video pattern (Boring et al. 2011). Users aim their device at the facade and observe it in live video, while can point through the display at the facade. Touch input occurring on the mobile device is projected onto the facade, giving the impression that users directly touch the surface of the building (Boring et al. 2011). This approach requires a direct line of sight and is therefore limited to the visible part of the facade. With facade maps, Gehring and Krüger introduced an approach to interact with media facades having 3D form factors

(Gehring/Krüger 2012). They apply cartographic map projections to make the whole facade visible at once on a map of its surface. This map is displayed on a mobile device, where users can interact with the facade with touch input on the mobile device's screen.

A common problem of such installations is they are often both stationary and highly tailored to the one specific setting and usage scenario. This limits their applicability as general input techniques to interact with media facades.

3.4 Remote

We are investigating *direct* interaction with media facades in a sense that to be able to interact with a facade, the user has to be within the potential interaction space in front of the facade. Especially for high resolution facades displaying advertisements, operators can remotely interact with the facade over web interfaces or dedicated software in order to provide the displayed content. Although they are interacting with the facade, we do not address this form of interaction since it can be instead considered as pure provisioning of content and it does provide passersby with the opportunity to interact with the facade. However, there exist different approaches providing people with a remote interface to interact with a media facade without the requirement of being within the potential interaction space or even the display space. While the aforementioned installations focused on allowing the people within the display space to interact with the facade, providing remote interfaces is usually driven by different design intentions. First, providing remote interfaces does not particularly focus on the people within the display space. It allows a wider range of people to interact with a facade while the interaction could be either limited to a particular group of people like for example all inhabitants of the city, or it could be allowed to all people that can access the remote interface (e.g., over the internet). Second, media facade installations providing remote interfaces often do not focus on continuous interaction. They rather provide means for sharing content with a media facade (e.g., by uploading images, videos or animations) or to participate by expressing yourself and visually branding or customizing a building.

One of the first installations is the *Blinkenlights* project (Haeusler 2009). The upper eight floors of an office building were turned into the at that time world's biggest interactive computer screen. They created a window raster animation facade by equipping the windows of the building with 144 individually controllable lamps in total, which resulted in display with 8x18 pixels. To control the content, people had to call a dedicated phone number with their mobile phones. Once connected, they could either control a virtual cursor on the facade or activate previously uploaded animation with a code also entered with the key pad of the mobile phone. The world's first interactive RGB media facade, the *Marnix* facade in Brussels, Belgium, allows people to participate by taking control of the media facade's content (Haeusler et al. 2013). The operators of the facade provide a free-to-download animation interface, with which people can create and upload their own animations from anywhere in the world. This installation is very popular and frequently used from people around the world to share content from wedding proposals, to political statements, to artful animations. The media facade of the *Rundle Lantern* building in Adelaide, Australia was built with *"the vision of creating an experience that would capture the imagination of the city and add beauty to peoples' lives"* (Haeusler et al. 2013). This low-resolution media facade consists of more than 700 individually controllable RGB panels that are wrapped around the building. To control the content of the facade, people can use a web interface to create and upload their own animations. With its frequent use, this installation has developed into a tool for continuous community engagement.

The aforementioned installations mostly have a playful, performative or artistic orientation. The interaction as well as the applied input techniques and devices were particularly designed for the specific installation. Besides the playful and artistic character of the installation, an important aspect when interacting with a media facade is its resolution and form factor. As we have seen, the resolution can easily vary from screens with 144 pixels to high-resolution screens capable of displaying sophisticated content. Furthermore, the majority of the presented installations require a direct line of sight between user and facade to interact. This would leave a user with only a part of the actual facade as an interactive screen. When developing novel interaction techniques, we need to address these issues in order to exploit the media facades' full potential as urban screens.

4 Characteristics of Interactive Media Facades

Media facades are commonly built to fulfill a particular purpose. They are based on different technologies and are situated in unique, dynamic settings. This makes a comparison of different media facade installations a challenging task. Interactive media facade installations usually apply different input modalities utilizing a wide range of input devices with various technical requirements. Furthermore, the technical properties and spatial arrangement of the interactive space itself influence the applicability of technologies to provide user input.

4.1 Context of the Setting

Media facades are usually situated in a dynamic setting with unique characteristics making it difficult to compare installations and situations that arise from them. Nevertheless, there are characteristic properties such as instrumentation of the space or spatial aspects in the context of a media facade's deployment space which have a strong influence on the applicability of different technologies. Furthermore, the intended interaction style (i.e., performative interaction) also introduces constraints. The properties can be brought in to categorize and compare different media facade installations in different contexts.

4.1.1 Spatial Aspects

Fischer et al. analyzed spatial aspects – the spatial configuration of the space around the installation – in the design of shared encounters for interactive media facades with respect to the spatial configuration in relation to the structuring of interaction (Fischer/Hornecker 2012). In combination with the resolution of the media facade itself, as well as its underlying technology (e.g., pixel-based, projected, etc.), the configuration of the space around a media facade has more impact on the appropriateness of content than on the general applicability of particular interaction techniques. Size and configuration of the space determine distances and angles from which users can see the facade and its content. To allow the users to perceive the displayed content as a whole from within this space, the content must be designed with respect to the spatial configuration of the setting. When dealing with multiple users interacting simultaneously with the facade, the spatial configuration of the potentially interactive space can further determine if the particular users can see each other directly or if they are at least aware of each other. The spatial aspects also influence the communication between the users and hence, the social configuration of the setting.

Concerning different interaction techniques, the spatial configuration of the setting represents a scaling factor rather than a criterion for the general applicability of a particular technique. Regarding the physical space that is required to perform an interaction, interaction techniques in the context of media facades in general only require minimal space – the immediate space around the user – to be applicable at all. For interaction that does not involve whole-body movement of the user, the minimal space is usually represented by the space required to operate the input device. When involving interaction techniques such as direct pointing, it further requires a direct line of sight between the user and the particular target area on the facade. Concerning whole body interaction, size and spatial arrangement of the involved spaces determines the possible scale of the mapping between body movement and reaction on the facade. Furthermore, it influences the potential number of maximum users that can interact simultaneously, since each user requires a certain amount of the available space. In summary, we can say that the spatial configuration of the setting represents a scaling factor rather than a criterion for the general applicability of a particular technique and therefore has no direct influence on the general applicability of a particular interaction technique. Hence, we only assign it a minor role in our taxonomy.

4.1.2 Instrumentation

The technical instrumentation of a media facade's environment has a direct influence on the applicability of different interaction techniques. Different interaction devices and interaction styles require the instrumentation of the potential interaction space to different extents. If users can interact with the media facade from a single place, usually only a small space needs to be instrumented, e.g., by providing wifi, installing a camera or providing an input device. If users can interact from anywhere within a given space, usually the whole space needs to be instrumented with the necessary technologies. While this is not a big deal when using wifi and the users' mobile phones as input devices, this can result in a very complex setting when for example the users' body movements need to be tracked within large spaces. In the following, we point out the influence of different characteristic properties of interactive media facade installations on the technical instrumentation of the potential interaction space.

4.1.3 Interaction Style

Interaction with media facades can be designed in various ways, resulting in interaction with different characteristics. This requires the potentially interactive environment to be instrumented to a different extent:

1. *Performative interaction* is usually realized by tracking the body posture or movement of a user. This is usually achieved by instrumenting the potentially interactive space with additional hardware such as cameras or sensors.

2. *Direct interaction* – such as direct pointing – requires either tracking the current position of the user, as well as the direction he is pointing at, or tracking the location of a cursor on the facade, initiated by a pointing device (e.g., a laser pointer). The latter is usually realized with cameras pointed at the facade and hence requires less instrumentation than tracking a user's body movements within a large open space.

3. *Indirect* or *relative interaction* techniques (e.g., using a mobile device's built-in inertial sensor to relatively control a pointer on the facade) usually do not require an extensive instrumentation of the potentially interactive space. The technical capabilities required to determine the user's input are usually provided by the input device itself (i.e., a mobile device or an interactive terminal placed in the space in front of the facade).

4.1.4 Connection

When using dedicated input devices (e.g., custom-built hardware or smart phones), there is the requirement for a permanent data connection between input device and media facade. With the increasing availability of public *wifi* networks and data plans for mobile devices, the demand for connectivity can be considered as a minor concern, and not as a dedicated instrumentation of the space around the media facade.

4.1.5 Number of Users

Aside from the interaction technique itself, the number of supported users is influenced by the technical instrumentation of the potentially interactive space. The instrumentation can be either a permanent installation of stationary hardware, the distribution of mobile input devices, or both. For example, if we consider whole body interaction where the user's movements are tracked with a camera, the number of users is limited to the number of users trackable by the available cameras. To allow for more users, the number of cameras has to be increased. For the sake of simplicity, we omitted the required computing power to process the actual camera data in this example, since this again depends on the particular algorithms, update rates and the detailed realization. Similarly, when using dedicated input devices, the number of users is limited by the number of provided devices and can be increased by distributing more devices up to a certain limit given by the application itself. In general, we can say that issues related to number of users can be handled either by hardware, software or a combination of the two.

4.1.6 Interaction Distance

As mentioned before, interacting with a media facade usually implies interacting at a distance. As can be seen when comparing techniques for interacting at a distance, such as *SMSLingshot* (Fischer et al. 2010) or *LaserTag* (Klanten et al. 2011), they require different minimal viewing distances and they can potentially work from great distances. Depending on the desired interaction distance, this can require the instrumentation of large spaces. On the flip side, if a designer aims for interaction from very short distances within the direct proximity of the facade, some interaction techniques are not applicable if the intended interaction distance is below the required minimal distance.

4.1.7 Location Awareness

The degree to which an installation can be aware of a user's position within the potential interactive space is also determined by the instrumentation of the environment. In the least constrained case, the application only needs to be aware of whether a user is within the potential interaction space or not. Since this is covered anyway by the chosen interaction technique, as a user needs to be within the potential interaction space for the technique to work, we can treat this as though the installation not being aware of the user's location and this case therefore does not need further instrumentation. If the facade needs to be aware of whether a user is within its direct proximity – which is often the case for interactive media facades installed at ground level – only the immediate space around the facade needs to be instrumented. If the exact location of a user within the potential interaction space needs to be known, the amount of required instrumentation increases with the size of the space and of course the accuracy with which the location needs to be provided.

The spatial configuration of the potentially interactive space again only plays a minor role for the general possibility of instrumenting it with different technologies. The size of the space simply indicates the amount of resources required. Or, conversely, the available amount of resources determines the size of the space that can be instrumented.

4.2 Input Modalities

When designing interactive installations for media facades, the applied interaction techniques in combination with the utilized input devices shape the interaction and have a huge impact on the usability and the user experience. Furthermore, they determine the technical requirements for the instrumentation of the potential interaction space in front of the facade. When choosing a particular input modality (e.g., touch, pointing, etc.) and a particular interaction technique (e.g., camera tracking, interaction through live video, etc.) there is always a trade-off between the technical requirements for utilizing the particular input modality and the granularity of the input and the triggered experiences. Hence, the utilized input modalities are an important factor for a systematic approach to categorize interaction with media facades. While we reviewed interactive media facade installations grouped by the input modality they use, in the following, we will investigate the characteristics of the particular input modalities as well as their influence on the installation.

4.2.1 Whole Body Interaction

With whole body interaction approaches, the human body itself is used as an input device, such an approach requires tracking body movement within the potential interaction spaces. Hence, those spaces have to be instrumented with different technologies, depending on the accuracy and the extent to which movements are supposed to be tracked. With the instrumentation of the space, and turning every body entering the potential interaction space into an input device, this input modality is especially suited for reactive media facade installations where the communication with the facade happens implicitly. Whole body interaction also turned out to be well suited for performative interaction within an artistic or playful context (Brynskov et al. 2009; Fritsch/Dalsgaard 2008; Haeusler 2009; Haeusler et al. 2013). In this context, mapping body movement within a particular space – physically running around within the space – to motion on the media facade is a common pattern. This allows for a continuous interaction through the whole potential interaction space. Furthermore, to passersby, users seem to *perform* in front of an audience, which usually draws attention and encourages passersby to engage in the social and physical setting (Brynskov et al. 2009; Fischer/Hornecker 2012).

For whole body interaction, the accuracy of the tracking and hence of the interaction itself heavily depends on the utilized tracking technologies, the speed of the movement, and environmental conditions such as lighting conditions. From this, we argue that whole body interaction is more suited for coarsely grained interaction where the accuracy of input is not of great importance. This is especially the case for low-resolution media facades that are not capable of displaying complex content. For fine-grained, precise interaction with complex content, we need more accurate interaction modalities. Concerning the number of users, whole body interaction is suitable for multiple users interacting simultaneously. It is only limited by the technical capabilities of the utilized tracking technologies and the size of the instrumented space.

4.2.2 Pointing

Direct and indirect pointing are further common techniques for interacting with a media facade (Klanten et al. 2011). Both usually require a dedicated input device with which the user points at the facade in order to interact (e.g., to control a pointer). While for direct pointing the movement of a visual cue that is initiated by the pointing device – usually a laser pointer – is tracked on the facade with the help of cameras, in the indirect approach, the input device itself calculates the relative movement or in some cases the position of the pointer and communicates it to the facade. Hence, the amount of required instrumentation of the potential interaction space is rather low, reducing the effort needed to set up the installation, while allowing for fine-grained interaction with complex content at the same time. The low instrumentation makes such an approach highly suitable for portable, non-permanent media facade settings.

It is common to use direct or indirect pointing in combination with non-permanent, projected media facades (Klanten et al. 2011; Scheible/Ojala 2009). In the case of direct pointing, a camera can be mounted onto the projector for observing the facade and tracking pointers. In the case of indirect pointing, the pointing can be realized with a portable mobile input device while no further hardware – the projection system aside – is required. It is common to use a projector which is connected to a mobile computer. For direct pointing, the most common pointing device is a laser pointer which also might be mounted onto or integrated into custom input devices. The position of the pointer on the projected facade is then usually determined with the help of a camera mounted onto the projector. For indirect pointing, a common input device is a standard mobile phone, which allows for calculating the relative pointer movement based on the movement of the device itself or based on touch input on the mobile device's screen. Since in both cases dedicated input devices – usually portable – are needed, such an approach usually needs an ongoing monitoring of the setting.

Although multiple users could interact with the media facade in parallel, this is hampered by two factors: (1) Every user needs an input device. Hence, the number of potential users is limited by the number of input devices. However, if the user's own mobile phone is used as the input device, then this is less of an issue. And (2), when using direct pointing with a laser pointer-like device, distinguishing between respective users is challenging. Such a system usually only detects a certain number of laser pointers on the screen, but it is not aware of how many lasers they are coming from and which pointer belongs to which user. To match a pointer to a particular user, further instrumentation of the input device is needed.

4.2.3 Touch and Gestures

Gestural user input by direct touch is a widespread approach often used with permanent installations. When applying touch as the input modality of choice, dedicated input devices are needed. This is a common approach utilized in various permanent media facade installations of various resolutions (Haeusler 2009; Haeusler et al. 2013). For such installations, a stationary input device (e.g., a input terminal or an interaction booth) is usually provided within viewing distance of the facade. While this comes with the benefit of keeping the required instrumentation at a minimum (e.g., only the stationary input device needs to be installed and usually no instrumentation of the further environment is required), this comes with the disadvantage of usually limiting the number of users to one or two. Furthermore, this leads to stationary settings, not exploiting the spatial aspects of interaction with media facades. While interacting, users are required to be within the direct proximity of the stationary input device. This can also turn into an advantage when realizing complex interactions requiring specialized or dedicated input hardware to address the peculiarities of a particular setting. Concerning the resolution of the facade, this approach is in general highly suitable for both low- and high-resolution facades.

4.2.4 Web and Remote Interface

A further approach to allow users to interact with the content of media facade is providing external – usually web-based – interfaces to upload and modify the displayed content (Klanten et al. 2011). While such an approach does not require instrumenting the environment in front of the media facade, it also does not particularly address the passersby in front of the facade within the display space. Furthermore, users do not get immediate visual feedback on their interactions. The main focus of such approaches lies in supporting a one-directional interaction, allowing a wide range of users to provide content for the media facade pushing this approach more in the direction of being reactive rather than being interactive. By providing remote interfaces, the target audience for interacting with the facade facade can be maximized since basically every person around the globe with access to the internet could potentially interact. However, we believe that this does not go along with the main idea of interacting with a media facade. It rather constitutes pushing content onto a media facade and we consider this as the minimal amount of participation that can be allowed.

5 Taxonomy

The goal of this chapter is to derive a taxonomy of interaction with media facades using different technologies. The aforementioned properties and characteristics of interactive media facade installations determine the applicability of different approaches for allowing interactivity with different characteristic traits. In addition to determine suitable approaches for particular settings, we can consult the taxonomy to compare interactive media facade installations in different contexts. In general, we address the following properties in the taxonomy, since – as it occurred when reviewing existing installations – they have proven to influence the characteristics of an installation as well as the applicability of different interaction approaches:

Instrumentation versus no instrumentation of the potential interaction space: The technical realization of interaction can require instrumentation of the potential interaction space in front of the facade to different extents. This can vary from providing custom input devices to equipping the space with complex infrastructure.

Utilized input modalities: Different input modalities usually come with different technical requirements. They vary in the level of user engagement they require. Furthermore, depending on their characteristics, there are input techniques more suitable for high-resolution media facades and some that work well with low-resolution facades.

Stationary versus mobile interaction: Interaction can be carried out in either a stationary or a mobile way. For stationary interaction, users are either provided with a stationary input device, or the interaction requires the user to remain in a particular place. When mobile interaction is possible, users usually can move around within the potential interaction space and interact from arbitrary places. Furthermore, they often can continuously interact while moving around the potential interaction space. The particular movement of the user can also be a part of the interaction itself.

Resolution of the media facade: Media facades can have different resolutions, ranging from very low resolutions of less than 200 pixels to high-resolution screens with several million pixels. This for example influences the options for displaying visual feedback such as pointers or controls necessary for particular input techniques, as well as the complexity of the displayable content. Furthermore, when the interaction is carried out while moving around within the potential interaction space, perceived resolutions might change dynamically.

The media facade's form factor: Different forms of interactivity can involve the presence of a user in various ways. Users can be required to be within a certain distance from the media facade in order to interact with its content in general. A user could also explicitly interact with a media facade by changing his distance from the facade. Furthermore, when providing means for remote interaction, a media facade might not require a user to be present at all. When considering the media facade as a whole and not only the particular part visible from a user's current point of view, the form factor of a media facade can introduce additional complexity. With interaction techniques requiring a direct line of sight between the user and the target area on the facade, interacting with all parts of the facade is not possible without relocating and moving around the facade. Furthermore, the media facade's content might never be completely visible as a whole to a user, which also can constrain the interaction.

The aforementioned properties are dependent on each other in different ways. We combine them into a taxonomy of interaction with media facades as follows: We initially classify the interactive installation according to the utilized input modality and whether it requires the instrumentation of the potential interaction space or not. Regarding input modalities, we consider whole body interaction, pointing, touch and gestures and remote interaction. We subdivide the installations into stationary ones, where the position from which a user interacts is fixed, and mobile ones, where a user can interact from different locations and also especially when moving between location. For the input modalities, we subdivide the applicability of the particular input modality for low- and high-resolution media facades. For each installation, we point out the number of supported users. This results in the spatial layout of the taxonomy as depicted in Figure 3. The layout was inspired by the taxonomy for mobile device input on external displays, presented in (Boring 2010).

Based on the introduced taxonomy, we revisited existing interactive media facade installations and categorized them accordingly as depicted in Figure 3. It turned out that whole body interaction usually demands static instrumentation of the potential interaction space, usually resulting in interaction from a static position with a limited number of users. Furthermore, the classification revealed that whole body interaction is usually applied in combination with low-resolution media facades. Pointing as well touch input also require the instrumentation of the potential interaction space. Even in the case of using a laser pointer as the pointing device, a camera is still required to track the pointer movement.

While pointing installations usually address high-resolution media facades, touch and gestural input are regularly applied for both low- and high-resolution media facades, which we believe involves using additional input devices, handling the mapping between input and facade resolution. Manipulating a media facade's content through remote interfaces (e.g., web interfaces) does not require

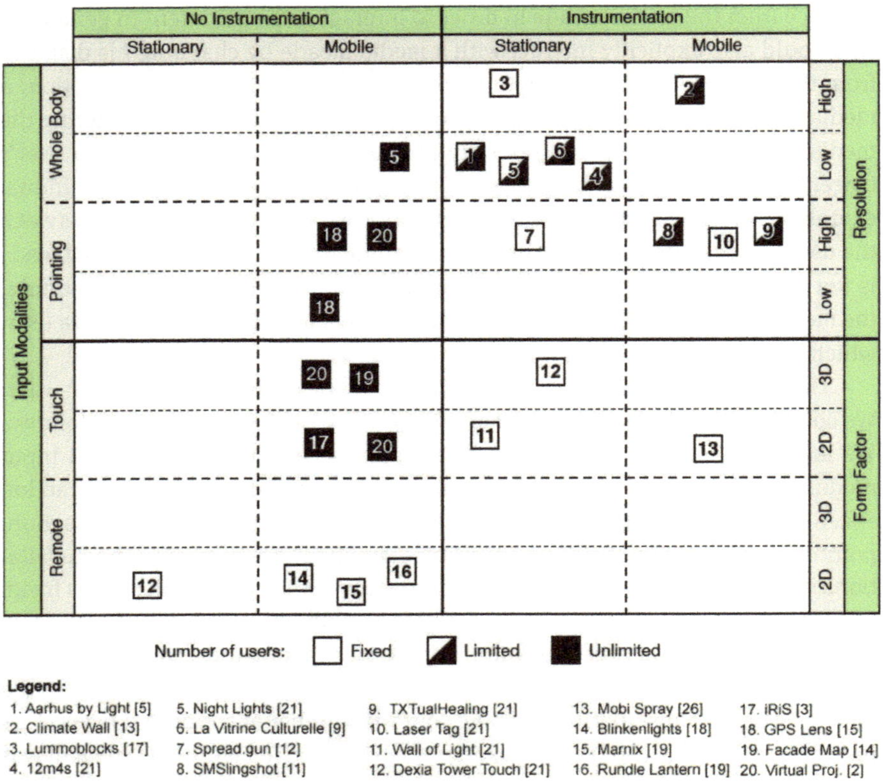

Fig. 3: Classification of the interactive media facade installations reviewed in this chapter. Installations can appear in more than one category.

the instrumentation of the space in front of the media facade, but it usually also does not require a user to be present within the display space near the facade.

6 Discussion

To our knowledge, this is the first taxonomy of interaction with media facades that comprises the unique properties and characteristics presented by media facades in general. It aims at the *interactivity* of media facades to go beyond considering them purely as information broadcasters. Upon review of existing media facade installations, it becomes apparent that such an installation does not require any instrumentation, allows for the users' mobility (and potentially mobile input) and is independent of the facade's form factors. Generally, fewer installations can be found that do not require instrumentation of the space the facade is located in. This limits the deployment of such facades as the instrumentation is often cumbersome and cost-intense. The taxonomy further reveals that – so far – installations that follow these characteristics only allow for controlling pointers. While this is an acceptable implementation of an interactive display, media facades are a separate device class (i.e., they are enormous in size and allow for a large number of users) and it is thus questionable whether pointing (as known from personal computers) is the appropriate and meaningful way for interacting with such displays. *Virtual Projection* presents an exception to interacting with pointers (Boring/Baur 2013). Although it has not been implemented on media facades, their implementation allows for a more direct coupling between personal mobile devices (e.g., mobile phones) and a large display, which may well be an entire media facade as in the case of (Boring et al. 2011).

6.1 Using the Taxonomy

Our taxonomy is targeted towards practitioners and designers who aim at deploying an interactive media facade installation. We consider two approaches: (1) defining the level of instrumentation based on desired input modalities; and (2) basing the input modality on the level of instrumentation present and more importantly *possible* in the space. In the first approach, for example, a designer may choose to have whole body interaction as the dominant input modality. This limits the space for deployment in question to one that can be instrumented (with the exception of *Night Lights* (Klanten et al. 2011)). In the case where the level of instrumentation is fixed, practitioners and designers can thus select from a range of techniques that have been deployed before. For example, if instrumentation is not possible and users are mobile, there are almost no limits with respect to the input modality. Yet, when an unlimited number of users is required, for example, some techniques appear more suitable than others.

Overall, we believe that our taxonomy, filled with a broad variety of existing installations, allows designers and practitioners to choose the best possible candidate for a new installation. In addition, the taxonomy enables researchers to fill in the gaps in case new combinations within the taxonomy are required (e.g., a stationary, mobile, whole body interaction with high tracking resolution).

6.2 Limitations

Our taxonomy was based on an extensive review of both literature as well as existing media facade installations, yet with the intent of being generally applicable to future installations. However, we are aware of limitations that arise from their public and outdoor nature. First and foremost, the taxonomy does not capture a facade's visibility. For example, a facade may only be partially visible due to other passersby or other buildings obstructing (parts of) the facade from a given viewing location. Additionally, the technical implementations may be affected by changing light conditions (e.g., daylight versus night). Finally, our taxonomy does not capture other external influences such as traffic in a given space that may interrupt a given interaction temporarily.

While these factors naturally affect interaction with media facades, they are highly unique to a given environment. We consider them part of the architectural planning. Our taxonomy helps in that certain aspects can be excluded before designing an interactive experience based on the layout of the space the media facade is located in.

Bibliography

Boring, S. (2010): "Interacting Through the Display: A New Model for Interacting on and Across External Displays". Dissertation, LMU München. Fakultät für Mathematik, Informatik und Statistik.

Boring, S.; Baur, D. (2013): "Making public displays interactive everywhere". Computer Graphics and Applications, IEEE 33:2, 28–36.

Boring, S.; Gehring, S.; Wiethoff, A.; Blöckner, A.M.; Schöning, J.; Butz, A. (2011): "Multi-user interaction on media facades through live video on mobile devices". In: Proceedings of the SIGCHI Conference on Human Factors in Computing Systems, CHI '11. New York, NY: ACM, 2721–2724.

Bouchard, D. (2007): "Embodied Emergence: Distributed Computing Manipulatives". PhD thesis, Massachusetts Institute of Technology. Dept. of Architecture. Program in Media Arts and Sciences.

Brynskov, M.; Dalsgaard, P.; Ebsen, T.; Fritsch, J.; Halskov, K.; Nielsen, R. (2009): "Staging urban interactions with media façades". In: T. Gross; J. Gulliksen; P. Kotz; L. Oestreicher; P. Palanque; R. Prates; M. Winckler (eds.): Human-Computer Interaction INTERACT 2009 (Lecture Notes in Computer Science 5726). Berlin u.a.: Springer, 154–167.

Bullivant, L. (2006): Responsive Environments: Architecture, Art and Design. London: V&A.

Dalsgaard, P.; Dindler, C.; Halskov, K. (2011): "Understanding the dynamics of engaging interaction in public spaces". In: P. Campos; N. Graham; J. Jorge; N. Nunes; P. Palanque; M. Winckler (eds.): Human-Computer Interaction INTERACT 2011 (Lecture Notes in Computer Science 6947). Berlin u.a.: Springer, 212–229.

Dalsgaard, P.; Halskov, K. (2010): "Designing urban media façades: cases and challenges". In: Proceedings of the SIGCHI Conference on Human Factors in Computing Systems, CHI '10. New York, NY: ACM, 2277–2286.

Dalsgaard, P.; Halskov, K.; Nielsen, R. (2008): "Towards a design space explorer for media facades". In: Proceedings of the 20th Australasian Conference on Computer-Human Interaction: Designing for Habitus and Habitat, OZCHI '08. New York, NY: ACM, 219–226.

Fischer, P.T.; Hornecker, E. (2012): "Urban HCI: spatial aspects in the design of shared encounters for media facades". In: Proceedings of the SIGCHI Conference on Human Factors in Computing Systems, CHI '12. New York, NY: ACM, 307–316.

Fischer, P.T.; Zöllner, C.; Hoffmann, T.; Piatza, S. (2010): "VR/Urban: SMSlingshot". In: Proceedings of the 4th International Conference on Tangible, Embedded, and Embodied Interaction, TEI '10. New York, NY: ACM, 381–382.

Fischer, P.T.; Zöllner, C.; Hornecker, E. (2010): "VR/Urban: Spread.gun – design process and challenges in developing a shared encounter for media façades". In: Proceedings of the 24th BCS Interaction Specialist Group Conference, BCS '10. Swinton, UK: British Computer Society, 289–298.

Fritsch, J.; Dalsgaard, P. (2008): "Media Façades beyond interaction". In: Proceedings of the 20th Australasian Computer-Human Interaction Conference, OZCHI '08. New York, NY: ACM, 8–12.

Gehring, S.; Krüger, A. (2012): "Façade map: continuous interaction with media façades using cartographic map projections". In: Proceedings of the 2012 ACM Conference on Ubiquitous Computing, UbiComp '12. New York, NY: ACM, 471–480.

Gehring, S.; Lander, C. (2013): GPS Lens: "GPS based controlling of pointers on large-scale urban displays using mobile devices". In: Proceedings of the 2nd ACM International Symposium on Pervasive Displays, PerDis '13. New York, NY: ACM, 115–120.

Greenfield, A.; Shepard, M. (2007): Urban Computing and its Discontents. New York, NY: The Architectural League of New York.

Guitiérrez, C.; Canet, M.; Puig, J.; Lloret, J. (2015): "Lummoblocks." http://www.lummo.eu/lummotetris.html. Accessed: 2015-10-19.

Haeusler, H.M. (2009): Media Facades – History, Technology, Content. Stuttgart: avedition.

Haeusler, H.M.; Tomitsch, M.; Tscherteu, G. (2013): New Media Facades – A Global Survey. Stuttgart: avedition.

Halskov, K.; Ebsen, T. (2013): "A framework for designing complex media facades". Design Studies 34:5, 663–679.

Klanten, R.; Ehmann, S.; Hanschke, V. (2011): A Touch of Code – Interactive Installations and Experiences. Berlin: gestalten.

Korsgaard, H.; Hansen, N.B.; Basballe, D.; Dalsgaard, P.; Halskov, K. (2012): "Odenplan: a media façade design process". In: Proceedings of the 4th Media Architecture Biennale Conference: Participation, MAB '12. New York, NY: ACM, 23–32.

Moere, A.V.; Hill, D. (2009): Research through design in the context of teaching urban computing. Street Computing Workshop (co-located with OZCHI '09), Melbourne.

Moere, A.V.; Wouters, N. (2012): "The role of context in media architecture". In: Proceedings of the 2012 International Symposium on Pervasive Displays, PerDis '12. New York, NY: ACM, 12:1–12:6.

Reeves, S.; Benford, S.; O'Malley, C.; Fraser, M. (2005): "Designing the spectator experience". In: Proceedings of the SIGCHI Conference on Human Factors in Computing Systems, CHI '05. New York, NY: ACM, 741–750.

Scheible, J.; Ojala, T. (2009): “MobiSpray: mobile phone as virtual spray can for painting big anytime anywhere on anything”. Leonardo 42:4, 332–341.
Schoch, O. (2006): “My building is my display”. In: Proceedings of the Conference on Education and Research in Computer Aided Architectural Design in Europe: eCAADe’06, eCAADe, Wien.
Seitinger, S.; Perry, D.S.; Mitchell, W.J. (2009): “Urban pixels: painting the city with light”. In: Proceedings of the SIGCHI Conference on Human Factors in Computing Systems, CHI ’09. New York, NY: ACM, 839–848.
Shamma, D.A.; Scheible, J.; Sheppard, R.M. (2009): “Graffiti dance: interaction of light, information, and environment”. In: Proceedings of the 7th ACM Conference on Creativity and Cognition, C&C ’09. New York, NY: ACM, 479–480.
Terrenghi, L.; Quigley, A.; Dix, A. (2009): “A taxonomy for and analysis of multi-person-display ecosystems”. Personal and Ubiquitous Computing 13:8, 583–598.
Weiser, M. (1992): “The computer for the 21st century”. Scientific American 265:3, 94–104.
Winograd, T. (2001): “Interaction Spaces for Twenty-First-Century Computing”. In: HCI in the New Millenium. New York: Addison-Wesley, 259–276.

Anke von der Heide and Heinrich Hußmann

Media Façades and Narratives for Public Spaces

In an effort to sustain XXIst century cities, technologies are given a significant role to compose a novel urban environment. Today's smart city approaches, driven by technology and information, are considered to be the answer for the transformation of a noxious milieu into a habitable ideal environment. Unfortunately, in an attempt to achieve such high-level goals, technologies are often put into the urban environment in an uncontrolled manner (Greenfield and Shepard 2007). In many cases, ad-hoc deployed technological applications are detached from public activities. For instance, apps on mobile devices often do not consider local conditions, information displays with standard proportions (like 16:9) re-format the image of the city outside any architectural concept, and city authorities lack regulations for media content in urban spaces.

To understand such phenomena, researchers of various fields are forming interdisciplinary groups. In Media-Architecture and Urban-Design studies, groups, or events such as UrbanIxD in Aarhus, Denmark, MediaCity in Weimar, Germany, or Media Architecture Biennale, architects mingle with computer scientists, city planners with sociologists or media designers. Out of this interdisciplinary work new domains evolve, and media architecture is one of them. As with many other appearing fields, not much is known about the changes this brings to urban environments and our daily life. These groups have started to go beyond the naïve digital-, intelligent-, or smart-city idea, which is that designers and planners simply have to incorporate technology to provide the best city planning strategies. Thoughts on how to design for the *Human City* through HCI means will be discussed in more details in the chapter "Media Architecture for Shared Encounters" by Fischer and Hornecker.

Even if enhancing cities with technology, we need to design devices and architecture for the needs of people (Carr 1992). In many ways this is already happening. But at the same time researchers describe the overload of information in public spaces or the deliberate ignoring of displays by passers-by (Memarovic et al. 2015; Huang et al. 2008; Müller et al. 2009). Memarovic et al. found out that not many people look at displays in public spaces, and if they do their time of attention is short. They explain this tendency of ignorance by peoples' expectation of uninteresting and boring content. Considering this trend, we ultimately need to ask if it is necessary to add more media to the urban space? However, giving up on media in public will not happen in the near future. Instead the current situation

DOI 10.1515/9783110453874-011

should be seen as an opportunity towards creating new narrations for the public environment.

The concept of narrations as part of the public environment is a well-known concept in architecture. Often buildings quote the history of their location or are enhanced with visible indications of their purpose or context. The idea that public places and buildings tell stories can be brought onto a new level with digital enhancements of the city. There exists the term 'Urban storytelling', which is well-suited for this idea. However, this term is often used for a planning method directly involving citizens. This term may be redefined or extended (Mager and Matthey 2015) from a "selective retelling of political communication" (Salmon 2007) or "a means of ensuring the collective governmentality of citizens" (Matthey 2014) towards a possibility to design public spaces with meaningful content taking into account interactive media devices and displays. We will use the term "urban storytelling" in this text in this broad sense.

Therefore, when thinking of media for urban spaces, we first need to ask questions such as which stories do we want to tell and how these narratives have to be designed? Classical design, architecture, or urban planning rules can provide a fundament to create urban storytelling. But how can these classical rules be combined with rules covering moving images or software-controlled architectural elements? Which set of rules will provide the best impact for telling stories in an urban environment? In this essay, we would like to explore whether classical design strategies and rules are applicable to media architecture or if we need to adjust them towards a complex integrative design strategy. This article first surveys several sets of rules for designing media, architecture, and urban environment. Afterwards three typical examples of narrative media architecture projects are presented, including one in which the lead author was involved. They provide the base to discuss challenges and strategies for urban storytelling on latest media architecture examples. Starting from these insights, we finally offer an outlook into future research.

However, we are not investigating design methods and tools for concepts or media architecture prototypes like Dalsgaard and Halskov are descripting in their chapter "Designing Media Architecture: Methods and Tools", but rather emphasize on the composition of architecture with media content towards a holistic design of a narrated story in the urban context.

1 Designing Media Architecture and Urban environments

Media and architecture imply two entirely different materialities and complexities. While architecture existed way before Common Era, technological 'mass' media as known today appeared in the late 20th century due to the invention of communication technologies like radio, cinema, television etc. Over time architecture implemented comforts like running water, windows, and central heating, later on followed by amenities like electricity, the usage of which already turned into a design element through the design of city and building lighting. Today, we experience another wave of technology being integrated into architecture, with various kinds of controllable and smart additions to private homes and business buildings. This relates also to communication networks, traditionally like telecommunication, and new inventions within the internet of things. Urban planning and design thinking changed in a similar way from industrial- to garden-city and further to car-oriented city approaches. Today's planning schemes need to cope with this unsustainable heritage and try to implement new "smart" technologies to measure, control, and observe for a livable and human environment.

Media architecture is one of the latest developments in the integration between architecture and technology. Bringing together the different domains "media" and "architecture" provides a very serious challenge, since these two domains do not only differ in their physicality, design language, and use, but they also work with entirely different time dimensions. Media 'plans' for the moment, is permanently changing, entertains, or informs with the obsession to keep the audience's attention through exiting stories. On the other hand, architecture is a very static matter, not meant to change but rather built to last at least the next thirty or fifty years.

The temporal issue of technology is not only in contrast to the goals of architecture. More generally, technological evolution is highly disruptive for the daily life of citizens. Technology is changing very fast, producing a permanent wave of new products and standards. Once the cinematograph entertained a whole society, and then the TV became the families' evening ritual. The LP-record was invented around 1900, replaced by the CD (1980s) and again replaced by MP3-files (1990s). The latter is again being superseded by web based sharing and streaming platforms like SoundCloud or Spotify. This fast pace adds new standards permanently, sometimes with adaptability and compatibility problems, not only due to novel equipment. Maintaining outdated technology and at the same time transiting successfully to state-of-the-art technology has become a challenge for citizens, in particular in the media sector.

Additionally, each of the fields relevant for this discussion (media, architecture, and urban planning) have their own rules defining the perception of aesthetics, static or moving images, or in large-scale architectures. Norms and standards regulate the best practices of architecture, while research on social and human behavior helps to configure and shape public areas. Questions that need to be asked are: Which of these rules and practices can help or be adapted towards interdisciplinary media architecture approaches? Can the concept of storytelling in an urban environment be a possibility to cope with the desire to combine technology, architecture, and (narrated) content? To respond to these questions, the following chapter is investigating concerns like: To which extent are moving images differently perceived on a large façade than on a smaller screen? Does the urban environment change the perception of a medium that is made for a living room perspective? Which set of design rules is valid or can help in designing media architecture? In the following, we will discuss several design rules and strategies in detail and give suggestions how they can support design and research in the area of media architecture.

1.1 Perception and Design Rules in General

Media design experienced a reorientation towards multimedia and intermedia design (Schaub 1989). Rautberg and Schlagenhauf describe that this phenomenon leads to liquidation and revision of traditional design rules in all participating fields: text, image, sound, and film/video. For the design of media architecture, this list needs to be extended towards new media and material products like architecture, urban environment, etc. (Rauterberg and Schlagenhauf 1993).

Perception

The human perception, however, has not changed over centuries. We distinguish different perception senses as visual, acoustic, olfactory, and gustatory, and skin related senses like pain, temperature, pressure, haptics, etc. Moreover, cognitive memory processes increase the observer's perception (Ware 2008)). Original and image, real and fake need to be logically explained. Figure 1 shows a tree and Figures 2 and 3 a metaphor of the same tree, one extremely pixelated and the other cropped. This illustrates how our cognitive abilities allow us to deal with high levels of abstraction and therefore relate very different images to the original tree, at least to a certain extent.

(Lochers (2006)) showed in eye tracking studies that only 61% of a picture is actually perceived. Wilson and Chatterjee (2005) assume that only specific organizational structures create an aesthetical experience and readability while others do not. Observers of a picture filter the relevant information, based on context and previous knowledge, to form a subjective perception, and in the end an opinion. Different composition rules therefore are a tool for artists and designers to make important information being perceived faster (Wilson and Chatterjee 2005).

Fig. 1: The original and the image of same tree.

1.2 Specific Rules

Rules of Composition

Composition rules for pictures describe the role of basic elements like points, lines, and areas. These elements imply characteristics like textures, colors, contrast, forms, and size. Graphic designers apply additional rules to fonts, signs, and symbols. Rules of balance, proportion, and visual hierarchies explain how to order all elements to create a spatial experience. They combine all elements of a picture to one narrative statement and allow the observer to understand the picture (Locher 2006; Tyler 1998).

Symmetry is often experienced as boring due to an excessive similarity of picture elements (McManus, et al. 1985). Instead Euklid von Alexandria's mathematical formula for a proportional asymmetry, the golden ratio, is used to define the exact relation between two parts, a smaller and a bigger one. During the Renaissance this golden ratio played an important role in philosophy and arts. Later, i.e., in19th century, the golden ratio served Adolf Zeising as a main proportional principle for aesthetic theories applied until today in art, crafts and architecture (Zeising 2015).

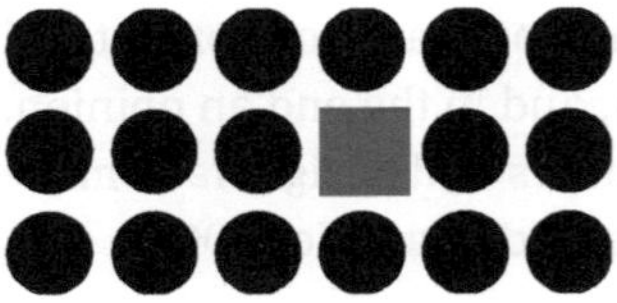

Fig. 2: Focal Points

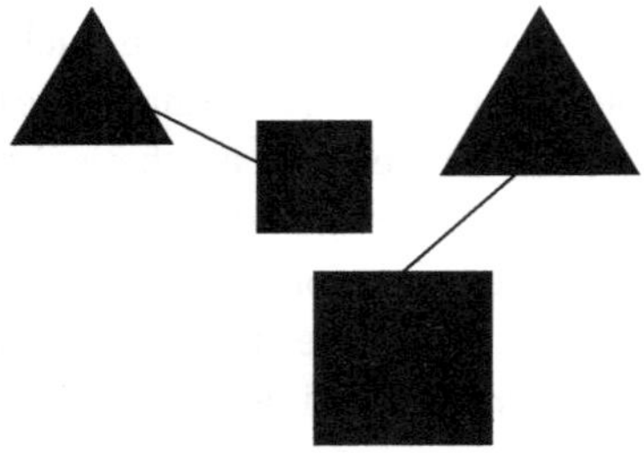

Fig. 3: Lines

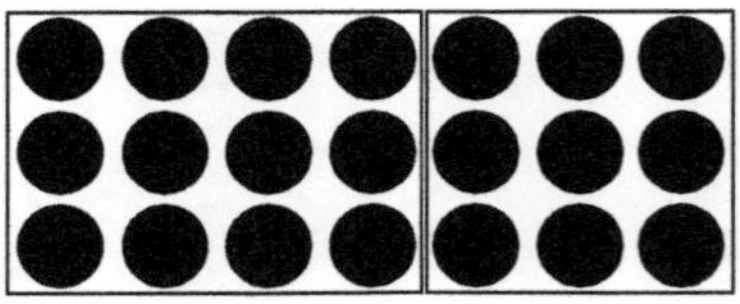

Fig. 4: Areas

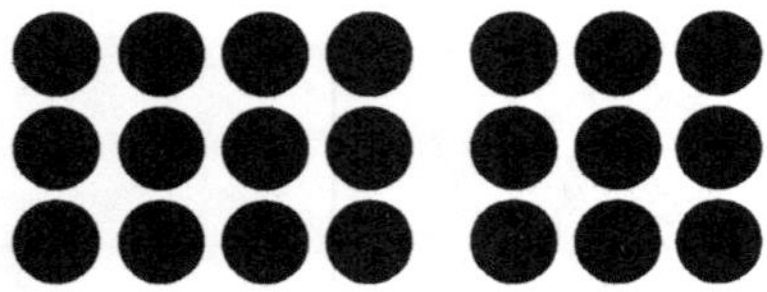

Fig. 5: Proximity

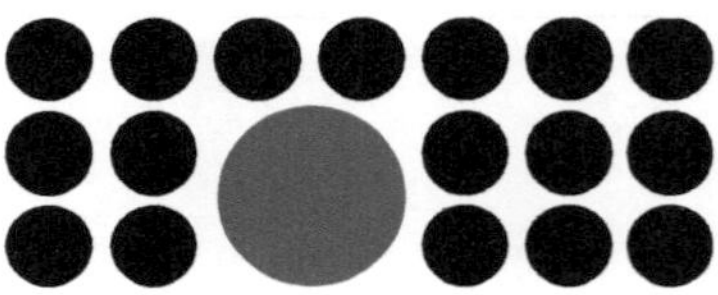

Fig. 6: Dominance and Subordination

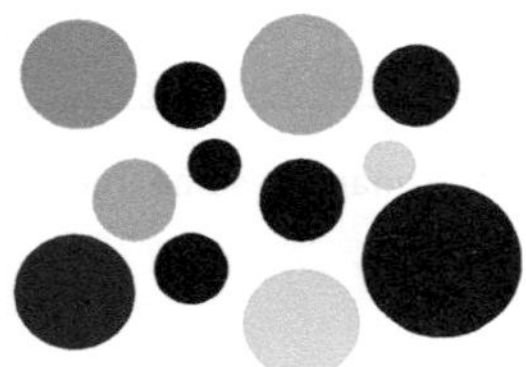

Fig. 7: Coherence

Fig. 8: Balance

Fig. 9: Positive and Negative Space

Fig. 10: Rhythm

The appearance of color is defined as object colour, a reflection of light on an object, and light colour, composed by adding or subtracting coloured light sources of the visible spectrum. (Bendin et al. 2011) Recent research in lighting design introduces questions of different perception of object and light color, e.g., blue in a projected picture is differently or even oppositely perceived than the blue colour of the same picture as a printed photo. (Ruland 2015) Colour is often used to define the main subject. Different intensities are additionally creating an illusion of depth.

Other composing rules are:

- **Focal Points**: to create attraction
- **Lines**: to guide the audience's gaze and connect elements
- **Areas**: to connect elements in enclosed regions
- **Proximity**: to combine or separate elements
- **Dominance and Subordination**: to control the attention each element receives (through size and colors)
- **Coherence**: to form a significant unity (by color, shape, and size)
- **Balance**: to establish relations between visual elements through the concept of placement and perceived weight. (Brightness corresponds to low weight)
- **Positive and Negative Space**: to create shapes and figures by separation of foreground and background
- **Rhythm**: to construct regular repetitive structures of different patterns, like in music.

Visual Directions

Understanding the reading gravity path of people allows placing important information in the best readable sequence of design elements or to emphasize visually elements placed in weak areas of the layout. Rudolf Arnheim's structural net describes the natural flow of how our eye moves on a rectangular canvas. (Arnheim1996) He explains that the center and the four corners are like magnets. Besides these focal points, axes are important connectors allowing the eye to move along them and from one focal point to another like in Gutenberg´s diagram developed by Edmund C. Arnold for text-heavy content purposes (Arnold 1981).

Eye-tracking and heat map methods (Nielsen and Pernice 2009) found that while reading the eye follows a Z-pattern or F-pattern. The Z-pattern refers to the reading path in books and additionally to Gutenberg's diagram, it also concerns the fallow areas. The F-pattern concerns mainly webpages and suggest a rather scanning reading path from left to right edge and further down the side. In general, all reading patterns suggest a layout that follows the natural flow of eye movement, depending on cultural background (in Western context, usually from left to right).

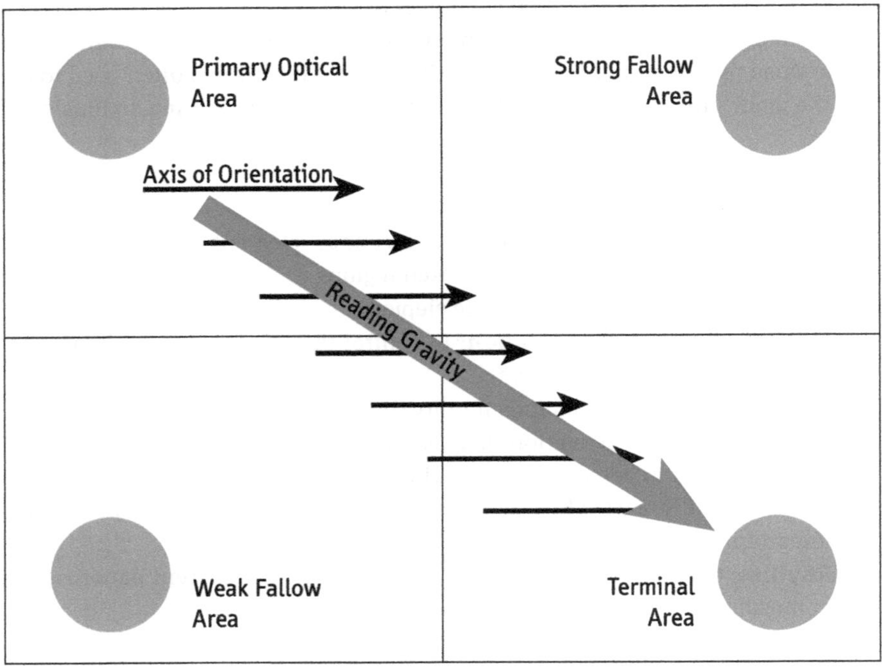

Fig. 11: Gutenberg's diagram (from left to right reading directions).

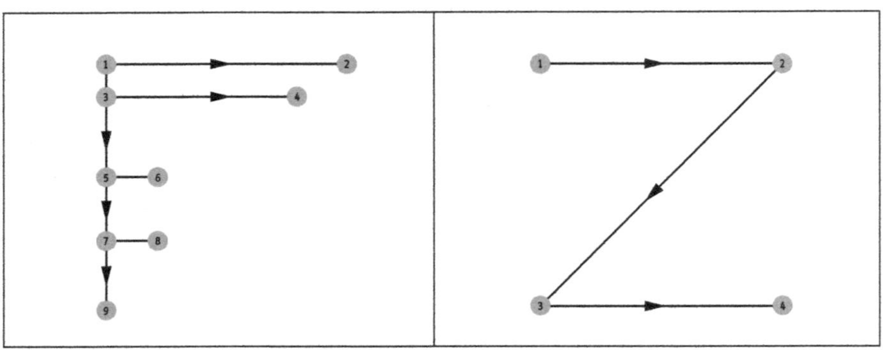

Fig. 12: Z- and F-pattern.

Rules for Moving Images

Chronological sequences of consecutive static pictures create moving images through the principles of dynamics, speed, and rhythm. Additionally, they enhance, beyond the visual impression, an inner sensation. This sensation is developed through a differentiated cognitive processing mechanism, the visual impression, and memory.

Rhythm is needed to regulate the speed and flow of composition elements, while intervals in-between form rhythmic patterns and let our eyes follow the structure visually, in a similar way like our ear follows the rhythm of a song. Elements may move in horizontal, vertical, or diagonal directions. Their scale lets them appear on short or long distances and on straight, curved or complex paths. The appearance of the elements can be defined by color hue, saturation and brightness, complexity, contrast, camera focus, zoom, and angle. (Bradley 2015)

Speed is an important factor for moving images which is derived from repetition and therefore related to rhythm. It is composed by repetition (tempo, rate or pace, continuity, interpolation), and variation (acceleration, accent, order, nesting, irregularity), e.g., slow motion adds drama while acceleration requests attention and suggests excitement (Wakefield 2008).

Rules for Interaction Design

Moving images today have the advantage that they can be produced inexpensively for nearly every audience. However, compared with TV or video, interactive systems can enhance the quality of presentation through control mechanisms that let the observer actively intervene. Designing the maximum usability is the main goal of interaction design and implies that the learning period for the systems' functions should be as short as possible. This can be achieved through a good match of experience and expectation, a sufficient consistency in design, simplicity of design, and by limiting functionality. The system should assist the user in reducing his "thinking work" or cognitive load and keep him engaged. (Rauterberg and Schlangenhauf 1993)

Architectural Rules

The Ten Books on Architecture by Vitruvius state that architecture depends on order, arrangement, symmetry, propriety, and economy. Palladio, a Renaissance architect, later describes three similar rules of arithmetic, geometric, and harmonic, derived from Pythagoras' mathematical rules. Different to the design rules of a picture he describes three dimensions, width, length, and height. (Suppes 1991) Later, in mid 18th century, Hume, Burke, and others state that a certain beauty and aesthetics can not be mathematically explained and object the traditional thoughts on the relation between proportions of the human body and architecture. However, there is no existing rule of how to achieve such aesthetics in modern architecture. Architect's Data (1936), also called "the Neufert" became the reference book for every young architect today. Ernst Neufert precisely explains all spatial requirements to form a framework for building projects and site planning. However, this has nothing to do with the aesthetics but rather with the function of elements. (Neufert and Neufert 2000)

1.3 Storytelling in Public Spaces

Public Space Strategies

Jan Gehl says, "A good city is like a good party". "You know it's working when people stay for much longer than really necessary, because they are enjoying themselves." (Mitra 2013) Over the years, through observing and researching public lives, Gehl, just like Jane Jacobs, the "grandmother" of humanistic planning, draws attention to the relevance of human scale. (Jacobs 1961) Both Gehl and Jacobs observe that the qualities of public spaces where people like to meet, stay, sit, or play – the "life between buildings" – need to be treated carefully by architects, urban designers, and city planners. (Gehl 2011) Stephen Carr in his book "Public Space" explains the main guidelines for such livable public spaces as follows: Human needs should be met, a right to use should be given, a meaning should be communicated, and maintenance should be provided. (Carr 1992)

Storytelling

Storytelling in the past referred to books and movies, but today it also plays an important role in marketing and public relation and further in all design disciplines. The term "storytelling" labels the optimization of compositional flow by presenting information in the right order or following a readable design hierarchy. Narrative, or story structure, in film theory refers to a temporal global-structure or as Wakefield says: "the highest level of unity and contrast". The plot of the story is usually composed by an exposition or beginning, conflict and climax or middle, and the resolution or end. The story line is a graph of progression marking exposition, conflict, climax, and resolution in different intensities over time. (Wakefield 2008) In a broader sense a story can be anything that is told through linked true or fictitious events and happenings. Stories allow us to share, assess, and interpret certain events, experiences, and concepts. They are the foundation of memory, learning, and knowledge. (Anon 2005)

Urban Storytelling

The term "urban storytelling" is used in this text as a way of remembering, narrating, and re-connecting urban environments with the communities, or like Jane Jacobs and Jan Gehl describe, "urban life is full of stories of the past, the present, and the future". In 1984 Bernardo Secchi drew the attention to an active planning technique called the 'urban planning narrative' (Secchi 1984). Throgmorton, Sandercock and others later describe the efforts to combine this technique with storytelling to establish an illustrative and even obligatory model for planning practices (Throgmorton 2003; Sandercock 2003; van Hulst 2012). As earlier mentioned it is part of the bottom up planning and "democratic communication" approaches (Matthey 2014; Matthey 2014b) and regional renewal actions (Devisme 2005; Laurent Devisme). As stated earlier, we refer to a broader usage of the term, which is also present in the literature. Belinda Redondo for instance puts urban storytelling in the public art context in which the urban project and its artistic implementation build an alliance around a "narrative process" on "the logic of attractiveness and competitiveness of territories" (Redondo 2015). Florence Bétrisey exploits local myth and legends to produce a sense of belonging (Bétrisey 2014). She divides storytelling in four phases: 'mythification, identification, emotionalisation, personification'. The diversity of urban narrative systems becomes evident in the context of 'conflict' for example in 'humanitarian urban planning' for improving living conditions.

In this sense the 'telling' part is all about the emotional stories literally 'lying on the streets'. Picking up on this allegory, we can consider the creation of urban stories similar as the creations of movies. So during the creative act of writing a plot it is important to know all elements of the story: the audience, the location, room, street, square, the elements to design with urban furniture, screens, displays, interaction devices, etc.

According to the Digital Storytelling Lab (DSL) at Columbia University School of the Arts, adding digital media as a new element of the urban setting makes it possible to combine and co-create new stories. It will not only change the perception of the audience but also evolve possibilities to incorporate multiple actors and narratives. DSL states that "Digital technologies also create the capacity to bring into view new perceptions, new publics and new assemblages of urban relations. (Anon n.d.)

2 Investigation of Three Narrative Media Architecture Examples

The following three media architecture examples depict different challenges and strategies of creating narrations for media architecture. The first is the waste-to-energy power plant in Roskilde, Denmark, by the Dutch architect Erick Van Egeraat. The second is the the St. Pauli Klubhaus in Hamburg, Germany, a concept by akyol kamps:bbp architects and the projection mapping specialists URBANSCREEN. The third is an example of castle-sized interfaces, an interactive façade mapping created temporarily for the 100th commemoration of Duke George II, in Meiningen, Germany, by media architecture and media informatics students of Bauhaus-University Weimar.

In this section, we introduce the three examples, with an emphasis on the narrative aspect. In the following section we will proceed with an analysis of challenges in urban storytelling.

2.1 Waste-to-Energy Power Plant in Roskilde

The waste-to-energy power plant in Roskilde, designed by the architect Erick van Egeraat and completed in 2014, expresses its combustion function onto the low-res media façade through individually controllable colored lights (RGBW LEDs). The shape and brick color of the building reflect historical factory buildings. A 100 meter high tower without direct function accumulates the metaphorical story of a burning flame that gradually grows from a smoldering ember into a flame relieved with glowing smoke through the spire.

This simple story creates a total work of art by considering and combining the function of the building and the design of the architecture, the chosen material (metal) and colored lighting – it becomes a Gesamtkunstwerk. The whole building is covered by one large media façade. (Van Egeraat 2014) The power plant is widely visible, since it is located in an industrial area close to a six-lane highway. So it has the potential to become a permanent landmark for the area. It was conceived as a light sculpture that stands out of the surrounding industrial lighting. Considering the location within a non-accessible industrial area and the dangerous highway separating the power plant from farmland it had to be built widely visi-

Fig. 13: Waste-to-Energy Power Plant in Roskilde, Photographer: © Tim Van de Velde.

ble for an audience that arrives from the open countryside into the city Roskilde. Consequently, the story is incomprehensible to a close standing person as only a few pixels are visible when standing right in front of the building.

2.2 St. Pauli Klubhaus in Hamburg

After the opening of the St. Pauli Klubhaus in 2015, designed by akyol kamps : bbp architekten and the media artist URBANSCREEN, this media façade reveals certain challenges of using different lighting materials for one large moving image. While the low-resolution media façade of the waste-to-energy power plant tells only one story of a growing energy discharged into the sky, the authors of the Klubhaus wanted to adjust stories accordingly to cultural activities. Abstract stories are the "core visuals" and will reflect the identity of the building; advertisements will be displayed for financial reasons.

A future challenge will be to produce and curate those stories after the first euphoric sentiment has passed. However, due to the novelty of the building and

Fig. 14: Rendering St. Pauli Klubhaus in Hamburg, © akyol kamps : bbp / moka studio (left). Opening of the St. Pauli Klubhaus in Hamburg 23.09.2015, Photographer Christian O. Bruch (right).

the beginning of the cold seasons not much can be said about the impact and changes of use of the surrounding environment. (Dalsgaard and Halskov 2011) This has to be researched further.

The Klubhaus is situated at Spielbudenplatz, a central place at Hamburg's Reeperbahn, the main entertainment quarter. Spectators mostly visit the area in the evening and due to the central location eventually pass by on their way from one end to the other. The permanent media façade is totally integrated in the building and unfolds into a 3D sculpture of different rectangular boxes with differing depths. The light material varies from glassed LED panels for a translucent elevator well, to LED mesh, projections, and LED panels. All are controlled by one integrated system that allows playing videos especially arranged for this façade. Additionally, the system allows visitors to upload twitter messages and photos or to play games. (Kirst 2012) This way the building tells the story of being a part of a community of people outside the building. However it will remain a challenge to maintain this system in the long term, especially for changing users.

In an interview with the light designers (Roland Greule and Johan Gielen), they expressed that the main challenge was the combination of different light sources with different levels of resolution and brightness. This became evident when reality had to match the ideas of the architectural renderings, which gave the impression of a façade covered with a homogenous light surface. This is not easy to realize in practice: One can imagine that projectors illuminate every part of the screen with the same brightness, while LED meshes of individual pixels create a different appearance.

2.3 Castle-Sized Interface at Elisabethenburg in Meiningen

The narration of this Gesamtkunstwerk, developed by MediaArchitecture and HCI students at Bauhaus University Weimar, tells the fictional story of sketches of a previously unknown theatre machine drawn by Duke Georg II of the city Meiningen that were discovered recently in the cities archive. This machine has been recreated and allows the audience to interact with the façade mapping. The mapping illustrates symbolically the 12 principles of classical theatre, which the Duke developed. So there is the basic story of the creative work on this machine and on theatre theory which has happened at this location, which is probably unknown

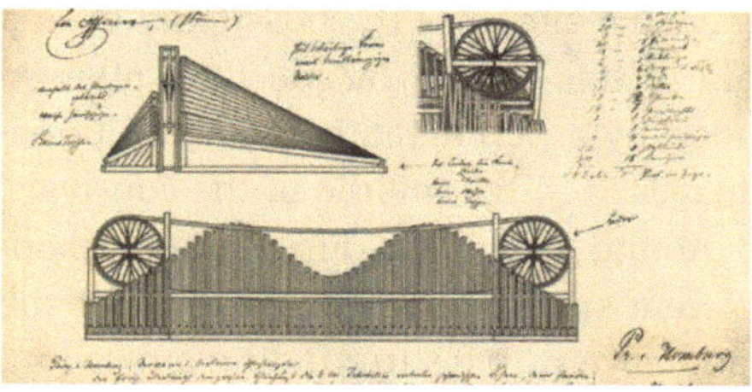

Fig. 15: Drawing of the Theater Machine by MediaArchitecture Students 2013.

Fig. 16: Castle-Sized Interfaces at Elisabethenburg in Meiningen, Photographer Candy Welz.

to most visitors. This is supplemented by more detailed "stories" about the functioning of the machine.

The installation was conceived as a temporary happening in the courtyard of the castle Elisabethenburg and consisting of: a reactive entry installation in the central access archway, a mapping onto a 120 meter long curved façade, a choreography performance by school children, and an interactive "theatre machine" as an architectural interface (Behrens et al. 2014). (Fischer et al. 2015) One of the main challenges in this project was to combine these different elements to one consistent storyline, the exact functioning of the Gesamtkunstwerk during the event and rouse the interested of the possible audience for the event during the one year production time

The horseshoe shape of the façade gave the audience the possibility to step into the projection. The impressive scale of this curved façade then allowed the impression of being almost surrounded by a permanently changing three-dimensional architecture. This feeling increased in the middle of the courtyard where the 'theatre machine' was placed around a fountain. Fischer at al. mentioned that this setting created three different spatial atmospheres, one for the distant observer, one that immerses the audience with a surrounding projection, and the last that allows becoming part of the story through interacting with the machine.

3 Challenges and Strategies for Narrative Media Architecture and Urban Storytelling

Creating narratives for media architecture and urban storytelling can encompass a variation of challenges assigned by the different disciplines involved. This short list categorizes identified challenges and strategies for design, from own and related work. However, research in this field is still young and needs further investigation and discussed.

3.1 Perception of Moving Images on Large-Scale Media Façades

In general, when designing for media façades, the flow of images over 3D objects and large-scale architecture elements requires new compositional thinking, deviating from the "canvas" or 16:9 size to endless format possibilities. How people perceive images on a large-scale media façade needs to be further investigated, but what we can say from our own research are that speed and rhythm of moving images matter a lot, fast or slow speed is seen relatively to the screen size and was differently perceived on a 1:100 model than on the actual façade. (Fischer et al. 2015) The speed perception is additionally dependent on the viewer's distance to the screen and content size. In this regard, information capacities need to be considered as well when designing for low-resolution or high-resolution façades (Hoggenmüller and Wiethoff 2014).

3.2 Composition of Architecture with Media Content

Vitruvius' statements on architectural order, arrangement, symmetry, and propriety might be used as architectural strategies to reveal different aesthetical content and illusions. The distance and angle of the observer towards media content on a façade can create various perceptions of the same image. Figure 17(a) shows a pixelated tree with black gaps and Figure 17(b) shows the same tree perceived from a different point of few, extruded and showing rather lines than separated pixels. Thus, the surrounding lighting, the size of the content and the size of the pixel allows perceiving some content either as an ornament or an architectural element (Figure 18(a) ornament and 18(b) architectural element).

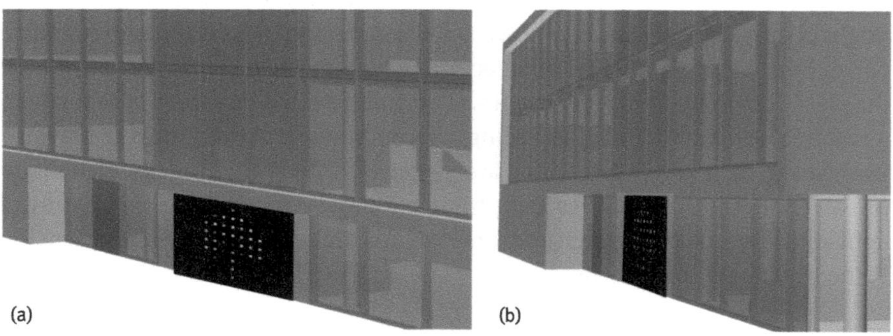

Fig. 17: (a) Building with almost frontal perspective with a projected pixilated tree. (b) Building with extreme perspective on a projected tree, perceived as an arrow.

Another challenge is to identify the right size or color of content elements, which cannot be exactly determined on a computer display or an architectural model. Hence, testing in reality becomes necessary. Chosen colors might change when mixing with the original color of the façade. Sizes of fonts and images might be judged differently due to the different viewpoint and angles that reveal when ac-

Fig. 18: (a) Building with pixilated tree, perceived as projected ornament. (b) Building with, a "Gestalt" rectangle, perceived as architectural element.

tually standing in front of the building. However, this can be only examined on existing buildings. (Dalsgaard and Halskov 2010). Consequently, size and color are important for the told story, because designing content only for the model might lead to different intentions and accentuations within the story. So for this aspect, the traditional sets of rules remain valid, but they have to be modified to create adequate subjective perception by the viewers.

Another challenge is when designing with light (façade projection in Meiningen) to also consider shadow. This applies to light design as well as to video mapping. Depending on the accentuation of the shadow, the set light appears to be bright or dark. This allows creating new illusionary dimensions through cognitive perception, physically, when architectural elements create shadows or through the play of shadows in moving images. (Thorsten Bauer, Genius Loci Weimar Symposium (2013)) Additionally, according to recent research and contrary to previous knowledge, light and object colors are perceived differently. This research might reveal new design possibilities in the future. (Ruland 2015) Anyway, the mixture of light and object colours which appears in media architecture makes an extension of the traditional rule sets necessary.

3.3 Designing Visual and Spatial Directions

The technique to accentuate light allows creation of focal points, just like in theater situations where a spotlight helps directing the focus of the audience. However, the possibilities for enhancing visual directions on large-scale façades need further research. For instance, in contrast to traditional theater, the audience is moving around in a media architecture setting and therefore may be guided to physically move to a focal point. Controlled movement of the audience with the help of light was shown to be working well in the Meiningen event. During the three event-phases, façade projection, choreography, and interactive machine, different light atmospheres emphasized the different parts in different areas of the courtyard. This is an example for a completely new design element in media architecture for which traditional rule sets can be applied only to a very limited extent.

3.4 Adapting Rules for Moving Images for Media Architecture

Keeping the story simple while increasing the complexity through adding diverse means of media, architecture, and technology can be achieved through a consistent design language or story line. For example, the constant image recreation of the "theatre machine" at the event in Meiningen took form in visuals and sound (gear wheals, clattering noises), and physically in the machine interface. So traditional design principles like consistency are useful also in media architecture settings, but need to be generalized to a multitude of media expression options.

Just like in movies, sound manipulates emotions and mood, can also help to interpret the story. During the interactive part of the Meiningen event, a constant gear moving sound helped the audience to understand that they were moving the wheels of the machine. The soundtrack, developed by Markus Rom, used a mix of effects and often gave the impression of a sound moving along the façade, which increased the spatial impression. (Fischer et al. 2015) This is an example of applying traditional design rules from cinematic design.

3.5 Spatial Aspects and Urban Elements

Most important for the design of media architecture is to identify viewpoints and obstructions like other buildings, trees, light, etc, and the placing of the media façade on ground or top level. Do the observers stand right in front of the media intervention or do they have a distant position? When standing right in front of a façade the height and width of the building has to be considered.

Design rules to cover this aspect may take the form of a (relatively complex) formula or a program taking into account all relevant parameters: distance and angle between observer and façade in relation with the façade's scale, to be applied to image, pixel, or font size. The results of such a calculation might give guidance to determine whether a low-resolution picture is understandable from a given viewer distance or not. It would also allow the creation of strategies of cognitive perception to complete missing parts of the image. (Dalsgaard and Halskov

2010) therefore suggest to integrate these interventions into the existing surrounding.

Designing for passers-by, observers, or an interacting audience needs also to consider other distractions like mobile phones, happenings, noise, cafés, playing kids, etc. Being louder and more obtrusive is arguably not a feasible option. Narrative media interventions in public space need to attract by other means. An option could be informative, playful, or participatory elements. Other options are to investigate the missing parts of the urban area, e.g. benches or shadowing elements that allow to stay longer, and add them to the design. This again is an example of new design elements and rules which barely are covered by traditional rule sets.

Designing narrations for media architecture can also mean to consider the history or other identifiers of the building and reflect them in the story. But as (Memarovic et al. 2015) mentions, the main challenge is to tell stories that create interest in order to overcome display blindness in public space. So a well-developed theory on attraction of viewers by media displays has to be incorporated into an adequate design rule set.

In order to overcome display blindness needs for comfort, relaxation, passive and active engagement, and discovery have to be met, according to (Carr 1992). This can be achieved through free access, freedom of action, change, and meaningfulness, among others. However, adding new technology to public spaces can "cause disruption and transform social relations and protocols, and can emerge in "unforeseen use of places and systems". (Dalsgaard and Halskov 2010) But it can also add new values or enhance social participation, communication among strangers, political and community engagement.

3.6 Integration of Interactive Elements

The chosen interaction needs to match the content to develop a consistent storyline on the screen or façade. In order to engage people a public interface should be simple and immediately understandable. This can be achieved through a limitation of functions.

Media architecture can be seen as a highly complex system combining a variety of technological materials. The main challenge, discussed by (Dalsgaard and Halskov 2011), is therefore the high need for 'robustness' and stability in open-air settings. A technical setting with drop-outs does not tell a story. The work on the castle-sized interface revealed that prototyping, in particular in 1:1 scale and testing, as well as in-situ work, were elemental for success. (Fischer et al. 2015)

Placement of technology like LEDs, projectors, or sensors might be constrained, not just for health and safety reasons, but also because of structural issues. Maintenance of technology and architectural elements is required. According to (Carr 1992) this can include also a constant change of content.

4 Lessons Learned and Outlook for Future Research on Storytelling for Media Architecture

Storytelling through media interventions as a Gesamtkunstwerk combines a multitude of different parts, i.e., audience, location, urban elements, media content, and devices into a coherent ensemble. As described above it can pose a challenge but also a possibility to create attractive places or to enhance communication between strangers. Additionally it can become part of the bottom up planning and "democratic communication" approaches as Matthey describes, or it can lead (Matthey 2014) to regional renewal actions (Devisme 2005) One common element of these stories is the emotional effect, which allows people to relate to them. This manipulative impact is the key of a good story.

How to design those stories is the main challenge. It starts with understanding which story is the right one for each place and does not end with simply putting all elements together. As (Memarovic et al. 2015) describes, the challenge is that display blindness needs to be overcome. This could be either through a good permanent story with a "lighthouse" effect like in the case of the waste-to-energy plant in Roskilde or through a well curated program of different stories as for the Klubhaus at Reeperbahn Hamburg.

An additional challenge is that each of the earlier mentioned rules and strategies are justified only within each of the individual design disciplines. But not much is known about the combination of disciplines, e.g., the perception of moving images on large-scale media façades and the integration of interactive elements. The observations made above are only a first step in this direction.

Furthermore each of the disciplines has its own ballast to cope with. The understanding of how new buildings will be accepted aesthetically and socially is difficult because architects work with models that do not reflect reality. Diagrams like Gutenberg's, the Z or F pattern are intended for layout on paper or flat interfaces but not to design content for the irregular surface of a façade. Previous research also shows that the perceptional speed of moving images is different between the 1:100 model and the real façade. (Fischer et al. 2015) But does this also apply to the distance of the observer to the media façade? How does form and shape, 16:9 urban screens or large-scale façades, curved or flat, matter in order to design content?

We also need to consider the architecture and the surrounding public space when creating a storyline between the interface and the screen/façade. The chosen interaction needs to match the content and the cultural knowledge of the users. In the end we need to consider for whom the media façade is meant, the passers-by near the building or does it rather serve as a light house image for the city and will be visible from kilometers away?

The observed challenges and strategies reveal many open questions of how media architecture will change our urban surroundings and how they might be designed to add value for people. How can further research help to develop a framework for an interdisciplinary cooperation which can put together "this current helpless mix of elements", namely architecture, design, lighting, video, sound, informatics, etc. (Schaub 1989)? This article intends to start an intensive discussion within the community, with experts in sociology, psychology, and others. This can not only help creating a framework for the design but also help in formulating strategies or regulations to curate media architecture in the future. Those media architecture curators would have to constantly research the needs of the community and the urban space and negotiate them with different stakeholders.

Bibliography

Hetherington M, Hakcett C. (2005): "What is storytelling". In: HTR Storytelling sub group paper. Storytelling as the vehicle? Conference report, Dunadry 12.

Anon. Columbia Digital Storytelling Lab – exploring the future of storytelling. http://www.digitalstorytellinglab.com/

Arnheim, R. (1996): Die Macht der Mitte – eine Kompositionslehre für die bildenden Künste. Köln: DuMont.

Arnold, E.C. (1981): Designing the total newspaper. 1st ed. New York: Harper & Row.

Behrens, M.; Valkanova, N.; Schieck, A.F. gen.; Brumby, D.P. (2014): "Smart CitizenSentiment Dashboard: A Case Study Into Media Architectural Interfaces". In: PerDis '2014. Copenhagen, Denmark: ACM: 19–24.

Bendin, E.; Bachmann, U.; Michel, R. (2011): Zur Farbenlehre. Studien – Modelle – Texte. Zürich: Die Verlagsgesellschaft.

Bétrisey, F. (2014): "De l'eau et des hommes: les coopérations induites par des paiements pour services hydriques en Bolivie", XIVe Rencontres du Réseau Inter-Universitaire de l'Economie Sociale et Solidaire, Lille.

Bradley, S. (2015): "Design-principles-compositional-flow-and-rhythm". Smashing Magazin.

Carr, S. ed. (1992): Public space. Cambridge, England; New York, NY, USA: Cambridge University Press.

Dalsgaard, P.; Halskov, K. (2010): "Designing Urban Media FaçAdes: Cases and Challenges". In: Proceedings of the SIGCHI Conference on Human Factors in Computing Systems, CHI '10. New York, NY, USA: ACM, 2277–2286.

Dalsgaard, P.; Halskov, K. (2011): “3d projection on physical objects: design insights from five real life cases”. In: Proceedings of the SIGCHI Conference on Human Factors in Computing Systems. Vancouver, BC, Canada: ACM, 1041–1050.

Devisme, L. (2005): La ville décentrée figures centrales á l’épreuve des dynamiques urbaines. Paris: L’Harmattan.

Greenfield, A.; Shepard, M. (2007): “Urban Computing and its Discontents”. Situated Technologies Pamphlets 1: Urban Computing and its Discontents. New York, NY: The Architectural League of New York.

Hulst, M. van (2012): “Storytelling, a model of and a model for planning”. Planning Theory 11:3 (August 2012), 299–318.

Egeraat, E. van (2014): “Towering Inferno”. Mondo Arc Mag. October/November, 77–79.

Fischer, P.T. et al. (2015): “Castle-Sized Interfaces: An Interactive Façade Mapping”. In: Proceedings of the 4th International Symposium on Pervasive Displays, PerDis ’15. New York, NY, USA: ACM, 91–97.

Gehl, J. (2011): Life between buildings: using public space. Washington, DC: Island Press.

Hoggenmüller, M.; Wiethoff, A. (2014): “LightSet: enabling urban prototyping of interactive media façades”. In: Urban Scenes, DIS (2014). Vancouver, BC, Canada: ACM, 925–934.

Huang, E.M.; Koster, A.; Borchers, J. (2008): “Overcoming Assumptions and Uncovering Practices: When Does the Public Really Look at Public Displays”? In: J. Indulska; D.J. Patterson; T. Rodden; M. Ott (eds.): Pervasive Computing. Berlin, Heidelberg: Springer Berlin Heidelberg, 228–243.

Jacobs, J. (1961): The Death and Life of Great American Cities. New York: Random House.

Kirst, N. (2012): “Neues für den Kiez: Das Klubhaus”. In: Page Magazin, Ebner Verlag GmbH & Co KG, Hamburg.

Laurel, B.; Mountford, S.J. eds. (1990): The Art of human-computer interface design. Reading, MA: Addison-Wesley Pub. Co.

Locher, P.J. (2006): “The usefulness of eye movement recordings to subject an aesthetic episode with visual art to empirical scrutiny”. Psychology Science 48, 106–114.

Mager, C.; Matthey, L. (2015): “Tales of the City. Storytelling as a contemporary tool of urban planning and design”. Articulo. Journal of Urban Research (2015), Special issue 7.

McManus, I.; Edmonson, D.; Rodgers, J. (1985): “Balance in pictures”. British Journal of Psychology 76, 311–324.

Memarovic, N.; Clinch, S.; Alt, F. (2015): “Understanding Display Blindness in Future Display Deployments”. In: Proceedings of the 4th International Symposium on Pervasive Displays (PerDis ’15). New York, NY, USA: ACM, 7–14.

Matthey, L. (2014): Building up stories: Sur l’action urbanistique à l’heure de la société du spectacle intégré. Genève: A•Type éditions.

Mitra, A.-O. (2013): “Cities for people Jan Gehl”. In: Assemble Papers, Blueprint City, Victoria, Australia, http://assemblepapers.com.au/2013/06/13/cities-for-people-jan-gehl/.

Müller, J. et al. (2009): “Display Blindness: The Effect of Expectations on Attention towards Digital Signage”. In: H. Tokuda; M. Beigl; A. Friday; A.J. Bernheim Brush; Y. Tobe (eds.): Pervasive Computing. Berlin, Heidelberg: Springer Berlin Heidelberg, 1–8.

Neufert, E.; Neufert, P. (2000): Neufert’s Architects’ Data. 3rd ed. Oxford, UK: Blackwell Science.

Rauterberg, M.; Schlangenhauf, K. (1994): “Gestaltung multimedialer Informationssysteme”. In: Nutzung und Technik von Kommunikationsendgeräten, ITG-Fachtagung (1994). Berlin u.a.: vde-verlag gmbh.

Redondo, B. (2015): "The partnership project public art/tram: for which city narrative(s)?" Tales City articulo. Journal of Urban Research 7,13.
Ruland, D. (2015): "Wirken Lichtfarben und Körperfarben unterschiedlich"? In: Lux Junior 2015, 11. Internationales Forum für den lichttechnischen Nachwuchs, HAWK Hildesheim.
Salmon, C. (2007): Storytelling. La machine à fabriquer les images et à formater les esprits. Paris: La Découverte.
Sandercock, L. (2003): "Out of the Closet: The Importance of Stories and Storytelling in Planning Practice". Planning Theory & Practice 4:1 (January 2003), 11–28.
Schaub, M. (1989): DuMont's Handbuch Kreative Entwurfsarbeit am Computer. Köln: DuMont.
Secchi, B. (1984): Il racconto urbanistico. Turin: Einaudi.
Suppes, P. (1991): "Rules of Proportion in Architecture". Midwest studies in Philosophy 16, 352–358.
Throgmorton, J.A. (2003): "Planning as Persuasive Storytelling in a Global-Scale Web of Relationships". Planning Theory 2:2, 125–151.
Tyler, C.W. (1998): "Painters centre one eye in portraits". Nature 392,:6679, 877–878.
Wakefield, G. (2008): "Theory Time". In: UCSB's festival of contemporary arts and digital music, University of California. University of California, http://www.mat.ucsb.edu/~wakefield/amv/theory-time.htm.
Ware, C. (2008): Visual Thinking: For Design. San Francisco, CA, USA: Morgan Kaufmann Publishers Inc.
Wilson, A.; Chatterjee, A. (2005): "The Assessment of Preference for Balance: Introducing a new test". Empirical Studies of the Arts 23, 165–180.
Zeising, A. (2014): Neue Lehre von den Proportionen des menschlichen Körpers. Reprint of original from 1854, Vero Verlag, Nordersted, Germany.

Soenke Zehle

Exploring Distribution as a Condition: Elements of a Minor Metropolitanism

Urban design has long foregrounded the visual in the *mise-en-scene* of experience, from the sites of sovereignty to the street as stage for the collaborative constitution of urban multitudes. Reflecting on media architectures from within the horizon of contemporary processes of informatization, this essay takes as its point of departure the ways in which ambient media is woven into the fabric of the everyday, in terms the need to analytically grasp this distribution as a condition (Hansen 2015). To the extent that it engages with this condition, media architecture research moves beyond the visual and its attendant socio-technological ensembles to explore the material conditions of possibility that frame everyday experience. Many of these developments are rooted in "imperial infrastructures" that cut across sovereign territories and establish shared frames of reference and responsibility, of imagination and intervention. At the same time, they occur across a wide variety of sites that are difficult to comprehend in relation to specific models of urbanization. In the spirit of an ecology of practice open to transfer and translation, the essay therefore proceeds provisionally, making the case for a minor metropolitanism attentive to the limited reach of analytical approaches and political propositions.

1 Object Worlds, Infrastructural Relationalities

We often encounter design as that which structures the everyday, from individual objects of use to the layout of urban systems that provide pathways to organize our lives. Here, I begin with the design of objects since it is at the level of design that key decisions are made regarding the future relationality of these objects, including the degree of their connectivity, their openness to reappropriation, the choice of raw materials and sourcing strategies, the parameters of production, the scope and structure of value chains. All of these decisions affect the way in which the object operates. And one way of comprehending these interdependencies, of bringing into focus the "total configurations" (Rams) around these objects, is to explore the perspective of an object's constitution – its creation and endowment with a wide range of properties, its insertion into different architectures and ecologies.

DOI 10.1515/9783110453874-012

To focus on objects is not meant to simply shift our perspective toward "the object" but to facilitate a design-driven comprehension and exploration of infrastructures in relational terms. Analytically, the question is not only *what* an infrastructure is – its concrete materiality, its situation, but *when*, including the material conditions of possibility of its operation, since "infrastructure is a fundamentally relational concept. It becomes infrastructure in relation to organized practices. ... Thus we ask, when – not what – is an infrastructure" (Star/Ruhleder 1996: 113). Such a concern for the contingency of infrastructure "de-emphasizes things or people as simply causal factors in the development of such systems; rather, changes in infrastructural relations become central" (ibid.). To focus on the *when* of infrastructure not only calls attention to the complexity of the social worlds of which they are a part, but also to the possibilities for reuse and reappropriation. Hacking, for examples, is less an act of infrastructural transformation than an attempt to affect a shift in the social world (in this case, alternative conceptions of intellectual property as always-already-common) framing specific infrastructural ensembles: "the hacker makes something new out of property that belongs to everyone in the first place" (Wark 2013; Powell 2016). We move from exploring the object from the perspective of its distribution to the contingent relationalities of infrastructures.

When we explore how objects affect our individual and collective agency, we have to take into account both their discreetness and their distribution across vast systemic architectures. Such an methodological interest in "scaling our senses" (Zehle 2015), an interest in shifting analytical attention from individual objects to the socio-technological assemblages that constitute them, is ultimately related to the question of use. How can we act, what kinds of usage are possible, and how do these possibilities define and determine our agency more generally? What comes into view as we explore distribution as a condition is the "distributedness" (Veran 2016) of our own agency, a comprehension of agency in terms of the material continuity of effects across vast spatial and temporal scales (Latour 2014). All of the decisions that affect (and govern) the constitution of objects are potential sites of intervention and collaborative creation to reshape not only these objects, but the relationalities of the infrastructures through and within which they exist and operate. To affect the shift of an object from one infrastructural constellation into another is easier said than done. Yet while fair foods are still far more common than fair phones, for example, disciplines such as ecological economics or systems toxicology suggest that the interest in comprehending objects from within such "total configurations" is already changing the way we organize research – including research on media architectures.

2 Ambient Media, Ecologies of Practice

What media architecture research can do as it reflects on the emergence of ambient media is, above all, to remind us of the extent to which we are, and will continue to be, attached to material worlds. Instead of culture-nature dichotomies that designate distinct spheres of experience, there is only a continuity of material effects (Zehle 2016). Such a focus on continuity is shared across a variety of urban ecologies (Mostafavi/Doherty 2010), comprehensions of architecture as dynamic organization of matter (Abraham 2015), and the analytical approaches to "ecologies of practice", understood as the process of "inventing systemic and dialectical units of analysis" (Star 2016).

Research on media architectures exist in this context, from open technology exercises that focus on environmental monitoring to engage citizens in the politics of urban development (https://smartcitizen.me, https://arrayofthings.github.io) to the large-scale collaborative interventions of "city making" (Brynskov et al. 2014; Hemmersam et al. 2015). Open to diverse communities, these processes of collaborative prototyping offer a form of communication above and beyond language (Gale/Ruecker 2010). The design of objects to facilitate specific forms of collaboration can be described in terms of the engineering of "boundary objects", i.e. "objects that are both plastic enough to adapt to local needs and constraints of the several parties employing them, yet robust enough to maintain a common identity across sites" and facilitate cooperation across social worlds (Star 1989; Bowker and Star 1999), but also as "boundary-negotiating objects" that shift these boundaries (Lee 2007; Halpern et al. 2013; Pennington 2010). Acknowledging that collaborative design should itself be approached as a distributed activity (Bjørn/Boulus-Rødje 2015), such efforts are also open to the multiplicity of futures and the co-creation of speculative scenarios (Dunne/Ruby 2013, Forlano/Mathew 2014). The design of objects plays a key role in these dynamics of collaboration, and they exemplify the shift in focus that takes the constitution of objects as its point of departure not simply to create new objects, but to comprehend worlds and generate visions of system design (Dubberly/Pangaro 2015). In a sense, this is media architecture research as a form of reverse engineering – an invitation to explore the constitution of these objects, explore the worlds that made them, and comprehend the rules that govern their operation.

3 Urban Scenographies, Imperial Imaginaries

Whether electricity, light, glass, or mobile communication networks, infrastructures have always operated as material conditions of possibilities for new modes of cognition and perception, changing the complex relation between the demands for the *mise-en-scene* of economic and political power and the design of architectures to operate as stages for such display (McQuire 2006, Coutard/Rutherford 2015). As we configure our communication devices for individual use, we also locate ourselves in configurations so expansive that they call for a new understanding of experience, a space of experience that is neither exclusively social nor technological, neither exclusively human nor non-human. It is through the sensing of the scope of this space of experience that we develop a comprehension of the political, of the epistemological and material conditions of possibility that can facilitate or foreclose specific instances of politic intervention. Which is why, if media architecture research is to reflect on agency and the possibilities of different kinds of politics, it will have to be attentive to the structural transformation of use. How do we compare the exercise of individual and social freedom, how do we decide what extent of co-design we wish to be part of our understanding of use? The question of agency is directly linked to the question of interfaces. If media architectures confront us with new possibilities for participation, it is the design of interfaces – from mobile technologies open to re-appropriation and re-use to commons-based models of self-organization linking local sites in translocal networks – that structures our sense and scope of participation.

The “becoming-environmental” (Zehle 2016) of media is not a self-organizing process, a peaceful dynamic of technological progress that simply unfolds. It has always been a process of conflict and contestation. The history of informatization, for example, is by no means limited to the short historical horizon of the digital but deeply intertwined with the installation of imperial infrastructures, from undersea cables connecting colonial economies and metropolitan consumers (Mattelart 2003) to satellite networks triggering the desire for cultural self-determination and the design of a New World Information and Communication Order (Zehle 2012). These processes are imperial in more then one sense; while they have often been tied to processes of economic or cultural colonization, they are also imperial in that they cut across the conceptual and political boundaries of sovereignty understood in statist terms (Stoler 2006). While urban research has its academic origins in analyses of the dynamics of modernization in Europe and North America, attention to the “coloniality” (Mignolo/Escobar 2010) of these developments, e.g. the complex relationships of domination and exploitation whose reverberations continue to resound across the terrain of contemporary geopolitics, can assist media architecture research in contextualizing contemporary corporate visions of planetary connectivity.

While considering broader historical, geopolitical contexts makes research more complex, it also makes it more exciting: rather than assuming that we can operate with a model of agency and subjectivity as always already given, we attend to the parameters and processes of its constitution. As our own experience of media architectures affects our research, such research can therefore not only be framed in historical terms, as the continuation of a long process of reflecting on what happens to us as we inhabit our cities. It has to include a sense of contingency of our own analytical awareness, its scope and situatedness. We can, for example, continue to refer to the proudly imperial architectures established in the process of "Haussmannization" as paradigmatic media architectures, as they continue to guide our gaze toward the symbols of empire and have historically anchor a new sense of imperial citizenship in our experience of the everyday (Jordan 1995). Or we take the seemingly aleatory architectures of "arrival cities" (Sanders 2011) as alternative frame of reference. Collaboratively created by the people moving through them, these arrival cities are neither centrally planned nor stable in their architectural constellations. As more and more people experience the city as a space of transit rather than final destination, they engage new arrivals in a becoming-urban that cuts across the analytical dichotomies of city and country. These two examples illustrate different assumptions of who gets to determine and design the parameters of public experience. A 'minor' metropolitanism, attentive to the *mise en scene* of sovereign power as well as the subterranean practices that shape and sustain urban experience, suggests we focus on the latter, complementing canonical narratives of urbanization to come to terms with the actuality of urban life under the condition of distribution.

4 Working Futures, Social Machines

As neo-industrial paradigms (Industry 4.0, Industrial Internet) refashion our understanding of the factory, places of production are effectively turned into media architectures, suggesting we explore the encounter between current shifts in infrastructural relationalities and the future of work. This is not as much of a conceptual leap as one might expect. On the contrary, the very idea of ecologies of practice implies attention to the structural transformation of work: "The constitution of anyone's work is a mixture of human and nonhuman which can be analyzed ecologically. But the nature and quality of that composition will reflect back on the organization of work in important ways. ... To change the ecological mix with respect to my work organization means changing the organization in which I work. It is not merely an exercise of imagination, but a real political risk" (Star 2015). The analytical focus on work is not a matter of aligning media architecture research with labor studies; it is already contained in our own situation within the human-non-human assemblages that frame what we do.

In this context, it is maybe time to revisit the "Durkheim Test" suggested by Star to guide the design of boundary objects, "a test adequate to meet the challenges of distributed open systems" (Gießmann 2015). Because distributed systems can neither be tested locally nor assessed in their totality, "the very concept of the test must change in order to deal with such systems", i.e. a test that "would be communal, irreducible, distributed, and dynamic" (ibid.). "In order to understand the acceptance and use of a machine in and by a community, that community must be actively present as it evolves" (ibid.). During the decades since the initial publication of these suggestions, methods of citizen science, open and social innovation have been mainstreamed and even begun to transform the way we talk about innovation and our collective futures (De Waag 2015). But the "Durkheim Test" also speaks to the blurring boundaries of labor and the exercise of citizenship: "In an open, evolving system, the boundaries between design and use, between technology and user, between laboratory and workplace, necessarily blur" (ibid.). To conduct research from within distributed systems implies that, at least in principle, we are already engaging in a vast "Durkheim Test" that explores whether or not these systems speak to our present and future needs. Given that the open discourse of futurity currently risks being absorbed into the technical idioms of predictive analytics (Hansen 2016), claiming the right to an open, multiple future above and beyond any "technological solutionism" (Morozov 2012) is no small matter.

Such a focus on risk resonates with the perspective of "social machines", be it as a way to understand the dynamics of self-organization (Raunig 2010) or explore the algorithmic design of computational systems geared toward the production of sociality (Donath 2014). Both include injunctions to create truly social objects – distributed, open to reconfiguration, and operational across a variety of social worlds and infrastructural constellations. Today, the question of media architectures is necessarily part of a broader comprehension of the role of informatized urban infrastructures, and the current stage of informatization is widely perceived as a threshold moment. While we can isolate the devices that connect us to communication networks, the vast infrastructures that sustain their operation and position us in a complex constellation that extends from satellites to the semiotics of machine-to-machine communication (De Souza 2005, Lazzarato 2014) can only be comprehended in relation to a general condition of distribution. And as the factory turns into a media architecture, there is an urgency to broaden the scope of those involved in speculative design scenarios and take the methods of "material deliberation" (Forlano/Halpern 2015) into places of work.

5 Minor Metropolitanisms

Allowing our analytical gaze to wander beyond customary fields of vision, we may come to terms with distribution as a condition of contemporary existence, increasingly defined by infrastructural informatization and the algorithmicization of core cultural techniques. Above and beyond specific media architectural ensembles organized around specific forms of display, encounter, or interaction, the essay therefore uses the term "media architecture" to frame the situation we find ourselves in, inviting us to explore both the transformations of urban experience and the ways in which we change with it as we explore the role of media architectures in structuring and sustaining our experience.

To suggest a minor metropolitanism, an analysis that moves sideways rather than seeking vertical conceptual integration, is not to discount that changes in the relationality of imperial infrastructures require systemic interventions. But it is to say that such systemic effects may well occur as consequence of aggregated interventions rather than by imagining that change occurs only when actors act on a central stage, share a script, or agree on the scope of individual and collective agency. In fact, one of the tasks of such minor research is to imagine the *mise-en-scene* of agency in distributed systems, of creating the fantastic fictions of such stagings not in terms of the aesthetic economy of a revolutionary *Bildungsroman* but as a commons-based storytelling series, engaging each other in acts of translation across sites and situations. Finally, minor is meant as reminder of the subtle rhythms of urban change, over and against the ambitious and sometimes even heroic visions of "smart citizenship" that anticipate an expansion of agency as we embrace technologies of the future. Maybe the changes will not be quite as grand, yet significant all the same – adopting a minor perspective serves as a reminder to be attentive to the effects of exhaustion (Chun 2011) as well as empowerment. Given its capacity to attend to the aesthetic, economic, and political registers of urban experience, media architecture research can play a key role in the collaborative creation of the imaginary of such a minor metropolitanism.

Bibliography

Abraham, A. (2015): A New Nature: 9 Architectural Conditions Between Liquid and Solid. Zuerich: Lars Mueller.

Bjørn, P.; Boulus-Rødje, N. (2015): "The Multiple Intersecting Sites of Design in CSCW Research". Computer Supported Cooperative Work (CSCW) 24:4 (August), 319–351.

Bowker, G.C.; Star, S.L. (2000): Sorting Things Out: Classification and Its Consequences. Cambridge, MA: MIT Press.

Bowker, G.C.; Timmermann, S.; Clarke, A.E.; Balka, E., eds. (2016): Boundary Objects and Beyond: Working with Leigh Star. Cambridge, MA: MIT Press.

Brynskov, M., ed. (2014): Urban Interaction Design: Toward City Making. Amsterdam: FLOSS Manuals.

Chun, W. (2011): "Crisis, Crisis, Crisis, or Sovereignty and Networks". Theory, Culture & Society 28:6, 91–112.

Coutard, O.; Rutherford, J., eds. (2015): Beyond the Networked City: Infrastructure Reconfigurations and Urban Change in the North and South. London u.a.: Routledge.

De Souza, C. (2005): The Semiotic Engineering of Human-Computer Interaction. Cambridge, MA: The MIT Press.

De Waag et al. (2015): Growing a Digital Social Innovation System for Europe. A study prepared for the European Commission DG Communications Networks, Content & Technology by Digital Social Innovation, accessed April 30, 2016, https://waag.org/en/project/digital-social-innovation-dsi/.

Donath, J. (2014): The Social Machine: Designs for Living Online. Cambridge, MA: MIT Press.

Dubberly, H.; Pangaro, P. (2015): "Cybernetics and Design: Conversations for Action". Cybernetics and Human Knowing 22:2–3, 73–82, accessed April 30, 2016, http://www.dubberly.com/articles/cybernetics-and-design.html/.

Forlano, L.; Halpern, M. (2015): "Reimagining Work: Entanglements and Frictions around Future of Work Narratives". Fibreculture 26, accessed April 30, 2016, http://twentysix.fibreculturejournal.org/fcj-189-reimagining-work-entanglements-and-frictions-around-future-of-work-narratives/.

Forlano, L.; Mathew, A. (2014): "From Design Fiction to Design Friction: Speculative and Participatory Design of Values-Embedded Urban Technology". Journal of Urban Technology 21:4, 7–24.

Galey, A.; Ruecker, S. (2010): "How a prototype argues". Literary and Linguistics Computing 25:4 (December), 405–24.

Gießmann, S. (2015): "Der Durkheim-Test. Anmerkungen zu Susan Leigh Stars Grenzobjekten". Berichte zur Wissenschaftsgeschichte 38:3 (September), 211–226.

Halpern, M.; Erickson, I.; Forlano, L.; Gay, G. (2013): "Designing Collaboration: Comparing Cases Exploring Cultural Probes as Boundary-Negotiating Objects". In: A. Bruckman; S. Counts (eds.): CSCW 2013: Proceedings of the 2013 ACM Conference on Computer Supported Cooperative Work. New York, NY: ACM, 1093–1102

Hansen, M.B.N. (2015): Feed Forward: On the Future of Twenty-First Century Media. Chicago: University of Chicago Press.

Hansen, M.B.N. (2016): "Our Predictive Condition, or, Prediction in the Wild". In: R. Grusin (ed.): The Non-Human Turn. Minneapolis: University of Minnesota Press, 101–138.

Hemmersam, P.; Martin, N.; Westvang, E.; Aspen, J.; Morrison, A. (2015): "Exploring Urban Data Visualization and Public Participation in Planning". Journal of Urban Technology 22:4, 45–64.
Jordan, D.P. (1995): Transforming Paris: The Life and Labors of Baron Haussmann. New York: The Free Press.
Latour, B. (2014): "Agency at the Time of the Anthropocene". New Literary History 45:1 (Winter), 1–18.
Lee, C.P. (2007): "Boundary-Negotiating Artifacts: Unbinding the Routine of Boundary Objects and Embracing Chaos in Collaborative Work". Computer Supported Cooperative Work (CSCW) 16:3 (June), 307–339.
Mattelart, A. (2003): The Information Society: An Introduction. New York: Sage.
Mignolo, W.D.; Escobar, A. (2010): Globalization and the Decolonial Option. London u.a.: Routledge.
Morozov, E. (2012): To Save Everything, Click Here: The Folly of Technological Solutionism. New York: Public Affairs.
Mostafavi, M.; Doherty, G. (2010): Ecological Urbanism. Cambridge: Harvard University Graduate School of Design with Lars Mueller Publishers.
Pennington, D.D. (2010): "The Dynamics of Material Artifacts in Collaborative Research Teams". Computer Supported Cooperative Work (CSCW) 19:2 (April), 175–199.
Powell, A. (2016): "Hacking in the public interest: Authority, legitimacy, means, and ends". New Media & Society 18 (April), 600–618.
Raunig, G. (2010): A Thousand Machines: A Concise Philosophy of the Machine as Social Movement, trans. Aileen Derieg. New York: Semiotext(e).
Sanders, D. (2011): Arrival City: How the Largest Migration in History is Reshaping Our World. New York: Pantheon.
Star, S.L. (1989): "The structure of ill-structured solutions: boundary objects and heterogeneous distributed problem solving". In: M.N. Huhns; L. Gasser (eds.): Distributed Artificial Intelligence Vol. 2. Menlo Park, CA: Morgan Kaufmann Publishers Inc., 37–54.
Star, S.L. (2016): Revisiting *Ecologies of Knowledge*. In: Bowker et al. (pp. 1–36).
Star, S.L.; Ruhleder, K. (1996): "Steps Toward an Ecology of Infrastructure: Design and Access for Large Information Spaces". Information Systems Research 7, 111–134.
Stoler, A.L. (2006): "On Degrees of Imperial Sovereignty". Public Culture 18:1 (Winter), 125–46.
Veran, H. (2016): "Afterword: On the Distributedness of Leigh". In: G.C. Bowker; S. Timmermann; A.E. Clarke; E. Balka (eds.): Boundary Objects and Beyond: Working with Leigh Star. Cambridge, MA: MIT Press, 499–500.
Wark, M. (2013): "Considerations on a Hacker Manifesto". In: T. Scholz (ed.): Digital Labour: The Internet as a Playground and a Factory. Londonu.a.: Routledge, 69–75.
Zehle, S. (2012): "New World Information and Communication Order". In: G. Ritzer (ed.): The Wiley-Blackwell Encyclopedia of Globalization. Chichester, West Sussex u.a.: Wiley Blackwell, (n. p.).
Zehle, S. (2015): "Scaling our Senses: Type in Motion between Sentient Semiospheres and a Semiotics of Intensities". In: N. Jones; S. Skinner (eds.): The Act of Reading. Manchester u.a.: Corridor 8 and Torque Editions, 239–266.
Zehle, S. (2016): "Common Conflicts, Imperial Imaginaries: Exploring the Becoming-Environmental of Media". In: S. Pop; T. Toft (eds.): What Urban Media Art Can Do. Berlin: Public Art Lab, 420–28.

About the Authors

Dr. **Patrick Tobias Fischer** is a research associate in Human-Computer Interaction (HCI) at Bauhaus-Universität Weimar. His research is positioned in the crossfire of art, technology and urban life and was sparked in 2006 while he studied at University of Technology, Sydney at Ernest Edmond's Creativity and Cognitions Studio. Since then Fischer's passion for novel human-computer interfaces that reach beyond desktop guided him to research institutes such as Fraunhofer, Berlin and Microsoft Research in Cambridge. He holds a PhD from the University of Strathclyde, Glasgow. He sees the responsibility of research in conceiving and exploring alternative futures for urban spaces. In his opinion novel urban technology prototypes should be tested early in the field to see immediately its impact on urban life, citizens experience, and behaviour. This is what he has done in his PhD extensively through his media intervention SMSlingshot which has been exhibited in various cities around the world. For him MediaArchitecture is situation design through interface and interaction design.

Professor **Marcus Foth** is founder and director of the Urban Informatics Research Lab, i/Director of the QUT Design Lab, and Professor in Interactive & Visual Design, School of Design, Creative Industries Faculty at Queensland University of Technology. Marcus' research focuses on the relationships between people, place and technology. He leads a cross-disciplinary team that develops practical approaches to complex urban problems. He adopts human-computer interaction and design methodologies to build engagement around emerging issues facing our cities. Marcus has authored and co-authored over 150 publications in journals, edited books, and conference proceedings. He received a Queensland Young Tall Poppy Science Award 2013, and was inducted by the planning, design and development site Planetizen to the world's top 25 leading thinkers and innovators in the field of urban planning and technology.

Dr. **Sven Gehring** is a researcher at the German Research Center for Artificial Intelligence (DFKI) in Saarbrücken, Germany. For his doctoral thesis "Interaction with Media Facades – The design of interactive systems for large-scale urban screens", he received a PhD from Saarland University in Saarbrücken, Germany. His main research interests are interaction with digital systems in urban environments, as well as ambient notification environments. At the DFKI Sven Gehring is head of research and development of the Innovative Retail Laboratory (IRL).

Associate Professor **M. Hank Haeusler** Dipl.-Ing. (Fh) / PhD (SIAL/RMIT) is Discipline Director of Computational Design (CoDe) at Australian School of Architecture + Design at the University of New South Wales, Sydney; board member of the Media Architecture Institute, a non-profit organisation designed to complement the work of established universities and research institutions, and Lead CI of Encircle, an ARC Linkage Grant funded research group investigating responsive transport environments. Haeusler is known as a researcher, educator, entrepreneur and designer in media architecture, digital technology, interaction design and ubiquitous computing and author of seven books listing publications such as 'Media Facades – History, Technology, Content' (avedition, 2009), 'New Media Facades – A global Survey' (avedition, 2012); 'InterChanging' (Spurbuch, 2014); and over 40 book chapters and conference papers. He has lectured in Europe, Asia, North America and Australia and was appointed Visiting Professor at Central Academy of Fine Arts, Beijing in 2013. He was Co-Chair of the 2016 Media Architecture Biennale in Sydney. Twitter: UNSWCoDe

Kim Halskov is professor in interaction design at The Department of Digital Design and Information Studies at Aarhus University, Denmark where he in addition to being director of Centre for Advanced Visualization and Interaction, see CAVI.au.dk, also is co-director of the Centre for Participatory IT, see PIT.au.dk. In 2007 Kim Halskov established the media architecture research group at Aarhus University. Major media architecture cases include Aarhus by Light (2007), The Danish Pavilion at Expo(2010), and conceptual design of The Odenplan Metro Station(2012). Current projects include the CIBIS project, which explores creativity in co-design. From a background in participatory design Kim Halskov's research areas includes innovation processes, design processes, media architecture, and experience design.

Marius Hoggenmueller is an interaction designer and researcher working in the field of media architecture and urban informatics. He holds a B.Sc. in Media Informatics from the University of Munich, Germany. Currently he is a visiting scholar at the Design Lab at University of Sydney, Australia conducting his master thesis project. Marius Hoggenmueller worked on several media architecture installations for public art festivals, including Luminale in Frankfurt and Vivid Sydney.

Dr. **Eva Hornecker** is Professor of Human-Computer Interaction at the Bauhaus-Universität Weimar within the area of media informatics. Her work is located at the intersection between technology, design, and the social sciences. Her research interests are the design and user experience of 'beyond the desktop' interaction. In her research, she focuses on aspects of user experience and social interaction in the context of novel interfaces, often in the context of museum and heritage sites as well as public spaces, where she and her team investigate how to enrich urban spaces/architectures and encourage social interactions. She co-founded the ACM Tangible Embedded and Embodied Interaction conference TEI. She has researched and taught previously in Bremen (Germany), TU Vienna (Austria), the University of Sussex (UK); University of Canterbury (New Zealand), the Open University (UK) and the University of Strathclyde (Scotland, UK).

Dr. Heinrich Hußmann is full professor for Media Informatics at Ludwig-Maximilians-Universität München, Germany. He holds a doctoral degree from the University of Passau and a degree in Computer Science from Munich University of Technology. For several years, he was a systems engineer and team leader in the advanced development laboratory of the telecommunications division of Siemens, and he had a position as full professor of Computer Science at Dresden University of Technology, holding a chair for Software Technology. His current research interests are in general in the transformation of every day life through digital media, and specifically in usable privacy and security as well as technology support for collaboration. According to Google Scholar data, Heinrich Hussmann is author of over 200 publications with more than 3300 citations.

Dr. **Martin Tomitsch** is associate professor and Head of Design at the University of Sydney's Faculty of Architecture, Design and Planning. He is the Chair of the Design Lab, a research group that focuses on interaction design and creative technologies. Before moving to Australia, he studied informatics and worked as interaction designer in Vienna, Stockholm, Reykjavik and Paris. He is founding member of the Media Architecture Institute, co-chair of the Media Architecture Biennale 2016, state co-chair of the Australian Computer-Human Interaction Special Interest Group (CHISIG), and visiting lecturer at the Vienna University of Technology's Research Group for Industrial Software (INSO).

Dr. **Alexander Wiethoff** is a media architecture researcher and lecturer at the Ludwig-Maximilians University of Munich (LMU). He has published over 40 peer-reviewed publications on the topic and is a skilled presenter at top-ranked conference series that he partly co-organises. Since 2012 Alexander is an active member of the media architecture institute (Vienna/Sydney). He has a diverse skill set combining theoretical knowledge along with practical skills rooted in the industry that support the seamless transfer of gained insights to be practically applied in the urban environment. Alexander Wiethoff has a background in art and design and received a doctoral degree with emphasis in Human-Computer Interaction from the University of Munich. He lived abroad in Linz (A), Milan (I) and Copenhagen (DK), developing a keen sensitivity to people from diverse cultural backgrounds.

Anke von der Heide Dipl.-Des. BUW, M.Arch. Tongji University, M.Sc. Urban Design TUB, is an artist, designer, architect/urban designer, and curator and is interested in the intersection of the Urban, Technology, and Sociology. Most of her participatory art works in public deal with the possibility to create dialogs between strangers on societal, political or environmental topics. She gained a diploma in design at Bauhaus-University Weimar, accomplished a research project in Intermedia Art at Tokyo University of Fine Arts and Music and studied Urban Design at TU Berlin and Tongji University Shanghai. She work and presented in Tokyo, Kiriu fine arts biennale (Japan), Busan art biennale (South Korea), and India. She was a researcher at the architecture faculty of TU Berlin on the topic of Smart Cities and since 2013 is an associate professor in the domains of MediaArchitecture and Human-Computer Interaction in Bauhaus-University Weimar. She curated various festivals and symposiums among them the Façade-projection festival Genius Loci in Weimar and the Wear It in Berlin. She has been invited as a speaker to various academic and non-academic platforms. Currently she is a PhD candidate with the topic "Narrating public space through media interventions". She is a founding member of the Urban HCI Lab at Bauhaus University and the Creative Coding School for refugees in Berlin.

Drawing on perspectives from comparative literature, philosophy, and translation, Dr. **Soenke Zehle's** current media-theoretical research interests include the role played by media architectures in framing our communicative modes of relation and the dynamics of communing. Lecturer in Media Theory at the Academy of Fine Arts Saar and an Affiliate Researcher at the Ubiquitous Media Technologies Lab (UMTL) at the German Research Center for Artificial Intelligence (DFKI), he also co-initiated and currently works as Managing Director of the academy's xm:lab – Experimental Media Lab as well as K8, a non-profit company with a focus on educational research and critical design. He frequently co-develop arts-and-technology projects with his academy colleagues from Communication Design, Fine Arts, Media Art and Design, Media Informatics and Product Design with a particular interest in practice-based and transcultural approaches. He publishes frequently and is also active as a curator; current projects include two international exhibition series, one on the visual storytelling pioneer Frans Masereel and another on the literary artists Claire and Yvan Goll.

Bei Fragen zur Produktsicherheit wenden Sie sich bitte an:
If you have any questions regarding product safety,
please contact:

Walter de Gruyter GmbH
Genthiner Straße 13
10785 Berlin
productsafety@degruyterbrill.com